A FIELD GUIDE TO
TEXAS TREES

A FIELD GUIDE TO
TEXAS TREES

BY BENNY J. SIMPSON

Gulf Publishing Company
Houston, Texas

Gulf Publishing Company
P.O. Box 2608
Houston, Texas 77252-2608

10   9   8   7   6   5   4   3   2

Library of Congress Cataloging-in-Publication Data

Simpson, Benny J., 1928–
    A field guide to Texas trees / by Benny J. Simpson.
      p. cm. — (Texas monthly field guide series)
    Originally published: Austin, Tex.: Texas Monthly Press, c1988.
    Includes bibliographical references and index.
    ISBN 0-87719-113-1
    1. Trees—Texas—Identification. 2. Trees—Texas—Geographical
    distribution—Maps. I. Title. II. Series.
    [QK 188.S55 1992]
    582.1609764—dc20   92-8671
                                          CIP

Texas Monthly is a registered trademark of Mediatex Communications Corporation.

Printed and bound in the United States of America (Color pages printed in Hong Kong)

To the memory of Bake
and
to Una, who still walks
beneath the blue Quitaques

Table of Contents

Preface

From the cathedral stillness of the Big Thicket to the land across the Pecos River, from Padre Island to the big sky of the High Plains, from the waters of the Hill Country to the timbered bottoms of the fabled Blacklands, Texas has a native flora that, in sheer loveliness, is second to none.

Yet, the native greenery of Texas is little known except to professional botanists and taxonomists. Even these learned people were relatively slow to develop the taxonomic keys and other tools needed to understand partially the flora of this vast state. Not until 1937 did we have a checklist of the Texas native plants. V. L. Cory, a range botanist, and H. B. Parks, Chief, Division of Apiculture, with the Texas Agricultural Experiment Station, published their *Catalogue of the*

Flora of Texas in July 1937. Every student of botany and hunter of native Texas plants has worn out his copy of this first guide.

In June 1962 this checklist was revised and brought up to date by F. W. Gould, Department of Range Science, Texas A&M University. This was further refined in April 1969 and January 1975. In 1970 the Texas Research Foundation published the *Manual of the Vascular Plants of Texas,* and finally we had a set of taxonomic keys to all the known native ferns and flowering plants of Texas. This book by Donovan S. Correll and Marshall C. Johnston is a monumental work and highly technical and precise in its terminology. Yet, this manual is in need of revision to incorporate changes in nomenclature as well as newly discovered plants within the state.

Several local manuals for specific areas of the state have been published over the years as well as floristic treatments for certain shrubs, trees, grasses, and wildflowers. The works of Charles Sprague Sargent and Elbert L. Little, Jr., have been most helpful in understanding the Texan trees.

For 35 years I have wandered the prairies and hills of Texas searching for trees of beauty that I feel should become part of our planned landscape. I spent most of this time alone, for I work better setting my own pace and direction. However, in these latter years, the trail has become too steep and my knowledge needed expanding, so I have called upon friends for assistance, which was freely given. I am most thankful to the following:

Barton Warnock and Lynn Lowrey, who together should have written this book. Without the able help and direction of these two close friends and trail companions, I simply would not have come in contact with many of the rarer trees of Texas;

The many farmers and ranchers of Texas who have never barred their gates to me;

The Texas Department of Highways and Public Transportation, its director, and the many district engineers and maintenance supervisors who have never failed to call off the mowers and erect permanent barriers around rare and beautiful plants that I have brought to their attention;

The many dedicated personnel of the Soil Conservation Service and the Texas Forest Service who know the land and the trees;
The superintendents and naturalists of Big Bend and Guadalupe national parks;
David Riskind and all the many Texas Parks and Wildlife people who have tolerated my seed-hunting forays for these many years;
Longtime friends, too numerous to mention, but especially Ruel Warnock, Alpine; Dude and Inell Sproul, Fort Davis; Willis and Virginia Williams, Shafter; Travis and Polly Roberts, Marathon; and Jim and Ann Taylor, Garrison.

Extra special thanks go to my dear friends Jill Senior Nokes, Austin; the late Carroll Abbott, Kerrville; Bob Rucker, College Station; Roy Roddy, former agricultural writer for the *Dallas Morning News;* the late Edith McRoberts, horticultural editor for the *Dallas Times Herald;* the late Sir Harold Hillier of Winchester, England, nurseryman extraordinaire; and Christine Serkland, of Branch, who typed the first manuscript. They "tailed me up" many a day at the first writing of this book years ago before native plants became popular.

My deep appreciation is extended to Andy and Sally Wasowski for assistance on the first draft of the manuscript and to Barbara Reuter for final manuscript preparation and for herbarium work in the preparation of the distribution maps for the difficult genus *Crataegus.* These maps are from specimen records at the Southern Methodist University Herbarium at Dallas (thanks to Bill Mahler and Barney Lipscomb), the Tracy Herbarium of the Texas Agricultural Experiment Station at Texas A&M University, College Station (thanks to Stephen Hatch), and the University of Texas Herbarium at Austin (thanks to Marshall Johnston and Guy Nesom).

Introduction

There is not one uniform definition of a tree. In fact, the definitions often differ significantly from one author to the next. The definition of a tree, especially its height, most likely determines the number of trees listed for a region. Here, a tree is defined as having a single trunk or multiple trunks, growing to twelve feet or more in height, and being definitely woody.

This book describes the natural history and distribution range of 222 trees considered to be native to the state of Texas. This number could potentially be 305, as is shown in the chart below.

	Families*	Genera*	Species
Native trees of Texas	39	80	222
Possible additional trees of Texas			24
Plants from CUST‡ considered shrubs	9	17	51
Trees from CUST not accepted			2
Extinct (in Texas) or "lost" native trees of Texas		1	6
Totals	48	98	305

*Each family and genus listed only once
‡*Checklist of United States Trees*

These numbers will always be approximate because of differing opinions concerning scientific nomenclature and the definition of a tree. The standard list of Texas trees used in this book is the *Checklist of United States Trees* (CUST), by Elbert L. Little, Jr. However, the works of C. H. Muller were used for the genus *Quercus* (oaks). These standards are backed up by the *Manual of the Vascular Plants of Texas,* by Correll and Johnston, and other works listed in the bibliography. Distribution maps were compiled from the publications of Gould, Little, Lundell, Nixon, Turner, and Vines[1] and from my own knowledge of where these trees occur.

The continental United States has approximately 650 to 680 indigenous trees, that is, trees that grew here naturally before the arrival of European settlers. Texas has 33 to 45 percent of the native tree species of the United States, with approximately 30 species that have become naturalized, that is, they are not native to Texas but have escaped cultivation and are able to reproduce and survive in the wild.

Table 1 lists the trees that are native to Texas. I am not in agreement with the status of some of the trees listed in this table. For example, it is difficult for me to believe that *Prunus munsoniana* (Munson Plum) is a true species. In fact, several of the *Crataegus* (hawthorn) species will most likely be absorbed into some of the more common series when this genus is revised.

Ten trees are not listed as native to Texas in CUST, but I

believe they are legitimate species and are present in Texas. They are listed in Table 2. An additional 24 trees are not listed by CUST as being native to Texas (Table 3). With the exception of *Acer saccharum* (Sugar Maple), I am in agreement with this list. One of the most controversial aspects of dealing with trees is deciding whether they are trees or shrubs. In essence, it is an arbitrary decision. Many species are shrublike in one environment and treelike in another. The distinction is difficult to make. Plants from CUST that are considered shrubs by this author are listed in Table 4. *Amelanchier arborea* (Serviceberry) at Monroe, Louisiana, is a 25-foot-tall tree. Yet the only one I have seen in the wild in Texas was scarcely 3 feet tall and flowering profusely. Seedlings grown from the Texas species for ten years remain only 3 feet tall. A 25-foot-tall specimen of *Karwinskia humboldtiana* (Coyotillo) with a 12-foot spread, is growing at the Valley Nature Center in Weslaco. Yet, this plant is commonly a shrub of only 3 to 6 feet tall. A few specimens of *Sophora secundiflora* (Mescal Bean) grown in cultivation and in rich sites in the wild are over 20 feet in height. Yet the majority of these plants never grow above 3 to 10 feet tall. *Erythrina herbacea* (Coral Bean) is considered by some to be a tree and by others to be a shrub. Yet I have seen it in northeastern Texas where it is a true herbaceous perennial, freezing to ground level each year. *Sophora affinis* (Eve's Necklace) is usually a tree, yet in deep shade, it can become a high climbing vine.

Only two trees listed in CUST are unacceptable to me. Both are oaks. One is a putative hybrid, and the other is a controversial variety. These are listed in Table 5. It is speculated that *Quercus tardifolia* is an introgressed hybrid of *Q. hypoxantha* x *Q. gravesii. Q. hypoxantha* is a Mexican oak no longer found in the United States. *Q. falcata* is accepted as a highly polymorphic species or as having two, three, or four varieties (see individual write-up).

There are six tree species that were once thought to occur in Texas but are now considered extinct in the state. These are listed in Table 6. *Ilex cassine* (Dahoon Holly) and *I. myrtifolia* (Myrtle Holly) were once thought to occur along the coast in southeastern Texas. It is possible that *Populus angustifolia* is still in some hidden, well-watered canyon in Culberson County, but attempts to locate the tree originally sampled by Barton Warnock were futile. There is no doubt that it was once prevalent in the high country of the Trans-Pecos, for supposedly both the Lanceleaf and Hinckley cottonwoods are hybrids of this Narrowleaf Cottonwood.

V. L. Cory was superintendent of the Texas Agricultural Experiment Station at Sonora when he presumably collected a specimen of *Leucaena greggii* (Gregg Leadtree) at the headwaters of the Devils River in Crockett County. However, there really is no record of the specimen because the voucher for *L. greggii* at the SMU Herbarium contains no plant material. The Texas literature describes its white flowers, but in Mexico, where it is readily found, the flowers are bright yellow.

Gymnocladus dioica (Kentucky Coffee Tree) and *Crataegus douglasii* (*C. rivularis;* Black Hawthorn) have been rumored to occur in the Texas Panhandle, with the coffee tree in Hemphill County and Black Hawthorn in Dallam County. Kentucky Coffee Tree occurs in the valley of the Canadian River in Ellis and Roger Mills counties in Oklahoma, just across the Texas state line, so it could just as easily be found in Texas. However, I am extremely doubtful about finding the black hawthorn in Texas. This is a tree of the high country farther north and west. If found in Texas, it would probably be in a secluded area of Cold Water Creek or Rita Blanca Creek or perhaps a hidden canyon off the Canadian River.

There are approximately 30 species of trees that have become naturalized in Texas (Table 7). That is, they have escaped cultivation and become established in the wild. If they can reproduce and spread, they are said to be naturalized. In some instances, this is of no concern. However, there are 4 species and one genus with several species that are creating a problem in Texas because of their aggressive growth:

●*Elaeagnus angustifolia* (Russian Olive)—This tree is native to the cold, high country of Asia and is not a problem in most areas of Texas because of the hot climate. However, several of these trees were used in a park in the city of Canadian and escaped to the Canadian River valley, where they spread aggressively. Around Santa Fe, New Mexico, and the banks of the Rio Grande, the tree has taken over to such an extent that it is crowding out the native trees.

● *Poncirus trifoliata* (Trifoliate Orange)—Perhaps this tree is more bark than bite, but I see it in rather large patches in East Texas. The thorns are quite vicious, and it appears to be a problem tree.

● *Pyrus calleryana* (Callery Pear)—This is quite an attractive tree until it reaches about 25 to 30 years of age, when the wood becomes quite brittle and the branches break easily. Some of the cultivars of the Callery Pear produce fruit that is consumed by birds who then void the seeds in their droppings. These seeds germinate and produce thickets that crowd out the natural vegetation, especially in northeastern Texas.

● *Sapium sebiferum* (Chinese Tallow Tree)—In the next half century, the Chinese Tallow Tree will infest the Coastal Plain and southeastern Texas. It can already be found in extensive thickets.

● *Tamarix* spp. (Salt Cedar)—Several species of this genus, which is native to the steppes of Asia, have already become widely spread in Texas. Many of the western, central, and southern Texas waterways that contain any amount of salt are clogged with these trees.

[1] See bibliography.

Table 1
Checklist of the Native Trees of Texas

Species	Common Name	Vegeta-tional Area (see map)	Family
Acacia farnesiana	Huisache	2,3,4,6, 7,10	Leguminosae
A. greggii	Gregg Acacia	2,6,7,8,10	Leguminosae
A. roemeriana	Roemer Acacia	6,7,8,10	Leguminosae
A. tortuosa	Huisachillo	6,7	Leguminosae
A. wrightii	Wright Acacia	6,7,8,10	Leguminosae
Acer barbatum	Southern Sugar Maple	1	Aceraceae
A. grandidentatum	Bigtooth Maple	5,7,10	Aceraceae
A. leucoderme	Chalk Maple	1	Aceraceae
A. negundo	Box Elder	1,2,3,4, 5,6,7	Aceraceae
A. rubrum	Red Maple	1,2,3	Aceraceae
Aesculus glabra var. *arguta*	Texas Buckeye	1,3,4,5,7	Hippocastanaceae
A. pavia var. *flavescens*		7	Hippocastanaceae
A. pavia var. *pavia*	Red Buckeye	1,2,3,4, 7,8	Hippocastanaceae
Alnus serrulata	Smooth Alder	1,3	Betulaceae
Amelanchier utahensis	Utah Serviceberry	10	Rosaceae
Aralia spinosa	Devil's Walking Stick	1,2	Araliaceae
Arbutus texana	Texas Madrone	7,10	Ericaceae
Asimina triloba	Pawpaw	1,2,3	Annonaceae
Betula nigra	River Birch	1,3	Betulaceae
Bumelia celastrina	Saffron Plum, Coma	2,6	Sapotaceae
B. lanuginosa	Chittamwood	1,2,3,4,5, 6,7,8,10	Sapotaceae
B. lycioides	Buckthorn Bumelia	2	Sapotaceae
Caesalpinia mexicana	Mexican Caesalpinia	6	Leguminosae
Carpinus caroliniana	American Hornbeam	1,2,3	Betulaceae
Carya aquatica	Water Hickory	1,2,3,4	Juglandaceae
C. cordiformis	Bitternut Hickory	1,2,3	Juglandaceae

C. glabra var. *glabra* (*C. leiodermis*)	Pignut Hickory	1	Juglandaceae
C. illinoensis	Pecan	1,2,3,4, 5,6,7,8	Juglandaceae
C. myristiciformis	Nutmeg Hickory	1,2,3	Juglandaceae
C. ovata var. *ovata*	Shagbark Hickory	1,2	Juglandaceae
C. texana	Black Hickory	1,2,3,4, 5,6,7	Juglandaceae
C. tomentosa	Mockernut Hickory	1,3	Juglandaceae
Castanea pumila	Allegheny Chinquapin	1,2	Fagaceae
Celtis laevigata	Sugarberry	1,2,3,4,5, 6,7,8,9,10	Ulmaceae
C. lindheimeri	Lindheimer Hackberry	6,7	Ulmaceae
C. occidentalis	Hackberry	8	Ulmaceae
C. reticulata	Netleaf Hackberry	2,4,5,7, 8,9,10	Ulmaceae
C. tenuifolia	Dwarf Hackberry	1,2,3	Ulmaceae
Cercidium texanum	Texas Paloverde	2,6	Leguminosae
Cercis canadensis var. *canadensis*	Eastern Redbud	1,2,3,4	Leguminosae
C. canadensis var. *mexicana*	Mexican Redbud	7,10	Leguminosae
C. canadensis var. *texensis*	Texas Redbud	4,5,7,8	Leguminosae
Cercocarpus breviflorus	Hairy Cercocarpus	10	Rosaceae
C. montanus var. *argenteus*	Silver Mountain Mahogany	8,10	Rosaceae
C. montanus var. *glaber*	Smooth Mountain Mahogany	7,10	Rosaceae
Chilopsis linearis	Desert Willow	6,7,10	Bignoniaceae
Chionanthus virginicus	Fringe Tree	1,2	Oleaceae
Condalia hookeri var. *hookeri*	Brasil	2,6,7	Rhamnaceae
Cordia boissieri	Wild Olive	6	Boraginaceae
Cornus florida	Flowering Dogwood	1,3	Cornaceae
Cotinus obovatus	American Smoke Tree	7	Anacardiaceae
Crataegus berberifolia	Barberry Hawthorn	1	Rosaceae
C. brachyacantha	Blueberry Hawthorn	1,2,3	Rosaceae
C. calpodendron	Pear Hawthorn	1	Rosaceae
C. crus-galli	Cockspur Hawthorn	1,3,4,5,7	Rosaceae
C. greggiana	Gregg Hawthorn	7	Rosaceae

7

Table 1
(continued)

Species	Common Name	Vegetational Area (see map)	Family
C. marshallii	Parsley Hawthorn	1,3	Rosaceae
C. mollis	Downy Hawthorn	1,2,3,4,5	Rosaceae
C. opaca	Mayhaw	1	Rosaceae
C. reverchonii	Reverchon Hawthorn	4,5,7	Rosaceae
C. spathulata	Littlehip Hawthorn	1,2,3,4	Rosaceae
C. texana	Texas Hawthorn	2,3,6	Rosaceae
C. tracyi	Tracy Hawthorn	7,10	Rosaceae
C. viridis	Green Hawthorn	1,2,3,4, 5,7	Rosaceae
Cupressus arizonica var. *arizonica*	Arizona Cypress	10	Cupressaceae
Cyrilla racemiflora var. *racemiflora*	Leatherwood	1,2	Cyrillaceae
Diospyros texana	Texas Persimmon	2,3,4,5, 6,7,10	Ebenaceae
D. virginiana	Persimmon	1,2,3,4, 5,8	Ebenaceae
Ehretia anacua	Anacua	2,6,7	Boraginaceae
Esenbeckia berlandieri	Jopoy	6	Rutaceae
Fagus grandifolia	American Beech	1	Fagaceae
Forestiera acuminata	Swamp Privet	1,2,3,4	Oleaceae
Fraxinus americana	White Ash	1,2,3,4,5	Oleaceae
F. berlandieriana	Mexican Ash	2,6,7,10	Oleaceae
F. caroliniana	Carolina Ash	1,2	Oleaceae
F. cuspidata	Fragrant Ash	10	Oleaceae
F. greggii	Gregg Ash	7,10	Oleaceae
F. papillosa	Chihuahua Ash	10	Oleaceae
F. pennsylvanica	Green Ash	1,2,3,4, 5,6,7	Oleaceae
F. texensis	Texas Ash	4,5,6,7	Oleaceae
F. velutina	Velvet Ash	10	Oleaceae
Gleditsia aquatica	Water Locust	1,2,3	Leguminosae
G. triacanthos	Honey Locust	1,2,3,4, 5,6,7	Leguminosae

8

Halesia diptera	Two-wing Silverbell	1	Styracaceae
Helietta parvifolia	Baretta	6	Rutaceae
Ilex ambigua	Carolina Holly	1	Aquifoliaceae
I. coriacea	Baygall Bush	1	Aquifoliaceae
I. decidua	Possum Haw	1,2,3,4, 5,7	Aquifoliaceae
I. longipes	Georgia Holly	1	Aquifoliaceae
I. opaca var. *opaca*	American Holly	1,2,3	Aquifoliaceae
I. verticillata	Winterberry	1,2	Aquifoliaceae
I. vomitoria	Yaupon	1,2,3,6,7	Aquifoliaceae
Juglans major	Arizona Walnut	7,10	Juglandaceae
J. microcarpa	Nogalito	5,7,8,10	Juglandaceae
J. nigra	Black Walnut	2,3,4,5, 7,8	Juglandaceae
Juniperus ashei	Ashe Juniper	4,5,6,7	Cupressaceae
J. deppeana	Alligator Juniper	10	Cupressaceae
J. erythrocarpa	Redberry Juniper	10	Cupressaceae
J. flaccida	Weeping Juniper	10	Cupressaceae
J. monosperma	One-seed Juniper	8,9,10	Cupressaceae
J. pinchotii	Pinchot Juniper	5,7,8,9,10	Cupressaceae
J. scopulorum	Rocky Mountain Juniper	8,9,10	Cupressaceae
J. silicicola	Southern Red Cedar	2	Cupressaceae
J. virginiana	Eastern Red Cedar	1,3,4,5, 8,9	Cupressaceae
Leucaena pulverulenta	Great Leadtree	6	Leguminosae
L. retusa	Goldenball Leadtree	7,10	Leguminosae
Liquidambar styraciflua	Sweet Gum	1,2,3	Hamamelidaceae
Maclura pomifera	Bois d'Arc	1,3,4,7	Moraceae
Magnolia grandiflora	Southern Magnolia	1	Magnoliaceae
M. pyramidata	Pyramid Magnolia	1	Magnoliaceae
M. virginiana	Sweet Bay	1,2	Magnoliaceae
Malus angustifolia	Southern Crabapple	1	Rosaceae
M. ioensis	Prairie Crabapple	7	Rosaceae
Morus microphylla	Texas Mulberry	4,5,6,7, 8,9,10	Moraceae
M. rubra	Red Mulberry	1,2,3,4, 5,6,7,8	Moraceae
Myrica cerifera	Southern Wax Myrtle	1,2,3	Myricaceae

9

Table 1
(continued)

Species	Common Name	Vegetational Area (see map)	Family
Nyssa aquatica	Water Tupelo	1,2	Cornaceae
N. sylvatica var. *biflora*	Swamp Tupelo	1,2	Cornaceae
N. sylvatica var. *sylvatica*	Black Gum	1,2,3	Cornaceae
Ostrya chisosensis	Chisos Hop Hornbeam	10	Betulaceae
O. knowltonii	Knowlton Hop Hornbeam	10	Betulaceae
O. virginiana	Eastern Hop Hornbeam	1,2	Betulaceae
Parkinsonia aculeata	Retama	6,7,10	Leguminosae
Persea borbonia var. *borbonia*	Red Bay	1,2	Lauraceae
P. borbonia var. *pubescens*	Swamp Bay	1	Lauraceae
Pinus cembroides	Mexican Pinyon	7,10	Pinaceae
P. echinata	Shortleaf Pine	1,2,3	Pinaceae
P. edulis	Pinyon	10(9?)	Pinaceae
P. palustris	Longleaf Pine	1	Pinaceae
P. ponderosa var. *scopulorum*	Rocky Mountain Ponderosa Pine	10	Pinaceae
P. strobiformis	Southwestern White Pine	10	Pinaceae
P. taeda	Loblolly Pine	1,2,3	Pinaceae
Pistacia texana	Texas Pistache	7	Anacardiaceae
Pithecellobium flexicaule	Texas Ebony	2,6	Leguminosae
Planera aquatica	Water Elm	1,2,3	Ulmaceae
Platanus occidentalis	Sycamore	1,2,3,4, 5,6,7	Platanaceae
Populus deltoides var. *deltoides*	Eastern Cottonwood	1,2,3,4, 5,6,7,8	Salicaceae
P. deltoides var. *occidentalis*	Plains Cottonwood	4,5,7,8,9	Salicaceae
P. fremontii var. *mesetae*	Meseta Cottonwood	10	Salicaceae

P. fremontii var. wislizenii	Rio Grande Cottonwood	10	Salicaceae
P. tremuloides	Quaking Aspen	10	Salicaceae
Prosopis glandulosa var. glandulosa	Mesquite	1,2,3,4,5, 6,7,8,9,10	Leguminosae
P. glandulosa var. torreyana	Western Mesquite	10	Leguminosae
P. pubescens	Screwbean	10	Leguminosae
Prunus caroliniana	Cherry Laurel	1,2	Rosaceae
P. mexicana	Mexican Plum	1,2,3,4, 5,7	Rosaceae
P. munsoniana	Munson Plum	4,5,7	Rosaceae
P. murrayana	Murray Plum	10	Rosaceae
P. serotina var. eximia	Escarpment Black Cherry	7	Rosaceae
P. serotina var. rufula	Southwestern Black Cherry	10	Rosaceae
P. serotina var. serotina	Black Cherry	1,2,3,4	Rosaceae
P. umbellata	Flatwoods Plum	1	Rosaceae
Pseudotsuga menziesii var. glauca	Blue Douglas Fir	10	Pinaceae
Quercus alba	White Oak	1,2,3	Fagaceae
Q. arizonica	Arizona White Oak	10	Fagaceae
Q. drummondii	Drummond Post Oak	3,5,6	Fagaceae
Q. emoryi	Emory Oak	10	Fagaceae
Q. falcata	Southern Red Oak	1,2,3	Fagaceae
Q. fusiformis	Escarpment Live Oak	2,3,4,5, 6,7,8	Fagaceae
Q. gambelii	Gambel Oak	10	Fagaceae
Q. glaucoides	Lacey Oak	7,10	Fagaceae
Q. graciliformis	Graceful Oak	10	Fagaceae
Q. gravesii	Chisos Red Oak	7,10	Fagaceae
Q. grisea	Gray Oak	7,10	Fagaceae
Q. hemisphaerica	Coast Laurel Oak	2	Fagaceae
Q. hypoleucoides	Silverleaf Oak	10	Fagaceae
Q. incana	Bluejack Oak	1,2,3	Fagaceae
Q. laurifolia	Laurel Oak	1,2,3	Fagaceae
Q. lyrata	Overcup Oak	1,2,3	Fagaceae
Q. macrocarpa	Bur Oak	2,3,4,5, 7,8	Fagaceae

11

Table 1
(continued)

Species	Common Name	Vegetational Area (see map)	Family
Q. margaretta	Sand Post Oak	1,2,3,4, 5,6	Fagaceae
Q. marilandica	Blackjack Oak	1,2,3,5, 7,8	Fagaceae
Q. michauxii	Swamp Chestnut Oak	1,2	Fagaceae
Q. mohriana	Mohr Oak	7,8,9,10	Fagaceae
Q. muehlenbergii	Chinkapin Oak	4,5,7,10	Fagaceae
Q. nigra	Water Oak	1,2,3	Fagaceae
Q. nuttallii	Nuttall Oak	1	Fagaceae
Q. oblongifolia	Mexican Blue Oak	10	Fagaceae
Q. phellos	Willow Oak	1,2,3	Fagaceae
Q. pungens var. *pungens*	Sandpaper Oak	10	Fagaceae
Q. pungens var. *vaseyana*	Vasey Oak	7,10	Fagaceae
Q. rugosa	Netleaf Oak	10	Fagaceae
Q. shumardii	Shumard Red Oak	1,2,3,4,5	Fagaceae
Q. similis	Bottomland Post Oak	1,2	Fagaceae
Q. sinuata var. *breviloba*	Bigelow Oak	3,4,5,7,8	Fagaceae
Q. sinuata var. *sinuata*	Durand Oak	1,2,3	Fagaceae
Q. stellata	Post Oak	1,2,3,4, 5,6,7,8	Fagaceae
Q. texana	Texas Red Oak	4,5,7	Fagaceae
Q. turbinella	Shrub Live Oak	10	Fagaceae
Q. velutina	Black Oak	1,2,3	Fagaceae
Q. virginiana	Live Oak	1,2,3	Fagaceae
Rhamnus caroliniana	Carolina Buckthorn	1,2,3,4, 5,6,7	Rhamnaceae
Rhus copallina var. *copallina*	Shining Sumac	1,2,3,4, 5,6	Anacardiaceae
R. lanceolata	Prairie Flameleaf Sumac	4,5,7,10	Anacardiaceae
Robinia neomexicana	New Mexico Locust	10	Leguminosae

Sabal mexicana	Texas Palmetto	6	Palmae
Salix amygdaloides	Peachleaf Willow	8,9,10	Salicaceae
S. nigra	Black Willow	1,2,3,4,5, 6,7,8,9,10	Salicaceae
S. taxifolia	Yewleaf Willow	10	Salicaceae
Sambucus caerulea	Blue Elder	10	Caprifoliaceae
Sapindus drummondii	Western Soapberry	1,2,3,4,5, 6,7,8,9,10	Sapindaceae
Sassafras albidum	Sassafras	1,2,3	Lauraceae
Sophora affinis	Eve's Necklace	4,5,7	Leguminosae
Styrax grandifolius	Bigleaf Snowbell	1	Styracaceae
Symplocos tinctoria	Sweetleaf	1,2	Symplocaceae
Taxodium distichum var. *distichum*	Bald Cypress	1,2,3,4, 6,7	Taxodiaceae
T. mucronatum	Montezuma Bald Cypress	6	Taxodiaceae
Tilia caroliniana	Carolina Basswood	1,2,3,7	Tiliaceae
Ulmus alata	Winged Elm	1,2,3,4,5	Ulmaceae
U. americana	American Elm	1,2,3,4, 5,7,8	Ulmaceae
U. crassifolia	Cedar Elm	1,2,3,4, 5,6,7,8	Ulmaceae
U. rubra	Slippery Elm	1,3,4,5,7	Ulmaceae
Vaccinium arboreum	Farkleberry	1,2,3	Ericaceae
Vauquelinia *angustifolia*	Chisos Rosewood	10	Rosaceae
Viburnum rufidulum	Rusty Blackhaw	1,2,3,4,5, 7,8,10	Caprifoliaceae
Yucca carnerosana	Carneros Yucca	10	Liliaceae
Y. elata	Soaptree Yucca	10	Liliaceae
Y. faxoniana	Faxon Yucca	10	Liliaceae
Y. rostrata	Beaked Yucca	10	Liliaceae
Y. torreyi	Torrey Yucca	7,10	Liliaceae
Y. treculeana	Trecul Yucca	2,6,7,10	Liliaceae
Zanthoxylum *clava-herculis*	Hercules'-club	1,2,3,4,5, 6,7,8,9,10	Rutaceae

Table 2
Additional Native Trees of Texas*

Species	Common Name	Family
Aesculus pavia var. *flavescens*		Hippocastanaceae
Cercis canadensis var. *mexicana*	Mexican Redbud	Leguminosae
Cercocarpus montanus var. *argenteus*	Silver Mountain Mahogany	Rosaceae
C. montanus var. *glaber*	Smooth Mountain Mahogany	Rosaceae
Ilex verticillata	Winterberry	Aquifoliaceae
Prunus murrayana	Murray Plum	Rosaceae
Quercus drummondii	Drummond Post Oak	Fagaceae
Q. hemisphaerica	Coast Laurel Oak	Fagaceae
Q. oblongifolia	Mexican Blue Oak	Fagaceae
Vauquelinia angustifolia	Chisos Rosewood	Rosaceae

*These trees are not listed for Texas in *Checklist of United States Trees* but are listed by Correll and Johnston (with the exception of the newly discovered *Quercus oblongifolia*) and are included in this book (see Table 1).

Table 3
Possible Additional Native Trees of Texas*

Species	Common Name	Family
Acer saccharum	Sugar Maple	Aceraceae
Aesculus glabra var. *glabra*	Ohio Buckeye	Hippocastanaceae
Crataegus anamesa	Coast Hawthorn	Rosaceae
C. brachyphylla	Shortleaf Hawthorn	Rosaceae
C. brazoria	Brazos Hawthorn	Rosaceae
C. bushii	Bush Hawthorn	Rosaceae
C. cherokeensis	Cherokee Hawthorn	Rosaceae
C. engelmannii	Engelmann Hawthorn	Rosaceae
C. glabriuscula	Smooth Hawthorn	Rosaceae
C. invisa	Turkey Hawthorn	Rosaceae
C. limaria	Shiny Hawthorn	Rosaceae
C. pearsonii	Pearson Hawthorn	Rosaceae
C. poliophylla	Rosemary Hawthorn	Rosaceae
C. pyracanthoides	Pyracantha Hawthorn	Rosaceae
C. sabineana	Sabine Hawthorn	Rosaceae
C. stenosepala	Narrow-sepal Hawthorn	Rosaceae
C. sublobulata	San Augustine Hawthorn	Rosaceae
C. sutherlandensis	Sutherland Hawthorn	Rosaceae
C. viburnifolia	Viburnum-leaf Hawthorn	Rosaceae
C. warneri	Warner Hawthorn	Rosaceae
Halesia carolina	Carolina Silverbell	Styracaceae
Ilex montana	Mountain Winterberry	Aquifoliaceae
Magnolia fraseri	Mountain Magnolia	Magnoliaceae
Sambucus mexicana	Mexican Elder	Caprifoliaceae

*Although some authors list these trees as growing in Texas, they are not included in this book (see synonyms in *Crataegus*, Table 8).

Table 4
Plants From CUST That Are Considered Shrubs

Species	Common Name	Family
Acacia berlandieri	Guajillo	Leguminosae
A. rigidula	Blackbrush	Leguminosae
*Amelanchier arborea**	Serviceberry	Rosaceae
Asimina parviflora	Dwarf Pawpaw	Annonaceae
Avicennia germinans	Black Mangrove	Avicenniaceae
Baccharis halimifolia	Sea Myrtle	Compositae
Bauhinia lunarioides	Anacacho Orchid Tree	Leguminosae
Cephalanthus occidentalis	Buttonbush	Rubiaceae
C. salicifolius	Willowleaf Buttonbush	Rubiaceae
Citharexylum berlandieri	Fiddlewood	Verbenaceae
Cornus drummondii	Roughleaf Dogwood	Cornaceae
*C. racemosa** (C. foemina?)	Gray Dogwood	Cornaceae
C. stricta (C. foemina?)	Swamp Dogwood	Cornaceae
Crataegus uniflora	One-flower Hawthorn	Rosaceae
*Erythrina herbacea***	Coral Bean	Leguminosae
Euonymus atropurpureus	Wahoo	Celastraceae
Eysenhardtia texana	Texas Kidneywood	Leguminosae
Forestiera angustifolia	Texas Forestiera	Oleaceae
Guaiacum angustifolium	Guayacan	Zygophyllaceae
Hamamelis virginiana	Witch Hazel	Hamamelidaceae
Koeberlinia spinosa	Allthorn	Koeberliniaceae
Leitneria floridana	Corkwood	Leitneriaceae
Myrica heterophylla	Evergreen Bayberry	Myricaceae
Pithecellobium pallens	Tenaza	Leguminosae
Prunus angustifolia	Chickasaw Plum	Rosaceae
P. virginiana	Chokecherry	Rosaceae
Ptelea trifoliata	Wafer Ash	Rutaceae
Quercus havardii	Havard Shin Oak	Fagaceae
*Q. toumeyi**	Toumey Oak	Fagaceae
Rhamnus betulaefolia	Birchleaf Buckthorn	Rhamnaceae
Rhus choriophylla	Mearn Sumac	Anacardiaceae
R. glabra	Smooth Sumac	Anacardiaceae
R. microphylla	Littleleaf Sumac	Anacardiaceae
R. virens	Evergreen Sumac	Anacardiaceae
Sabal minor	Dwarf Palmetto	Palmae

Salix caroliniana	Coastal Plain Willow	Salicaceae
S. exigua	Coyote Willow	Salicaceae
S. lasiolepis	Arroyo Willow	Salicaceae
Sambucus canadensis var. *canadensis*	American Elder	Caprifoliaceae
Solanum erianthum	Mullein Nightshade	Solanaceae
Sophora secundiflora	Mescal Bean	Leguminosae
Stewartia malacodendron	Silky Camellia	Theaceae
Styrax americanus	American Snowbell	Styracaceae
S. platanifolius var. *platanifolius*	Sycamore-leaf Snowbell	Styracaceae
S. platanifolius var. *stellata**	Hairy Sycamore-leaf Snowbell	Styracaceae
Tecoma stans var. *angustata*	Esperanza	Bignoniaceae
Toxicodendron vernix	Poison Sumac	Anacardiaceae
Ungnadia speciosa	Mexican Buckeye	Sapindaceae
Viburnum nudum	Possum-haw Viburnum	Caprifoliaceae
Zanthoxylum fagara	Lime Prickly Ash	Rutaceae
Z. hirsutum	Toothache Tree	Rutacaea

*Not listed in Texas in *Checklist of United States Trees.*
**In northern Texas this plant is a herbaceous perennial.

Table 5
Trees From CUST That Are Not Accepted

Species	Common Name	Family
Quercus falcata var. *pagodifolia*	Cherrybark Oak	Fagaceae
Q. tardifolia	Lateleaf Oak	Fagaceae

Table 6
Extinct (in Texas) or "Lost" Native Trees of Texas

Species	Common Name	Family
Crataegus douglasii	Black Hawthorn	Rosaceae
Gymnocladus dioica	Kentucky Coffee Tree	Leguminosae
Ilex cassine	Dahoon Holly	Aquifoliaceae
I. myrtifolia	Myrtle Holly	Aquifoliaceae
Leucaena greggii	Gregg Leadtree	Leguminosae
Populus angustifolia	Narrowleaf Cottonwood	Salicaceae

Table 7
Naturalized Trees of Texas

Species	Common Name	Family
Ailanthus altissima	Ailanthus	Simaroubaceae
Albizia julibrissin	Mimosa	Leguminosae
Aleurites fordii	Tung Tree	Euphorbiaceae
Broussonetia papyrifera	Paper Mulberry	Moraceae
Caesalpinia gilliesii	Paradise Poinciana	Leguminosae
C. pulcherrima	Flower Fence	Leguminosae
Catalpa bignonioides	Southern Catalpa	Bignoniaceae
C. speciosa	Northern Catalpa	Bignoniaceae
Cinnamomum camphora	Camphor Tree	Lauraceae
Elaeagnus angustifolia	Russian Olive	Eleagnaceae
Leucaena leucocephala	Leadtree	Leguminosae
Ligustrum japonicum	Japanese Ligustrum	Oleaceae
L. sinense	Chinese Privet	Oleaceae
Melia azedarach	Chinaberry	Meliaceae
Morus alba	White Mulberry	Moraceae
M. nigra	Black Mulberry	Moraceae
Nicotiana glauca	Tree Tobacco	Solanaceae
Paulownia tomentosa	Royal Paulownia	Scrophulariaceae
Poncirus trifoliata	Trifoliate Orange	Rutaceae
Prunus persica	Peach	Rosaceae
Pyrus calleryana	Callery Pear	Rosaceae
P. communis	Pear	Rosaceae
Robinia pseudoacacia	Black Locust	Leguminosae
Sapium sebiferum	Chinese Tallow Tree	Euphorbiaceae
Schinus longifolius	Longleaf Pepper Tree	Anacardiaceae
S. molle	Pepper Tree	Anacardiaceae
Tamarix chinensis	Tamarisk	Tamaricaceae
T. gallica	French Tamarisk	Tamaricaceae
Vitex agnus-castus	Chaste Tree	Verbenaceae
Ziziphus jujuba	Jujube	Rhamnaceae

Vegetational Areas of Texas

When climate (rainfall, temperature, wind, and humidity), topographical factors (elevation and slope), edaphic factors (geology, parent material, soils, erosion by wind and water), and biotic factors (man, insects, diseases, grazing, and fire) have reacted with the force of time, broad belts of distinctive vegetation are formed. These areas have many different names, such as ecoregions, biotic regions, plant communities, plant associations, land resource areas, and vegetational areas. Each area has a unique combination of soils, climate, and other factors that create a flora distinct from all other regions. A knowledge of these vegetational areas in regards to soil, climate, and type of flora will be most helpful in the understanding of the trees of Texas.

Although all factors interact and are, more or less, of equal importance, there is little doubt that rainfall, or lack of it, is of prime importance in the creation and maintenance of the vegetational areas of Texas. The amount of rainfall increases from roughly 7 inches in El Paso to more than 55 inches at Orange in extreme southeastern Texas. Of great interest are the 25- and 30-inch rainfall lines, which for the most part occur between the 98th and 100th meridians. This is a rather narrow vegetational transition zone. According to some authors, the prairies in this area give way to plains, and forests become mere woodlands. Tall and mid grasses extend into this area from east of the 98th meridian, while the area west of the 100th meridian consists mostly of mid- to shortgrass prairies.

W. L. Bray did one of the first vegetational surveys of Texas in 1906. This was followed by B. C. Tharp in 1926 and 1939. In 1937, V. L. Cory and H. B. Parks divided Texas into seven plant areas. These divisions were very broad; they considered the Post Oak Savannah, Grand Prairie, East and West Cross Timbers, and Blackland Prairies as one entity and put the High Plains and Rolling Plains together in a vegetational area. In 1938, W. T. Carter proposed fourteen different areas of vegetation in Texas and eleven natural geographic divisions. In 1952, Tharp divided Texas into eighteen vegetational regions based on ecology and plant associations. In 1960, F. W. Gould, G. O. Hoffman, and C. A. Rechenthin separated Texas into ten vegetational areas and further refined them in 1962. The Texas Agricultural Experiment Station published its "General Soil Map of Texas" in 1973 and divided Texas into fifteen land resource areas. The Lyndon B. Johnson School of Public Affairs, of the University of Texas, sponsored the Winedale Conference in 1978. Here, an interdisciplinary group of scientists and laymen classified Texas into eleven natural regions, with 29 subregions (although 2 of the subregions are not delineated). In 1978, the Soil Conservation Service (SCS) divided Texas into six land resource regions with twenty land resource areas. The SCS land resource regions gave credence to agricultural use of the land,

and its land resource areas are subdivisions of the land resource regions.

By far, the most comprehensive vegetational mapping of Texas is found in *The Vegetation Types of Texas, Including Cropland*, published in 1984 by the Texas Parks and Wildlife Department. Forty-five vegetation types (plant associations) are mapped for the state.

The divisions outlined by Gould et al. in *Vegetational Areas of Texas* will be used here because they are simple and adequate.

VEGETATIONAL AREAS OF TEXAS

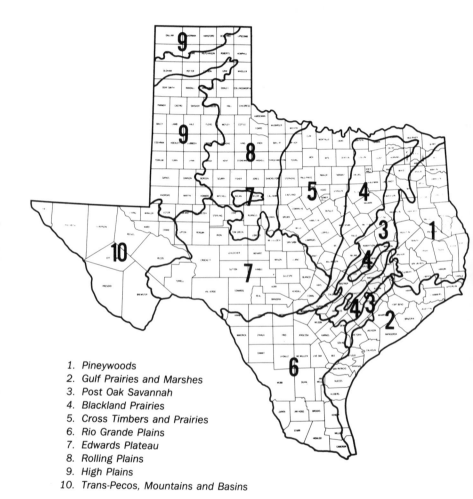

1. Pineywoods
2. Gulf Prairies and Marshes
3. Post Oak Savannah
4. Blackland Prairies
5. Cross Timbers and Prairies
6. Rio Grande Plains
7. Edwards Plateau
8. Rolling Plains
9. High Plains
10. Trans-Pecos, Mountains and Basins

Source: Adapted from F. W. Gould, G. O. Hoffman, and C. A. Rechenthin,
Vegetational Areas of Texas, Texas A&M University leaflet 492.

AVERAGE ANNUAL PRECIPITATION
(INCHES)

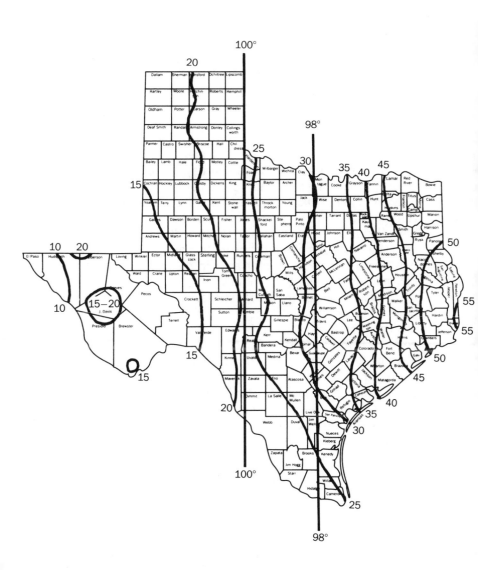

Pineywoods

The Pineywoods of east Texas contain about 15,000,000 acres of land. In the Big Thicket area of Polk, Tyler, Hardin, Liberty, and Orange counties, landforms are gently rolling to almost flat. Farther north, the land becomes quite hilly. Soils are usually sandy to sandy loam and acidic to highly acid. I am impressed by four distinct areas in the Pineywoods: the Big Thicket, the Longleaf Pine Forest, the Redlands, and the Sabine Uplift. The Big Thicket is an area of high rainfall and slow drainage, with many bogs and baygalls containing rare orchids. The Longleaf Pine Forest covers parts of Jasper, Newton, Tyler, Polk, and other counties. Anderson, Rusk, Nacogdoches, and San Augustine counties occur on the fabled Redlands of east Texas. These redland soils are the richest and consist of reddish loam to clay-loam soils high in iron. From the Sabine Uplift area in the north, east Texas becomes quite dissected and hilly.

Elevation ranges from near sea level to almost 500 feet. Rainfall totals about 45 inches on the west to almost 60 inches in southeast Newton County. The average annual temperature is roughly 66° F, with a growing season of 230 days near the Red River to more than 250 days in the south. East Texas is part of the Southeastern Mixed Forest, where pines are fire disclimax species. The Pineywoods have a rich tree flora with oaks, beech, magnolia, sweet gum, pine, maple, hickory, and elm. Today the land is largely used for timber and as pastures for cattle.

Gulf Prairies and Marshes

The Gulf Prairies and Marshes contain about 9,500,000 acres of land along the Gulf Coast of Texas. The marshes are narrow bands of vegetation on the coast, and the Gulf Prairies occupy the greater portion of the area inland. Elevation rarely exceeds 150 feet over the entire area. Soils of the marsh area are acid sands, sandy loams, and clay. The Gulf Marshes contain many plants that can tolerate large amounts of salts. The Gulf Prairies soils are quite rich in nutrients and contain more clay than the marsh areas.

Rainfall varies from around 25 inches near Brownsville to more than 55 inches at Sabine Pass. Annual average temperatures will range from 74° F in Cameron County to 70° F along the coast from Nueces to Jefferson and Orange counties. The growing season is quite long, lasting 365 days near Brownsville, 306 days at Corpus Christi and Victoria, 331 days on Galveston Island, and 312 days at Port Arthur.

The Gulf Prairies consist largely of tallgrass prairie with Big Bluestem, Little Bluestem, and Indian Grass. Notable trees are true *Quercus virginiana* (Live Oak), occurring along the eastern coast from the mouth of the Sabine to the Brazos River, *Juniperus silicicola* (Southern Red Cedar), and *Quercus sinuata* var. *sinuata* (Durand White Oak). The Gulf Marshes are used for pastureland, and the rich prairie soils are farmed in rice, cotton, grain sorghum, and corn. Many acres of both planted and native pasture are utilized by cattle.

Post Oak Savannah

The Post Oak Savannah occupies approximately 8,500,000 acres, and some people consider it part of the Pineywoods area. Here it is considered part of the true tallgrass prairie association. When first settled, the Post Oak Savannah consisted of prairie with trees occurring in widely spaced clumps (mottes). With the cessation of fires on the prairie, the trees increased in number, and today the savannah aspect is largely missing.

Landforms consist of small rolling hills, and elevations range from 300 to 500 feet. Soils are usually acidic, with sands and sandy loams on the uplands, clay to clay loams on the bottomlands, and a dense clay pan underlying all soil types. From west to east, rainfall varies from about 35 to almost 50 inches. Annual average temperatures range from 65° F north to 70° F south, with 222 days of growing season in the Red River Valley to almost 275 days south of Cuero.

Presettlement climax vegetation of the Post Oak Savannah consisted of widely spaced *Quercus stellata* (Post Oak) and *Q. marilandica* (Blackjack Oak) with an understory of tallgrasses such as Little Bluestem, Indian Grass, and Switch Grass. Almost assuredly Post Oak and Blackjack Oak are post-climax to this area. Today, the Post Oak Savannah is used largely for "improved" pasture, with vast acreages sodded to Bermuda Grass and seeded to Bahia Grass.

A few other trees of the Post Oak Savannah are *Sassafras albidum* (Sassafras), *Quercus falcata* (Southern Red Oak), *Cornus florida* (Flowering Dogwood), *Ilex opaca* (American Holly), *I. vomitoria* (Yaupon Holly), *Ulmus alata* (Winged Elm), and *Acer rubrum* (Red Maple).

POWELL'S CITY OF BOOKS
JC W BURNSIDE
L A ', OR 97209
728-876-7300   1-800-878-7323
728-4651

SKU	PRICE
1 Field Guide To Texas Trees	11.50

Total # of items in this sale: 1

Purchase

Total Sale   USD$ 11.50

Cash $15.00

Your Change $3.50

2/17/2018 1:18:34 PM
[Store: 1] [Register: 1] [Cashier: 553]

WE ACCEPT RETURNS WITHIN
30 DAYS OF PURCHASE
VINYL ALBUMS AND GAMES
MUST BE UNOPENED.

THANK YOU FOR SHOPPING AT
POWELL'S CITY OF BOOKS.

RETURN POLICY

We accept returns within 30 days of purchase with your receipt. Your refund will correspond to the original form of payment. Merchandise should be in the same condition as at the time of purchase; any and all media included with new books must be unopened.

Thank you for shopping at Powell's.

POWELL'S CITY of BOOKS | 800.878.7323 POWELLS.COM

RETURN POLICY

We accept returns within 30 days of purchase with your receipt. Your refund will correspond to the original form of payment. Merchandise should be in the same condition as at the time of purchase; any and all media included with new books must be unopened.

Thank you for shopping at Powell's.

POWELL'S CITY of BOOKS | 800.878.7323 POWELLS.COM

RETURN POLICY

Blackland Prairies

The Blackland Prairies contain approximately 11,500,000 acres of some of the richest, naturally fertile soil in the world. The land is nearly level to gently rolling and ranges in elevation from 300 to more than 800 feet. Soils of the Blackland proper are deep, black calcareous clay soils, high in organic matter (over 5 percent), rich in most nutrients but generally low in phosphorus. Transitional soils on the eastern border and in the Fayette and San Antonio prairies are lighter in color and slightly acidic. The San Antonio Prairie is the site of the Old San Antonio Road (Texas Highway 21 from near Bastrop east to the Trinity River) that linked San Antonio to the Spanish missions of eastern Texas. Little pristine prairie is left.

Rainfall varies from 32 inches in the west to more than 45 inches east of Paris in northeastern Texas. Average annual temperatures range from about 66° F near the Red River to 70° F near LaGrange in south Texas. The growing season is approximately 228 days at Paris to 276 days near Gonzales.

The Blackland is true tallgrass prairie, with little bluestem as the climax dominant. The waterways abound with trees such as *Quercus macrocarpa* (Bur Oak), *Q. shumardii* (Shumard Red Oak), *Q. muehlenbergii* (Chinkapin Oak), *Ulmus crassifolia* (Cedar Elm), *U. americana* (American Elm), *Maclura pomifera* (Bois d'Arc), *Gleditsia triacanthos* (Honey Locust), and *Carya illinoensis* (Pecan).

Cross Timbers and Prairies

The Cross Timbers and Prairies consist of about 17,000,000 acres in four land resource areas: the East Cross Timbers, the West Cross Timbers, the Grand Prairie, and the North Central Prairies. The East Cross Timbers contain approximately 1,000,000 acres, with 3,000,000 acres in the West Cross Timbers, 6,500,000 acres in the Grand Prairie, and 6,500,000 acres in the North Central Prairies. This land is hilly, rolling, deeply cut, and well drained. The East and West Cross Timbers have sandy to loam soils that are slightly acidic to quite basic. The North Central Prairies have dark brown sandy to clay loam soils that are generally neutral to only slightly acidic, while the Grand Prairie has shallow, well-drained, dark-colored calcareous clay soils.

Elevation ranges from about 600 to almost 1,700 feet. Rainfall varies from about 25 inches in the North Central Prairies to almost 35 inches in the East Cross Timbers. Average annual temperatures range around 66–67° F, and the growing season ranges from 228 days at Henrietta to approximately 243 days at Brownwood.

It is rather surprising that the vegetation in these areas is so similar in spite of the wide differences in the soils. However, the trees vary somewhat—the East and West Cross Timbers are true Post Oak Savannah with an overstory of Post Oak and Blackjack Oak widely spaced and Little Bluestem as the climax dominant understory. Post climax in these two areas is probably Post Oak–Blackjack Oak. Escarpment Live Oak (*Quercus fusiformis*) is prevalent in all but the East Cross Timbers, with Mesquite (*Prosopis glandulosa*) being especially prevalent in the Western Cross Timbers and North Central Prairies.

Rio Grande Plains

The Rio Grande Plains contain 20,000,000 acres of almost level to gently rolling land with elevations ranging from sea level to 1,000 feet. Soils are generally extremely basic to slightly acidic and range from deep sands in the Wild Horse Desert to tight clays and clay loams.

Rainfall varies from 16 inches in the west to almost 30 inches in the east. The Rio Grande Plains is a land of recurring severe droughts. The weather is usually quite balmy, with the average annual temperature ranging from 72° F in the north to more than 74° F around Brownsville. The growing season extends from about 254 days at Uvalde to 365 days in some years around Brownsville.

A distinctive part of the Rio Grande Plains is the area known as the Rio Grande Valley, or simply the Valley, which is in Cameron County, although some authors add Hidalgo and Willacy counties, and others add Starr County as well. The only true subtropical area of Texas is in Cameron County and to the south and east of Brownsville.

The Rio Grande Plains were once a rich grassland, or at least a savannah-type grassland. The savannahs consisted of *Quercus fusiformis* (Live Oak) and *Prosopis glandulosa* (Mesquite) with Seacoast Bluestem, Indian Grass, Switch Grass, and Sideoats Grama. The native palm *Sabal mexicana* (Texas Palmetto) still occurs in small colonies along the Rio Grande southeast of Brownsville.

Edwards Plateau

The Edwards Plateau has 24,000,000 acres of more or less rough, stony lands. This is the Hill Country of Texas. The spectacular canyons of the Balcones Escarpment, the Central Basin or Central Mineral Region, and Stockton Plateau are included in this area. The Lampasas Cut Plains area is considered by some as a northern extension of the Edwards Plateau, but others would consider it the southern terminus of the Cross Timbers and Prairies region. Elevations range from 1,000 to more than 3,000 feet.

Rainfall ranges from 12 inches in the Stockton Plateau area to almost 33 inches at the Balcones Escarpment line. Average annual temperatures are 64° F north to almost 67° F on the southern edge, and the growing season varies from 227 to 303 days. Soils range from neutral to slightly acidic sands and sandy loams in the Central Basin, to thin, rocky, highly calcareous clays and clay loams over the rest of the plateau area.

The Central Basin is a combination of Mesquite savannah and oak to oak-hickory woodlands. The western Edwards Plateau proper is Live Oak—Mesquite savannah grading into desert grassland on the Stockton Plateau. From the standpoint of diversity, the most interesting areas are the steep canyons and rocky ridges of the Balcones canyonlands on the eastern and southern edges of the plateau. Some of the trees found here are *Acer grandidentatum* (Bigtooth Maple), *Cotinus obovatus* (American Smoke Tree), *Quercus fusiformis* (Escarpment Live Oak), *Q. texana* (Texas Red Oak), *Arbutus texana* (Texas Madrone), *Q. glaucoides* (Lacey Oak), *Q. sinuata* var. *breviloba* (Bigelow Oak), *Prunus serotina* var. *eximia* (Escarpment Black Cherry), *Pinus cembroides* (Mexican Pinyon), and *Juniperus ashei* (Ashe Juniper).

Rolling Plains

The Rolling Plains consist of about 24,000,000 acres of rather rough topography. This area is part of the Great Plains region of the central United States. Most of the soils are neutral to slightly basic, and in some areas, outcroppings of Permian redbeds, gypsum beds, and saltbeds occur. All rivers flowing out of the Rolling Plains are high in salts that were picked up as they passed over the saltbeds.

Elevations range from 800 feet on the east to 3,000 feet in the northeast. The beds of the Red and Canadian rivers are of Permian origin and are part of the Rolling Plains. Rainfall varies from about 16 inches at Big Spring to about 27 inches at Wichita Falls. Average annual temperatures are 60° F in the Canadian River bottoms to almost 64° F in the southern Rolling Plains, with a growing season of 191 days at Follett and 233 days at San Angelo.

Originally, the vegetation was tallgrass prairie on the deep sands with dominant species such as Little Bluestem, Sand Bluestem, Indian Grass, and Switch Grass to midgrass prairie on the clay and clay loams with dominants such as Sideoats Grama, Blue Grama, Hairy Grama, and Western Wheat Grass. Mesquite has become quite severe after 100 or more years of grazing. Other trees occurring along the waterways and in the canyons around the Caprock are *Celtis reticulata* (Netleaf Hackberry), *Populus deltoides* var. *occidentalis* (Plains Cottonwood), *Quercus mohriana* (Mohr Oak), *Juniperus pinchotii* (Pinchot Juniper), *J. monosperma* (One-seed Juniper), and *J. scopulorum* (Rocky Mountain Juniper).

High Plains

The High Plains contain approximately 20,000,000 acres of sandy to heavy, dark, calcareous clay soils lying over an impervious caliche layer. This caliche layer is the fabled caprock and is usually 2 to 5 feet below the surface. The High Plains are dissected by the eastward-flowing Canadian River, and the Llano Estacado lies to the south of that river.

Approximately 10,000,000 years ago, the Rocky Mountains were much taller, perhaps 25,000 to 30,000 feet tall. The warm air from the Gulf of Mexico contained a lot of moisture, and when it reached the Rocky Mountains, the moisture condensed in the form of rain. This precipitation was great, some think as high as 800 inches per year. Erosion was tremendous, and as a result, the high, level plateau called the High Plains was formed. Sediments in the Llano Estacado alone are thought to be 6,000 cubic miles, which would be a mountain 300 miles long, 20 miles wide, and 5,000 feet high. This plateau most likely started eroding almost as soon as it was formed. The eastern edge of the Caprock escarpment once extended many miles farther east into Texas.

Present elevations in the High Plains range from about 4,700 feet in the northwest to 3,000 feet in the southeast. The average frost-free season is 225 days in the south and 179 days in the north. The average annual temperature is about 59° F.

A unique feature of these tablelands is the many playa lakes, which are shallow bodies of water that dot the plains and are usually dry. Rainfall ranges from 21 inches on the eastern edge to as low as 12 inches on the southwestern edge. Today the High Plains are irrigated from the vast Ogallala formation with some 200,000,000 acre-feet of fossil water.

At one time the High Plains was a vast pine woodland (perhaps 10,000 to 12,000 years ago), but today it is essentially treeless and is classified as shortgrass to midgrass prairie.

Trans-Pecos

The Trans-Pecos is 20,000,000 acres of mountains, deserts, and arid grasslands in far western Texas. The soils vary from deep sands to shallow stony clays. The Chisos, Davis, Chinati, Vieja, Quitman, Eagle, and lesser mountain ranges are igneous in origin with acidic soils. The Apache, Delaware, Diablo, Glass, Del Norte, and Guadalupe mountain ranges are limestone in origin with the soils being quite alkaline.

Elevation ranges from 1,700 feet in the valley of the Rio Grande in Brewster County to 8,751 feet atop Guadalupe Peak in Culberson County. Rainfall ranges from less than 8 inches in El Paso to around 20 inches at the summit of Mount Livermore in the Davis Mountains. The average annual temperature over the entire area is about 64° F, with a growing season of 240 days along the Rio Grande and less than 210 days in the mountain ranges.

Well over 2,000 species of plants can be found in the Trans-Pecos, with 1 out of every 12 species of the Texas flora endemic to the Trans-Pecos. The flora is exceedingly rich and varied, with plants coming in from the plains, the mountains, and Mexico. Some of the vegetation types found in the Trans-Pecos are Tobosa—Black Grama grassland, yucca-Ocotillo shrub, Creosote-Tarbush shrub, Creosote-Lechuguilla shrub, Creosote-Mesquite shrub, Four-wing Saltbush—Creosote shrub, Mesquite-Lotebush brush, Mesquite-Sandsage shrub, Mesquite-juniper brush, Havard Shin Oak brush, Gray Oak—Pinyon Pine—Alligator Juniper parks/woods, and Ponderosa Pine—Douglas Fir parks/forest associations.

The Native Trees of Texas

No book has been written about *all* the native trees of Texas. I hope that situation is now rectified and this will become a handbook because of its lists and distribution maps.

A word about the maps: If a distribution area covers an entire county, that tree does not necessarily occur everywhere in that county. Also, if the map shows the Escarpment Live Oak, for example, to be growing in Tarrant, Parker, and Palo Pinto counties but not in Denton, Wise, Jack, Young, and Throckmorton, the tree is not necessarily absent from those counties. It just means that this tree is so widespread that the different university herbaria simply don't have the space to house the same species from many locations. (Almost all distribution maps are constructed from herbarium specimens, although several of these maps are from the author's own records.) There will be many cases, however, where a tree is not shown in a county simply because it is not known to exist in that county; that is, a specimen has not been deposited in an herbarium.

The trees are listed alphabetically by genus, thus—*Acacia, Acer,* through *Zanthoxylum*—and then alphabetically by species within the genus, thus—*Acacia farnesiana, A. greggii,* through *A. wrightii.*

No climatic varieties have been listed, although several may be mentioned in the text.

Finally, not all the trees in Texas have been discovered. There will probably be no new species per se, but other trees known outside the borders of Texas may be in the state. As can be ascertained in this book, the trees that are in Texas now are but little understood. It is believed all the known trees of Texas are covered in this publication in one list or another. A consensus on correct nomenclature and identification was strived for. Failing that, the author of course is responsible for any missed diagnosis.

Acacia (acacia)

Leguminosae (legume family)

In Texas, there are 5 species of *Acacia* that are trees and 7 species that are shrubs or herbaceous perennials. The United States has 8 tree species, and worldwide there are possibly as many as 800 species. The Texas trees are mostly found in the Rio Grande Plains and the southern Trans-Pecos. However, Wright, Gregg, and Roemer acacias are also found on the western Edwards Plateau and southern Rolling Plains. Generally, acacias are found growing in dry, rocky limestone soils. Exceptions are the Huisache and Huisachillo, which can be found on sandy loams to heavy clay, neutral soils of the Rio Grande Plains.

The leaves of acacias are twice compound with very small leaflets. The flowers occur in round or globular inflorescences as in Roemer, Huisache, and Huisachillo acacia, or they might occur in definite spikes as on Gregg and Wright acacia. They are usually quite fragrant, with stamens numbering more than twenty. Colors range from bright gold on the Huisache and Huisachillo to a creamy light yellow or even white.

Acacias, with the exception of Huisache, are superb honey plants. Huisache is cultivated worldwide for its fragrant flowers, which are used in the perfume industry.

The fruit is a turgid legume and is usually linear. All acacias are lightly to heavily browsed. Acacia wood is hard, heavy, and hot burning.

Acacia farnesiana
(*Acacia smallii*)

Huisache

(Sweet Acacia, Cassie, Texas Huisache)

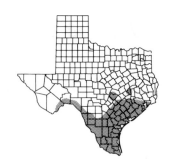

Huisache grows to heights of 20 to 30 feet and is found on the heavier, wetter clays and clay loams of the Rio Grande Plains and up the Rio Grande to Big Bend National Park in Brewster County. It has been planted all the way up the coast to Houston and has become naturalized in great thickets near Victoria in Victoria County and College Station in Brazos County. There is one small colony on the southern edge of Austin in Travis County. The trees in Austin and those at Bryan and College Station flower infrequently. There is one lone Huisache high up in the Basin in Big Bend National Park. This tree occurs above one mile in elevation and generally flowers quite well, but the severe weather in December 1983 froze more than half of the top of the tree.

Huisache is a lovely tree with an intense fragrance while in bloom. The globular inflorescences of bright gold flowers are borne in profusion from February through April. The leaves are twice compound with 2 to 8 pairs of pinnae and 10 to 25 pairs of small, dark green leaflets. The fruit pod is distinctive among the Texas acacias, for it is a rounded cylinder less than 3 inches long that does not shatter on ripening.

The wood is reddish brown, hard and dense, and makes excellent firewood. The branches are armed with paired spines up to 2 inches in length. Nevertheless, the young tender leaves and branchlets are heavily browsed by domestic livestock and wildlife. According to the late H. B. Parks, the pollen of Huisache is a good bee food, but the flowers contribute no nectar to the honey flow.

40

Acacia greggii

Gregg Acacia

(Devil's Claw, Texas Catclaw, Catclaw Acacia, Gregg Catclaw, Una de Gato, Catclaw)

Gregg Acacia is a large shrub of 5 to 6 feet to a small tree of 15 to 20 feet and is armed with catclawlike prickles on the branches and branchlets. It sometimes occurs in dense thickets, and because of these recurved prickles, the grove is impenetrable. It then becomes a haven for small mammals and birds. Gregg Acacia occurs in the western Edwards Plateau, southern Rolling Plains, High Plains, eastern Rio Grande Plains, and the Trans-Pecos. It is found on shallow caliche soils to deep sand that is almost always alkaline in nature.

Gregg Acacia and Wright Acacia are difficult to tell apart, both in the field and on a herbarium sheet, although Wright Acacia has leaflets about twice the size of Gregg Acacia and is usually a larger tree.

The seed pods of Gregg Acacia are quite contorted, and the seeds are fairly orbicular in outline. The short spikes of flowers are creamy white to creamy yellow, about one half to two thirds of an inch long, and are a source of excellent honey. The shrub form of Gregg Acacia lines the street leading to the schoolhouse at Robert Lee in Coke County. The tree form occurs on the deep sands between Kermit and Monahans in Winkler and Ward counties and in Loving County between Mentone and Kermit.

Cattle will browse on tender new growth of Gregg Acacia but only when other forage is lacking. It is extremely drought tolerant and is useful for landscape purposes in areas of light rainfall and short water supplies.

Acacia roemeriana

Roemer Acacia

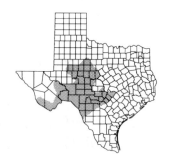

Roemer Acacia grows in dry limestone or gravelly soils from the northern Rio Grande Plains, across the Edwards Plateau to Jones and Taylor counties in the Rolling Plains, and west to Howard, Tom Green, Brewster, and Presidio counties in the Trans-Pecos. Anywhere that there is good, deep soil it grows to 15 or 20 feet. I have seen it in Edwards County as a scraggly shrub of 3 to 6 feet growing on thin limestone hillsides with pinyon. In dry creek beds in Crockett and Terrell counties it forms a tree of 10 to 12 feet, whereas at the mouth of Bee Cave Creek in the Chalk Mountains of Brewster County, it attains heights of over 20 feet and has a trunk diameter of 3 to 4 inches.

The leaves are bipinnately compound with one to three pairs of pinnae and three to eight pairs of leaflets. The small globe-shaped flowers are greenish white to white and are a good source of honey. It is drought resistant and fairly cold hardy, as are Gregg and Wright Acacia.

Acacia tortuosa
(*A. schaffneri* var. *bravoensis*)

Huisachillo

(Dwarf Huisache, Twisted Acacia)

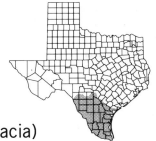

To most people, Huisachillo is a shrubby version of Huisache. Huisachillo regularly grows into a tree of 15 to 20 feet on the northern edge of the Rio Grande Plains near Spofford in Kinney County. It generally grows on limestone soils in the Rio Grande Plains and extreme southern edge of the Edwards Plateau. It seems to tolerate much more cold than its taller, more famous, and better-known relative, Huisache. The seed pod of Huisachillo is more than 2½ to 3 inches long and is covered with downy hairs, distinguishing it from Huisache, which is glabrous, less than 2½ to 3 inches long, and much more woody and rounded.

Acacia wrightii

Wright Acacia

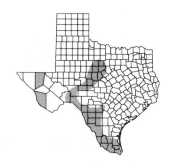

Wright Acacia grows from 20 to 30 feet in height, although in some areas it is a shrub. It grows on the Rio Grande Plains and Edwards Plateau; in Culberson, Presidio, and Terrell counties in the Trans-Pecos; and in Taylor, Jones, Shackelford, and other counties in the Red Rolling Plains to at least Stephens County in the Cross Timbers and Prairies. It occurs in dry, rocky limestone soils on prairies and plateaus. It reaches its maximum height in the Montell-Uvalde-Spofford area, especially in the Turkey Mountains and the dry washes of the west prong of the Nueces River. In the Abilene-Baird area it is generally a shrub, although it is a tree in protected locations.

Wright Acacia is the most cold-hardy acacia, having survived the winter of 1983 as far north as Abilene and Dallas when temperatures were below freezing for 296 consecutive hours. Wright Acacia is a superb honey tree and—along with Guajillo, Gregg, and Roemer acacias—is used to make Uvalde honey, which is a clear, mild, excellent honey of great repute. With its clusters of fragrant white flower spikes, feathery leaves, and relative freedom from insect pests and diseases, it is a welcome landscape tree for west Texas. It is highly drought tolerant and, once established, requires little supplemental water.

Acer (maple)

Aceraceae (maple family)

There are approximately 120 species of maple worldwide, with 13 in the United States and 5 in Texas. Chalk Maple and Southern Sugar Maple occur primarily in the Pineywoods, and Red Maple occurs in the Pineywoods and the eastern Gulf Prairies and Marshes. Box Elder is found in eastern and central Texas, with Bigtooth Maple occurring in secluded canyons of central Texas and in the mountain ranges of the Trans-Pecos.

The identification of maples is quite controversial, and in the latest interpretation of this problem, it has been decided that *Acer saccharum* (Sugar Maple) does not grow in Texas. However, in rather sterile, deep, sandy soils in southeastern Texas near Woodville in Tyler County and Burkeville in Newton County, 100-foot-tall trees appear to be *A. saccharum*. Relatively small Sugar Maples scarcely 30 feet tall occur on the Redland soils (the most fertile in east Texas) of the Pineywoods near Rusk in Cherokee County and Nacogdoches. These Redland trees seem to be *Acer barbatum* (Southern Sugar Maple). Recent taxonomy classifies both populations as *A. barbatum*.

Acer barbatum

Southern Sugar Maple

(Florida Maple)

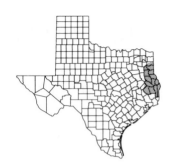

Many botanists have thought that Southern Sugar Maple is a small version, variety, or subspecies of *Acer saccharum* (Sugar Maple). However, taxonomists now claim that *A. saccharum* does not occur in Texas.

Southern Sugar Maple has diverse growth habits. On the deep, sterile sugar sands of the Blue Hills in Newton County, the Alabama-Coushatta Indian Reservation in Polk County, and Woodville in Tyler County, these lovely trees attain more than 100 feet in height. Around Rusk in Cherokee County, Nacogdoches in Nacogdoches County, and San Augustine in San Augustine County, these trees scarcely reach 30 feet in height even though they grow on the Redlands, which is the most fertile soil in all of east Texas.

Southern Sugar Maple is beautiful in autumn, with scarlet to crimson to orange to old-gold leaves. It can be tapped for sugar like Sugar Maple, but the flow is not nearly so pronounced.

Acer grandidentatum

Bigtooth Maple

(Sabinal Maple, Western Sugar Maple, Uvalde Bigtooth Maple, Canyon Maple, Southwestern Bigtooth Maple)

Bigtooth Maple is one of the most attractive and interesting Texas trees. Native to the sheltered canyons of the Edwards Plateau, the Lampasas Cut Plains, and the high country of the Trans-Pecos, it is a small tree up to 50 feet tall.

In the heart of the Hill Country, Bigtooth Maple occurs near Vanderpool in Bandera County in the Sabinal River valley along with its feeder canyons. Bigtooth Maple possibly occupied a much larger area of the Edwards Plateau before the end of the last great ice age 8,000 to 12,000 years ago. As temperatures increased and moisture became limited, Bigtooth Maple remained in only some of the deeper, well-watered canyons in Bandera, Kerr, Kendall, Real, and Uvalde counties. In those areas it is found in two confusing forms, *Acer grandidentatum* var. *grandidentatum* (Bigtooth Maple), which has three- to five-lobed, toothed leaves, and *A. grandidentatum* var. *sinuosum* (Uvalde Bigtooth Maple), whose toothless leaves are three-lobed. However, both types of leaves can sometimes be found on the same tree.

Bigtooth Maples grow on limestone in the north-south dry canyons of the Lampasas Cut Plains. They occur on the Fort Hood military reservation in Coryell County, which is 150 miles northeast of the Bigtooth Maples in the Hill Country. These healthy, magnificent small trees must be quite drought tolerant, for the canyons have no running water.

Across the Trans-Pecos, Bigtooth Maple occurs in the sheltered, usually dry canyons of the high mountains. Some authors believe that Bigtooth Maple once grew on the valley floors at much lower elevations but was cut for timber long ago.

Bigtooth Maple is found on igneous soils in the Chinati, Chisos, Davis, and Vieja mountains and on limestone soils in the Del Norte, Glass, and Guadalupe mountains. It reaches its largest size in the east-west canyons on the eastern flank of the Sierra Vieja, a rather surprising location for Bigtooth Maple because there the elevation is much lower than where the trees occur elsewhere in the Trans-Pecos.

Groves of *A. grandidentatum* var. *brachypterum* occur high in the upper reaches of the Davis Mountains, west by southwest of Star Mountain, and scattered throughout McKittrick Canyon in the Guadalupe Mountains. The trees are characterized by small winged seeds and leaves that are scarcely one fourth as large as those of typical Bigtooth Maple. Like the three-lobed leaves of Uvalde Bigtooth Maple, these smaller leaf and samara sizes cannot be reproduced readily in seedlings.

Acer leucoderme

Chalk Maple

(Whitebark Maple)

Texas' loveliest maple is also its rarest. Rumors persisted for years that Chalk Maple existed in Texas, probably in Newton County, but it was not positively identified until 1977. Volume 4 of Little's *Atlas of United States Trees: Minor Eastern Hardwoods* was published in 1977 and listed Chalk Maple as occurring in Jasper and Sabine counties. An immediate check confirmed that Chalk Maple does occur in those two counties as well as San Augustine and Newton counties. It is the dominant maple in the Sabine National Forest and is the most numerous of the Sugar Maple complex in that area.

Chalk Maple averages only 12 to 15 feet in height, although some individuals are 20 feet tall. It is almost always multitrunked and has pendent, drooping leaves, much like those of *Acer nigrum* (Black Maple), which occurs in the northern U.S. The undersides of the small leaves are a characteristic green with pilose pubescence that feels like fine velvet. The chalky bark so characteristic of this species farther east is not as pronounced in Texas.

Acer negundo

Box Elder

(Box Elder Maple, Ashleaf Maple, Red River Maple)

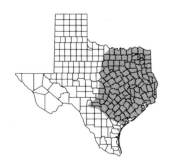

Box Elder grows to 45 feet in height and differs from all other maple species in having compound leaves with three, five, seven, or sometimes nine leaflets. The young trees and the branchlets and twigs on older trees are a bright olive-green. The trees can be easily recognized along watercourses because of their bright pea-green foliage.

Box Elders are widely distributed from the Eastern Seaboard onto the Great Plains. In Texas the tree occurs from the eastern borders of the state to west of a line between Dallas—Fort Worth and San Antonio in floodplain swamps and along waterways farther west. It is a "soft" maple, as are Silver and Red Maple, and the trees are seldom lumbered.

Box Elder was a favorite tree for shelterbelt plantings in the northern Great Plains, but it is intolerant of drought and should not be planted in the southern Great Plains. It is also susceptible to heart rot and many insects, especially box-elder bugs.

Acer rubrum

Red Maple

(Drummond Red Maple, Trident Red Maple, Swamp Maple, Water Maple, Scarlet Maple, Soft Maple)

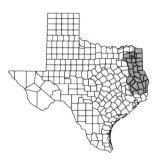

Red Maple reaches 90 feet in height and occurs in the wetter areas of the Pineywoods, Gulf Prairies and Marshes, and Post Oak Savannah.

It is aptly named because in any season it exhibits bright crimsons and scarlets. During winter the fat red buds brighten the dark, upper reaches of the bare forest canopy. In February, long before the leaves unfold, the stamens of the male flowers are rosy pink to bright red. The trees then produce flaming orbs of drooping clusters of bright pink and brilliant red samaras. The trees are the showiest in the fall, when the leaves turn to shades of crimson and scarlet.

There are several varieties of Red Maple, according to some authors. Drummond Red Maple, which has leaves that are densely pubescent underneath, and Trident Red Maple, which has three-lobed leaves, are probably the most frequently encountered Red Maples in Texas. Drummond Red Maple is quite common in southeastern Texas. Trident Red Maples are especially attractive in northeastern Texas. The leaves of most Trident Red Maples turn golden yellow in the fall, not red, as is typical of other Red Maples.

Aesculus (buckeye)

Hippocastanaceae (buckeye family)

There are thirteen species of buckeyes, or horse chestnuts, worldwide, with six species in the United States and three, or perhaps four, rather confusing taxa in Texas. The buckeyes in Texas are generally small trees (although Texas Buckeye sometimes approaches 50 feet in height) or quite large shrubs. They are easily distinguished by their palmately compound leaves and the large, shiny, tan to brown seed that resembles the eye of a deer and gives the genus its common name. Probably all parts of the plant are poisonous, so the tree is usually shunned by wildlife, although at least one account has been documented of deaths of bees that had been working buckeye flowers. Cattle losses occur in drought years when the young buds of Texas Buckeye are the only green forage.

Aesculus glabra var. *arguta*

Texas Buckeye

(White Buckeye)

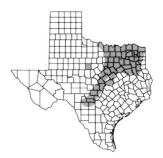

Texas Buckeye reaches its largest size (more than 40 feet) in the hard limestone of the central Edwards Plateau, although it also occurs in the northern Blacklands, Cross Timbers and Prairies, Pineywoods, and Post Oak Savannah and then as far southwest as Uvalde and Real counties on the Edwards Plateau.

Texas Buckeye has palmately compound leaves with seven to nine (sometimes eleven) leaflets. The leaves are usually lost in midsummer because of various fungal diseases. The flowers are creamy white to light yellow, appearing in terminal clusters after the leaves unfurl. They can be perfect or imperfect; if the flowers are perfect, the pistil will usually be sterile. The fruit, a leathery capsule with blunt spines, has one to three large shiny seeds.

It is possible that all parts of the plant are poisonous, but livestock graze only on the tender buds and young foliage and generally ignore older growth.

E. L. Little maintains that *Aesculus glabra* var. *glabra* (Ohio Buckeye) does not occur in Texas, but I have seen what I believe to be that variety on the northern East and West Cross Timbers and the acid sands of east Texas. The trees had the light yellow flowers and palmately compound leaves with five leaflets so typical of Ohio Buckeye.

Aesculus pavia var. *flavescens*

Aesculus pavia var. *flavescens,* a small tree up to 30 feet tall, differs from *A. pavia* var. *pavia* (Red Buckeye) only in having bright yellow flowers, as opposed to the red flowers of Red Buckeye. Yet, as Correll pointed out, flower color by itself is not sufficient to name a new variety. These plants are strictly limited to the Edwards Plateau, whereas Red Buckeye grows in east Texas on acid sands and in the Edwards Plateau in Travis, Hays, Bexar, and Comal counties. Where the two meet on the Edwards Plateau, they hybridize and produce offspring with red-streaked yellow flowers. The yellow variety then extends westward to Real and Edwards counties, becoming a major part of the disturbed-roadside flora along Ranch Road 337 from Medina to Vanderpool, Leakey, and Camp Wood.

Aesculus octandra already has the vernacular name "Yellow Buckeye." So, for the present, *A. pavia* var. *flavescens* has no acceptable vernacular name.

Aesculus pavia var. *pavia*

Red Buckeye

A tall shrub or small tree up to 30 feet in height, Red Buckeye produces showy clusters of bright red flowers in early to late spring. The palmately compound leaves have five leaflets and generally emerge before the flowers. As is true of other buckeyes in Texas, the leaves of Red Buckeye fall in mid- to late summer. The loss of leaves is usually associated with a disease complex, although it is not necessarily the primary cause. The defoliation is sometimes less severe in the partial shade of the eastern forests.

Red Buckeye occurs on slightly acid soils of the Pineywoods. It also occurs in Montgomery and Harris counties and comes across the Post Oak Savannah and Blackland Prairies to the eastern edge of the Edwards Plateau, where it hybridizes with *Aesculus pavia* var. *flavescens*. It is rare farther west on the Edwards Plateau and usually does not occur on the open prairies of the Gulf Prairies and Marshes.

Alnus (alder)

Betulaceae (birch family)

Approximately 30 species of alder are found world-wide, with 8 occurring in the United States and 1 in Texas. Alders are almost always found in low, wet areas, where they form dense thickets along streams and sloughs. They require full sun and are intolerant of even the slightest amount of shade. Alders are among the few nonleguminous plants that can fix atmospheric nitrogen via nitrogen-fixing bacteria in their root nodules. Alders are generally found in soils that are neutral to only slightly acid or alkaline.

Alnus serrulata

Smooth Alder

(Hazel Alder, Common Alder, Tag Alder, Black Alder)

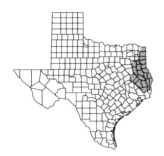

Smooth Alder is found in open, sunny areas of the east Texas Pineywoods. Requiring copious moisture and soils that are acid in reaction or at least neutral, it is most at home on the edges of ponds, streams, swamps, and sloughs. Smooth Alder is a small tree to 40 feet tall and is largely thicket-forming. The deciduous leaves are alternate, simple, and somewhat rounded. The flowers are borne in separate catkins. The male catkins are 4-inch-long cylinders, and the females produce aggregations of small nutlets that are ¼ to ½ inch long.

Amelanchier (serviceberry)

(Juneberry, Sarvis, Sarvisberry, Shadblow, Shadbush)

Rosaceae (rose family)

There are approximately sixteen tree species of *Amelanchier* worldwide, with four species occurring in the United States (four trees and five shrubs). Only one species in Texas is a tree, and two are shrubs. The genus has always been difficult to classify because species readily hybridize within the genus, and intergeneric hybridization occurs between *Amelanchier* and *Sorbus* (mountain ash).

Amelanchier utahensis

Utah Serviceberry

Utah Serviceberry reaches 16 feet in height and occurs in dry canyons and on slopes of the Guadalupe Mountains in Guadalupe Mountains National Park in Culberson County. Several small shrubs occur on the floor of South McKittrick Canyon, and trees grow at about 7,000 feet on Bear Spring Trail. The species probably occurs on the western side of the park in Hudspeth County and might also be in the Cornudas Mountains.

The plant is showy and ornamental when in full flower. White to pink flowers are produced in April and May or even later, depending on when it rains. The dark brown to purplish fruit matures in midsummer to early fall. The juicy pomes were widely used by the native Americans and are readily consumed by many species of birds. The foliage is a favorite browse for mule deer.

Aralia (aralia)

Araliaceae (ginseng family)

Of the approximately 30 species of *Aralia* worldwide, most are shrubs. The United States has 1 tree and 1 shrub species, both of which occur in Texas. *Aralia spinosa* is a small tree of the Pineywoods, and *A. racemosa* is an extremely rare shrub in the Davis Mountains.

Aralia spinosa

Devil's Walking Stick

(Angelica Tree,
Hercules'-club, Pigeon Tree,
Prickly Ash, Prickly Elder,
Shotbush, Toothache Tree)

Devil's Walking Stick, which grows to 40 feet tall, occurs in moist soil at the edges of woods in the Pineywoods, where it usually forms thickets by suckering. Its spiny trunk is only sparingly branched. The leaves are alternate and usually twice pinnately compound. Its white flowers, produced from July to August, are in terminal clusters of small umbels. The fruit, a black fleshy berry with purple juice, is eaten by many birds and other wildlife. The bark, roots, and berries were widely used in the frontier apothecary.

Arbutus (madrone)

Ericaceae (heath family)

There are ten to fifteen species of *Arbutus* worldwide, with three occurring in the United States. *Arbutus menziesii* grows on the Pacific coast, and *A. arizonica* grows in Arizona with small colonies in Grant County in the southwestern part of New Mexico. *Arbutus texana,* the smallest of these three trees, is found in the Edwards Plateau and sheltered mountain ranges of the Trans-Pecos and occurs in the Guadalupe Mountains of Eddy County, New Mexico.

Arbutus texana
(*Arbutus xalapensis*)

Texas Madrone

(Naked Indian, Lady's Leg, Texas Arbutus, Madroño)

Texas Madrone occurs in the Chisos, Davis, Del Norte, Glass, Vieja, and Guadalupe mountains of the Trans-Pecos and areas of the Edwards Plateau. It grows to 40 feet tall and, in early spring, produces clusters of the small, white, lantern-shaped flowers that are so typical of members of the heath family. The yellow-orange to bright red berries that ripen in the fall rival those of any female holly tree. The evergreen leaves are dark green above and paler on the underside. Perhaps the greatest beauty of Texas Madrone is its lovely exfoliating bark. When the older layers slough off, the newer bark is smooth and shows a wide range of colors. Some trees have white bark, others have orange grading through shades of apricot to tan, but the most outstanding are the dark reds. In the Hill Country it is called Naked Indian or Lady's Leg because of its smooth red bark. In the Guadalupes it is known as Manzanita, meaning "little apple" in Spanish, although this vernacular name more properly belongs to members of the genus *Arctostaphylos,* a shrubby relative of *Arbutus.* To most of us, it is familiar as Texas Madrone or simply Madrone or Madroño.

Other members of the Ericaceae, such as heathers and blueberries, grow on highly acidic soils in wet sites and cannot tolerate free calcium. But Texas Madrone grows in a more xeric climate, must have good drainage, and grows equally well on slightly acidic to alkaline soils. Across the Edwards Plateau it grows on soils with a pH of 7.5 to 7.8, while in the Chisos, Davis, and Vieja mountains it occurs on slightly acidic igneous soil. In the Del Norte, Glass, and Guadalupe mountains, it grows on alkaline or limestone soils. If it is to be used in a landscape situation, keep in mind that the amount of water it receives and the type of drainage are much more important than the type of soil in which it grows.

Asimina (pawpaw)

Annonaceae
(custard apple family)

Pawpaws are strictly plants of eastern North America. There are eight species, of which three are trees and five are shrubs. One tree, *Asimina triloba* (Pawpaw), and one shrub, *A. parviflora* (Dwarf Pawpaw), occur in Texas. The flowers are perfect, but the pollen sometimes matures before the pistil is receptive. Pollination is usually facilitated by flies, although the success rate is rather low. The fruit generally ripens after it falls from the tree, and it is consumed by many species of wildlife.

Asimina triloba

Pawpaw

(Custard Apple, Wild Banana)

Pawpaw is a tree of 30 feet in height occurring in the deep, rich soils of the bottomlands of the Pineywoods, Gulf Prairies and Marshes, and Post Oak Savannah. In former years, there were large drifts and thickets of Pawpaw, but now it is found as single, isolated understory trees, or in small groves.

The leaves of Pawpaw are up to 6 inches wide and 12 inches long, among the largest of any tree in America. They are alternate and simple and turn a rich butter yellow in autumn. The drooping flowers are 2 inches across and brownish to maroon red. The fruit is a banana-shaped berry (pawpaw), which might be up to 6 inches long. Pawpaws are edible in the fall after they have turned almost black and become soft.

Pawpaw is an interesting tree to use for home landscaping because it has a decidedly tropical appearance. It resembles its exotic tropical relatives in the magnolia family with its oversized leaves, rich flowers, sweet fruit, and aromatic foliage. Pawpaw is as close as Texans can get to growing ylang-ylang, sweetsop, soursop, or cherimoya.

Betula (birch)

Betulaceae (birch family)

There are roughly 50 species of birches in the northern temperate and arctic zones. The United States has 7 trees and 5 shrubs. *Betula nigra* (River Birch) occurs farther south than any other birch and is the only birch in Texas. Birches have smooth, exfoliating bark with long, narrow, dark lenticels (pores to allow gas exchange from the plant).

Betula nigra

River Birch

(Black Birch, Red Birch, Water Birch)

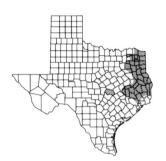

River Birch occurs in the wetlands of the Pineywoods and the Post Oak Savannah. It grows near the running water of rivers and creeks as well as the still waters of swamps, bays, and sloughs.

River Birch ranges from 20 to 30 feet in height, although some grow to 90 feet. It is usually not bothered by insects or diseases, but it is still a relatively short-lived tree.

The distinguishing characteristic of River Birch is its bark, which is dark red-brown to red-gray. There are thick scales at the base of the trunk, and the bark on the upper trunk and branches is shiny cinnamon in color and peels off in large papery sheets.

Young twigs and buds are browsed by whitetail deer; the seeds are favored by many species of birds.

Bumelia (bumelia)

Sapotaceae
(sapodilla family)

The species of *Bumelia* range from the southern United States through Mexico and Central America to Brazil. It is a genus of the tropics and the only member of the family that occurs in the northern temperate regions. There are roughly 25 species of *Bumelia*, with 4 tree and 2 shrub species in the United States and 3 tree species in Texas.

Bumelia celastrina

Saffron Plum

(Antswood, Coma, Downward Plum, Milk Buckthorn, Tropical Buckthorn)

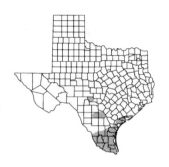

Saffron Plum is a small, thorny tree that grows to almost 30 feet in height. It is also a tall shrub of the southern Gulf Prairies and Marshes and the Rio Grande Plains, where it occurs most frequently from Matagorda County through Cameron County on the Texas coast. A disjunct population has been reported in Kerr County, although it is possibly a variant of some other species of *Bumelia*.

The leaves are persistent, usually lasting at least two years, and have obscure venation. Flowering occurs from May through November. The blue-black berries mature between April and June and are eaten by many species of wildlife, especially birds.

Bumelia lanuginosa

Chittamwood

(Gum Bumelia, Woolybucket
Bumelia, Gum Elastic,
Wooly Buckthorn,
Gum Woolybucket, Wooly Bumelia,
False Buckthorn, Shittamwood,
Ironwood, Coma)

Chittamwood grows to 80 feet in height and occurs in all areas of Texas except the High Plains. The thick, firm leaves are usually dark green on the upper surface; they appear white, gray, or tan on the underside because of the numerous hairs. The leaves often remain on the tree for more than one year. There are five varieties of Chittamwood, which are distinguished by the differences in the amount, length, and color of the hairs or fuzz on the underside of the leaves.

The small, inconspicuous flowers of Chittamwood have a sweet and penetrating odor. The large, 1-inch-long blue to black berries ripen in the fall and are eagerly eaten by wildlife.

Chittamwood is closely related to the Sapodilla Tree, which produces the latex or chicle used to make chewing gum. In fact, the sap that oozed from the cracks and wounds of Chittamwood was chewed by the children of early pioneers. The wood, though hard and heavy, is weak.

Bumelia lycioides

Buckthorn Bumelia

(Buckthorn, Smooth Bumelia, Ironwood)

Buckthorn Bumelia is a small tree (40 feet) or tall shrub occurring in wet areas such as swamp edges or riverbanks. It is usually thornless, and the leaves are narrow-pointed instead of rounded at the tips as in other *Bumelia* species.

This species is extremely rare in Texas and other areas west of the Mississippi River. In Louisiana, it was known for many years from only West Feliciana Parish but has since been found in six additional parishes. In Texas, C. S. Sargent recorded it near Beaumont in Jefferson County and Columbia in Brazoria County. E. L. Little, Jr., shows it in Newton, Jasper, Hardin, and Tyler counties, as well. Elray Nixon has an herbarium specimen of *Bumelia lycioides* from a palmetto bottomland area near the Neches River in Jasper County. This particular tree was 12 feet tall and flowered on June 6, 1970.

Caesalpinia (caesalpinia)

Leguminosae (legume family)

There are 60 to 200 species of *Caesalpinia* that occur in the tropics and subtropics around the world. There are 10 species native to the United States, with 1 tree and 9 shrubs in Texas. There are also 1 introduced tree and 1 naturalized shrub species. Some authors have merged *Caesalpinia* with the genus *Poinciana.*

Caesalpinia mexicana

Mexican Caesalpinia

(Mexican Poinciana)

Mexican Caesalpinia occurs only in Cameron and Hidalgo counties in the Rio Grande Valley. It grows best on sandy upland soils that are neutral to only slightly acid or alkaline in reaction. It is used sparingly as an ornamental in the subtropical areas of southern Texas.

This is a small tree of up to 30 feet in height, usually much smaller. The plant has no thorns or prickles and is grown for its highly fragrant, golden yellow flowers borne in clusters 3 to 6 inches long. Flowering occurs at any time of the year in a tropical to subtropical setting, depending primarily on the season of rainfall.

Carpinus (hornbeam)

Betulaceae (birch family)

There are 25 to 30 species of *Carpinus* occurring in the Northern Hemisphere. *Carpinus caroliniana* (American Hornbeam) is the only species occurring in the United States and Texas. These trees are more or less hardy and resistant to disease and insects, but they are rather slow growing.

Carpinus caroliniana

American Hornbeam

(Hornbeam, Ironwood, Blue Beech, Water Beech)

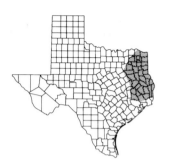

American Hornbeam is an airy, graceful understory tree to 50 feet in height. It grows in the Pineywoods, Gulf Prairies and Marshes, and Post Oak Savannah, preferring the moist, rich bottomlands of valleys and watercourses. These trees have no terminal buds, so new growth must occur each year from an axillary bud at the base of a leaf. This causes the tree to appear irregular and somewhat informal.

The simple, alternate leaves of American Hornbeam turn orange to scarlet in autumn. The bark is reminiscent of the bark of beech in that it is smooth and gray. However, unlike beech, it has broad ridges that curve up and around the trunk and branches, resembling a sinewy, muscular arm.

The fruits ripen in the fall; small nuts are borne at the bases of leafy bracts that radiate outward from the fruiting stem, which might be 5 to 6 inches long.

Carya (hickory)

Juglandaceae (walnut family)

There are only sixteen species of hickory worldwide. Eleven species occur in the eastern United States, and eight of them occur in Texas. These eight species are extremely difficult to distinguish from one another. Part of the difficulty is that the flowers are nondescript and are not useful for identification purposes. Vegetative keys use number of leaflets, number of bud scales, shape of bud scale scars, and thickness of the husk of the nut. These are difficult characteristics to use because they are so variable. There are also differences of opinion as to the sweetness or bitterness of the nuts within a species. To further complicate matters, hickories vary widely within species and readily hybridize between species.

Carya aquatica

Water Hickory

(Bitter Pecan, Swamp Hickory, Wild Pecan, Bitter Water Hickory, Bitter Hickory, Water Pignut)

Water Hickory, as a tree to 113 feet, is found in wet, poorly drained areas in east Texas from the Pineywoods, Post Oak Savannah, and Gulf Prairies and Marshes, west to Robertson and Burleson counties. There is also a disjunct population in Williamson County on the Blackland Prairies. It sometimes covers large areas and is a part of the Willow Oak—Water Oak—Black Gum forest association, Water Oak—elm-hackberry forest association, Bald Cypress—Water Tupelo swamp association, and the Loblolly Pine—Sweet Gum association.

Water Hickory has shaggy bark and leaves that are reminiscent of Pecan. The bitter, flattened nuts are readily eaten by wildlife such as wood ducks and mallards.

Carya cordiformis

Bitternut Hickory

(Bitternut, Swamp Hickory, Pignut, Pignut Hickory, Pig Hickory, White Hickory, Red Hickory, Bitter Walnut, Bitter Pecan)

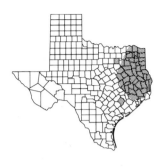

Bitternut Hickory grows up to 100 feet in height and occurs in low moist areas near the edges of swamps and streams. It also grows on rich, dry uplands in the acid soils of east Texas. It was thought to occur in Dallas County, but it most likely was misidentified and is actually *Carya texana* (Black Hickory) or perhaps a hybrid.

The nuts are extremely bitter, so much so that they are hardly eaten by wildlife. The shell is thin and easily crushed underfoot. The bark is a silvery reddish brown, thin, and sometimes broken up into platelets, but never shaggy. Bitternut Hickory is easily identified by its bright sulfur-yellow winter buds.

There are several Bitternut Hickories in Martin Dies, Jr., State Park in Jasper County.

Carya glabra var. *glabra*

Pignut Hickory

(Pignut, Sweet Pignut, Coast Pignut Hickory, Smoothbark Hickory, Swamp Hickory, Broom Hickory, Switch Hickory, Red Hickory, Switchbud Hickory)

Pignut Hickory has recently been merged with *Carya leiodermis* (Swamp Hickory). Pignut Hickory grows on well-drained sandy ridges, but Swamp Hickory grows in lower, wetter areas. It would seem to be equally adapted to such diverse habitats as the Shortleaf Pine—Post Oak—Southern Red Oak association, which is a relatively well-drained plant association, through the more mesic Loblolly Pine—Sweet Gum association to an inundated Bald Cypress—Water Tupelo swamp association. As with most hickories, different authors describe the nut as either sweet or bitter.

Pignut Hickory is very uncommon in Texas. E. L. Little, Jr., shows it in Titus, Liberty, and Chambers counties; Elray Nixon places it in Anderson, Nacogdoches, and Sabine counties; and I have collected it near Winnsboro in Wood County and in Upshur and Camp counties. The leaves on these north Texas clones are typically shiny and smooth, but the nuts look more like a pecan, which suggests hybridization.

Carya illinoensis

Pecan

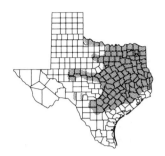

Pecan is native to all areas of Texas except the High Plains and the Trans-Pecos. In western Texas it is found in the valley of the Devils River in Val Verde County, on the Middle Concho River to Irion County, on the North Concho in Sterling County, and in the valley of the Colorado River to Coke County. In northern Texas, it occurs on Wanderers Creek in Hardeman County, where it was probably planted by the Comanche, for this area is just south of their revered Medicine Mounds.

Many of the trees inland in America were unknown for hundreds of years, but not so the Pecan. Less than 50 years after Columbus discovered America, Hernando de Soto dined on Pecan nuts, probably in Arkansas. Many years later, Pecan nuts were traded by trappers in the eastern United States, where they were known as Mississippi nuts or Illinois nuts.

Pecan grows to 90 feet in the fertile river valleys of Texas, where its deep taproot can reach perched water tables. It is the fastest-growing of all the hickories and can easily live 300 years or more.

Today, Pecans are marketed as improved papershell clones. These trees produce more meat per pound and have shells that can be hand crushed. Yet, in areas such as Edna Hill in Erath County, each family has its own native paper-shell, one that has been selected for ease of shelling and excellence of taste.

Carya myristiciformis

Nutmeg Hickory

(Swamp Hickory, Bitter Water Hickory, Bitter Waternut)

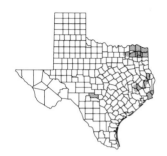

Nutmeg Hickory is a tree to about 70 feet tall that is uncommon within its narrow range across the southern portion of the state. The late Claire Brown listed it as uncommon in Louisiana on Tertiary black calcareous soils in Natchitoches and Winn parishes. In Texas, small stands can be found in Jefferson, San Jacinto, San Augustine, and Tyler counties in the southeast, Kerr County on the Edwards Plateau, and the Red River and the North and South Sulphur rivers drainageways in the northeast.

The nut looks like a small dark pecan; some people suggest that it looks like a nutmeg. Some of the vernacular names indicate that the nut is bitter, although most authors say it is sweet. Robert Vines calls it "sweet but tart."

Carya ovata var. *ovata*

Shagbark Hickory

(Carolina Hickory, Scalybark Hickory, Upland Hickory, Shellbark Hickory)

Shagbark Hickory is a component of the pine-hardwood forest association and reaches almost 110 feet in height. It grows in rich woodlands, flats, slopes, and hills of the Pineywoods in east Texas. Shagbark Hickory usually occurs singly or in twos, at most in small groups but never in drifts or thickets.

The nut from Shagbark Hickory is second only to the Pecan in sweetness and is the standard by which all hickory nuts are measured. It is difficult to collect many nuts because they are avidly consumed by many forms of wildlife.

Shagbark Hickory is rather easily identified in nature by its bark, which breaks into strips up to 12 inches long and 8 inches wide, with the ends bowing away from the tree. The compound leaves usually have five leaflets.

Carya texana

Black Hickory

(Buckley Hickory, Pignut Hickory)

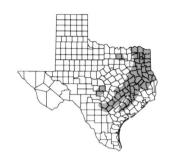

Black Hickory is by far the most widely adapted of all the hickories. It is a tree of almost 140 feet in height in the rich, moist bottoms of Sabine County in far east Texas, a small tree of 30 feet with a narrow crown in the East Cross Timbers of Denton County, and an even smaller tree on the granitic sands of Enchanted Rock in Llano County. Average annual rainfall in its area of growth ranges from 26 inches in the west to 52 inches in the east.

Black Hickory is the hickory I look for on dry, sandy, steep, eroded, rocky hillsides. I look for Post Oak and Blackjack Oak in all its area of adaptation, for it appears more at home on the thinner, well-drained areas.

The nut of Black Hickory is described as both very bitter and sweet. This characteristic probably does vary. What varies but little, however, is thickness of shell, or rather hardness of shell. Although Black Hickory has only a moderately thick shell, it is tough and extremely hard to crack.

Carya tomentosa

Mockernut Hickory

(Mockernut, White Hickory, Whiteheart Hickory, Hognut, Bullnut, Fragrant Hickory, Bigbud Hickory, Hardbark Hickory)

Black Hickory may be adapted over a wider area of Texas, but Mockernut Hickory is by far the most commonly encountered hickory in eastern Texas, where it is adapted. It is found on dry slopes and ridges but makes its best growth on rich, well-drained bottomlands of the Pineywoods and the Post Oak Savannah with more than 45 inches of rainfall annually.

Mockernut Hickory is long-lived, 300 to 500 years, and the tallest of its species in Texas is 115 feet in Polk County. The leaves are large, hairy, glandular, resinous, and fragrant, especially on warm moist days in deep woods. The wood is probably among the best of the hickories.

The nut is small and sweet but has a thick shell. The kernel is extremely difficult to extract, hence the name "Mockernut."

Mockernut Hickory is easily damaged by fire, but it sprouts from stumps and suckers freely.

Castanea (chinquapin)

Fagaceae (beech family)

The twelve species of *Castanea* are restricted to the Northern Hemisphere. Three species occur in the United States, one of which is the fabled American Chestnut (which was never in Texas). That species is almost extinct because of *Endothia parasitica* (chestnut blight), an imported fungus. The disease took less than 40 years to sweep from New York City down the spine of the Appalachian Mountains. Today, American Chestnut survives only as stump sprouts, and though they sometimes live long enough to produce nuts, they almost always succumb to the disease.

The other two American species occur in Texas. *Castanea alnifolia* (Chinquapin) is a shrub less than 6 feet tall. The other is *C. pumila,* Allegheny Chinquapin.

The fruit of American Chestnuts and Chinquapins are sweeter and considered superior in taste to those in the Old World and Asia. Chestnuts contain two to three nuts in each spiny ball, but the Chinquapin has only one.

Castanea pumila

Allegheny Chinquapin

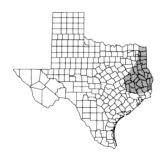

Allegheny Chinquapin is a large shrub or small tree. Some of the largest trees are just north of Houston in the city of Conroe in Montgomery County. Here, in at least one location, home builders left all of the native trees. Several of them are 15 to 20 feet tall.

Allegheny Chinquapin occurs on the deep sugar sands of the Pineywoods. It is one of the loveliest of all trees in late May and early June, when the ends of the branches burgeon forth with creamy white, fragrant male catkins. The spikes, 2 to 6 inches long, stand erect like white candles in a green holder. Soon after the male catkins are shed, the female flowers begin to show spiny burs that ripen in late fall to early winter. Generally, there is only one nut per bur. Chinquapin nuts are sweet and palatable, and they are preferred over chestnuts by people who have been fortunate enough to sample both. During the depression of the early 1930s, Chinquapin nuts were considered a rare delicacy and were sold and bartered on school lots across the South. The going price was five cents per handful, with the buyer allowed to use his or her hand, whatever the size.

The future of Chinquapin in Texas is uncertain. It is only moderately resistant to *Endothia parasitica* (chestnut blight), which almost caused the extinction of the American Chestnut. Each year there are fewer Chinquapins in Texas. Several years ago, there were stands of fair-sized Chinquapins in the deep sugar sands west of Garrison in Nacogdoches County. Today, there are only sprouts from the stumps.

Celtis (hackberry)

Ulmaceae (elm family)

There are 60 to 80 species of *Celtis* worldwide. The United States has 5 tree and 2 shrub species, with Texas having 5 tree and 1 shrub species.

Hackberries occur throughout Texas; two of the species occur in most vegetation areas. The leaves are simple, alternate, and deciduous. The inconspicuous male and female flowers are produced in early spring on the same tree. The fruit is a small, thin-fleshed, reddish brown drupe that is sweet and eagerly consumed by many species of wildlife, especially cedar waxwings and robins. The bark is smooth and gray with warty protuberances on the older wood.

Celtis laevigata

Sugarberry

(Hackberry, Sugar Hackberry, Texas Sugarberry, Southern Hackberry, Lowland Hackberry, Palo Blanco)

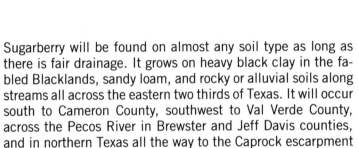

Sugarberry will be found on almost any soil type as long as there is fair drainage. It grows on heavy black clay in the fabled Blacklands, sandy loam, and rocky or alluvial soils along streams all across the eastern two thirds of Texas. It will occur south to Cameron County, southwest to Val Verde County, across the Pecos River in Brewster and Jeff Davis counties, and in northern Texas all the way to the Caprock escarpment and up Palo Duro Canyon to Randall County.

It is a tree that can attain upwards of 60 feet in height, by far the largest and most imposing of the Texas hackberries. It is the only species of hackberry found in all ten vegetational areas of the state.

Celtis lindheimeri

Lindheimer Hackberry

Lindheimer Hackberry grows to 40 feet and has a grayish cast due to its leaves. It is a little-known tree and was at one time thought to be endemic to southern Bexar County. It is closely related to the Netleaf Hackberry. C. S. Sargent lists it in Bexar, Comal, Hays, Travis, and Goliad counties, and Robert Vines also lists it in three locations in Coahuila in Mexico.

I have collected seed from this species at the post office at Fischer in northwestern Comal County. The tree is to be expected in Blanco and Kendall counties.

Celtis occidentalis

Hackberry

(Beaverwood, Northern Hackberry, American Hackberry, Common Hackberry, Sugarberry, Nettletree, False Elm)

"*Bois inconnu,*" the unknown tree, the early French settlers to America called it. "Hackberry," it was called by the earliest English-speaking immigrants to the New World. The name seems to be merely a corruption of Scottish "hagberry," a name reserved for the small-fruited bird cherry left behind in their far-off homeland. Even the generic *Celtis* is confusing, for it is a name that Pliny gave to a sweet-fruited lotus. Certainly the early inhabitants might have been even more confused if they had known that this runt tree was so closely kin to the regal elms.

My friends that had just moved to north Texas kept asking to see the "real Hackberry," and refused to accept the Sugarberry for what they sought. It was several months before I realized that the common species they grew up with in the north and east was *Celtis occidentalis,* a hackberry found only in the Panhandle in Texas and one that this author is unfamiliar with in its pure form. This "real" hackberry, with its elmlike toothed leaves, comes into Texas in Hemphill County through the valley of the Canadian River. In this area it will be around 20 to 30 feet tall and is a part of the cottonwood-Hackberry—Salt Cedar brush/woods association. The trees are growing with *C. reticulata* and appear to be extensively introgressed with this more common hackberry.

91

Celtis reticulata

Netleaf Hackberry

(Palo Blanco, Western Hackberry, Hackberry, Sugarberry, Netleaf Sugar Hackberry)

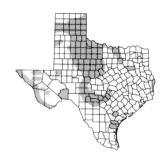

Netleaf Hackberry is a small tree, growing to 30 feet, although in west Texas it seldom reaches 20 feet in height. It occurs on the Rolling Plains, the Canadian River and Palo Duro Canyon Breaks in the High Plains, the Edwards Plateau, the Trans-Pecos, and Denton County in the East Cross Timbers. There is also a disjunct population in Newton County and in Nueces and San Patricio counties on the coast.

The upper surface of the leaves feels like rough sandpaper, and the lower surface has conspicuous netlike veins, hence the common name. The trees are strongly taprooted but also have many shallow roots. Some authors say it is short-lived (100 to 200 years), and when compared with a Bristlecone Pine (5,000 years), it surely is. It is a tree that can stand severe droughts, low fertility, and yearly temperature ranges of more than 140° F. Netleaf Hackberry is fairly resistant to disease and insects, although it is bothered some years by gall insects. It is also strongly tolerant of the cotton root rot fungus (*Phymatotrichum omnivorum*). The succulent fruit persists on the tree throughout the winter, and many species of birds that normally feed on seeds have been saved from certain starvation in January and February by eating these fruits.

Celtis tenuifolia

Dwarf Hackberry

(Georgia Hackberry, Upland Hackberry, Hackberry, Small Hackberry)

Dwarf Hackberry is a small tree of up to 25 feet in height, with short, narrow leaves. It occurs on hillsides and other dry, gravelly areas in Red River, Wood, and Upshur counties in northeast Texas; Nacogdoches, San Augustine, and Shelby counties in middle east Texas; and Jasper, Newton, Jefferson, Orange, and probably other counties in southeastern Texas. Some authors consider this to be a variety of *Celtis occidentalis*.

Cercidium (paloverde)

Leguminosae (legume family)

Cercidium is a small genus with seven to nine species occurring in arid to semiarid areas of the tropical and subtropical regions of North and South America. *Cercidium macrum* (Border Paloverde) is merged with *C. texanum* (Texas Paloverde). Texas Paloverde was considered a shrub, and Border Paloverde was considered a small tree.

Cercidium texanum

Texas Paloverde

(Border Paloverde, Paloverde, Retama China)

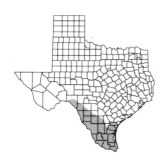

Texas Paloverde is found on alkaline sandy loam or clays. It is frequent in brushy plains from Val Verde County on the west to the tip of Cameron County in southern Texas. Inland, it extends from the Rio Grande to McMullen and Duval counties and up the coast to Kleberg, Nueces, and San Patricio counties. This species has long been confused with *Cercidium floridum* (Blue Paloverde) of Arizona.

Texas Paloverde grows to 25 feet in height and has green bark and short, straight spines. The leaves are twice compound, and bright yellow flower clusters occur in the axils of the leaves. The flowers have five unequal petals and usually bloom from March to November, although they will also bloom after a rain in any season of the year.

Some authors merge *C. texanum* and *C. macrum* into *Parkinsonia texana*. These two entities then become varieties, that is, *P. texana* var. *texanum* and *P. texana* var. *macrum*.

95

Redbud Complex

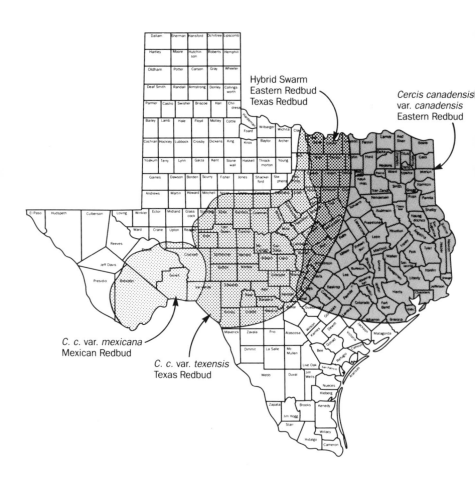

Hybrid Swarm
Eastern Redbud
Texas Redbud

Cercis canadensis
var. *canadensis*
Eastern Redbud

C. c. var. *mexicana*
Mexican Redbud

C. c. var. *texensis*
Texas Redbud

Cercis (redbud)

Leguminosae (legume family)

Two native redbuds occur in the United States, *Cercis canadensis* in eastern America and west Texas and *C. occidentalis* in California, Arizona, Utah, and Nevada. There are eight species worldwide, including *C. siliquastrum* (Judas Tree), and the blue-green-leaved *C. griffithii* of Afghanistan and Southeast Asia.

There are three varieties of *Cercis canadensis* in Texas. *C. canadensis* var. *canadensis* (Eastern Redbud) grows in east Texas where there are 35 inches or more of rainfall, *C. canadensis* var. *texensis* (Texas Redbud) grows on the thin limestone soils of central Texas in a 20-to-30-inch rainfall belt, and *C. canadensis* var. *mexicana* (Mexican Redbud) grows on alkaline soils in the 12-to-20-inch rainfall belt.

Eastern Redbud is available in the nursery trade in many forms, such as white-flowered, pink-flowered, double-flowered, and red-leaved. Recently, two different color forms of Texas Redbud have been introduced into the nursery business. They are 'White Texas,' which was a chance seedling discovered at the Germany Nursery in Fort Worth, and the bright rosy-red 'Oklahoma,' which was discovered by an Oklahoma nurseryman in the Arbuckle Mountains of southcentral Oklahoma. To date, no commercial strains of Mexican Redbud have been developed, although the Trans-Pecos has many striking individuals worthy of propagation.

Cercis canadensis var. *canadensis*

Eastern Redbud

(Redbud, Judas Tree)

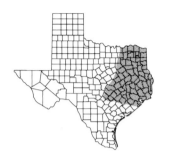

Eastern Redbud is present in the Pineywoods, Gulf Prairies and Marshes, Post Oak Savannah, Blackland and Grand Prairies, and West Cross Timbers. It is characterized by leaves that are thin, dull green, and large, sometimes up to 5 inches long and wide. Its flowers are generally purplish red, although individual trees might have flowers that are bright pink to red or occasionally white. This is the largest redbud, growing to 40 feet in height.

Eastern Redbud is usually single-trunked and grows as an understory tree on the well-drained sands and sandy loams from east Texas to the heavy black clays of the Blackland Prairies.

Cercis canadensis var. *mexicana*

Mexican Redbud

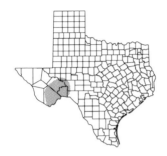

Mexican Redbud grows to 20 feet in height and is multi-trunked. It occurs on hard limestone soils and is an uncommon tree in Crockett, Pecos, Val Verde, Terrell, and eastern Brewster counties.

Mexican Redbud ranges from the western edge of the Edwards Plateau to the Trans-Pecos. The leaves of these trees are much smaller than those of Texas Redbud, an adaptation for conserving precious moisture in the dry west. The twigs and petioles are covered with dense fuzz, and the leaves are greatly crinkled around the edges.

Cercis canadensis var. *texensis*

Texas Redbud

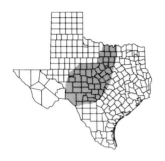

Texas Redbud is most common on thin, calcareous, well-drained soils of the Blackland and Grand Prairies and West Cross Timbers, Edwards Plateau, and Rolling Plains. Although individuals sometimes mix with Eastern Redbud on the Blackland and Grand Prairies and West Cross Timbers, Texas Redbud is usually west of the native habitat of its more eastern relative. It attains its most beautiful form on the Edwards Plateau around Blanco and Hays counties, where it produces flowers that are a salmon pink. Its leaves, which are thick and much smaller than those of Eastern Redbud, reflect the more xeric climate where it occurs. The upper surface of the leaves is waxy and glossy to help retard transpiration. Texas Redbud is usually multitrunked and smaller than Eastern Redbud.

Eastern Redbud occurs throughout Dallas County while Texas Redbud occurs on the whiterock soils in the western and southwestern areas of the county. Hybridization is common where these two mix. A similar area of much crossing and introgression is the area along the Balcones Escarpment on the eastern side of the Edwards Plateau.

Cercocarpus (mountain mahogany)

Rosaceae (rose family)

The ten species of mountain mahogany are shrubs or small trees and occur in western and southwestern North America. The taxonomy of this genus in Texas is confusing and needs further study. It appears that there are three taxa, either one species with two varieties or three varieties of a highly variable species. The wood is hard and heavy and makes excellent firewood. The leaves are evergreen or persistent, and the fruits have long silvery "tails." Most species are able to fix atmospheric nitrogen through the nodulation of a filamentous bacterium, *Actinomycetes,* although it is not known if the Texas plants have this symbiotic relationship.

Cercocarpus breviflorus (*Cercocarpus montanus* var. *paucidentatus*)

Hairy Cercocarpus

(Hairy Mountain Mahogany, Wright Mountain Mahogany, Shaggy Mountain Mahogany)

Hairy Cercocarpus grows to 15 feet and occurs in the Chinati, Chisos, Davis, Del Norte, Franklin, Glass, Guadalupe, Quitman, and Vieja mountains of the Trans-Pecos. It grows in dry, rocky soils on the mountain slopes at altitudes of one mile or more. It appears to be equally adapted to limestone and igneous soils. This species is easily identified by its tiny flowers and small narrow leaves. Easiest accessibility to this plant is along U.S. Highway 62/180 at the entrance to the Pine Springs camping area in the Guadalupe Mountains in Culberson County.

Cercocarpus montanus var. *argenteus*

Silver Mountain Mahogany

(Mountain Mahogany, True Mountain Mahogany)

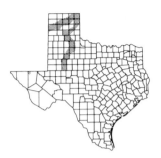

Silver Mountain Mahogany is a large shrub or small tree of 12 to 15 feet in height. Its evergreen or persistent leaves are 1 inch long and ¾ inch wide. They are dark green above and covered with a dense white wool on the underside. It is most beautiful in late summer and fall, when the sharp-pointed fruit matures and resembles a threaded needle or an extremely narrow, delicate feather. The seeds can be blown many yards, and the heavy sharp end lands first and helps to anchor the seed in the soil.

Silver Mountain Mahogany is palatable to all browsing livestock; thus, its treelike form is seldom seen. Its wood is dense and hard, though extremely brittle.

Silver Mountain Mahogany occurs on the limestone soils of the Rolling Plains and northern Trans-Pecos. This small tree of the rose family is not closely kin to the great mahogany of commerce, *Swietenia,* and professional foresters stubbornly refer to it as merely cercocarpus. Because of its small size, evergreen foliage, and attractive fruiting habits, it should be more widely grown, especially where yard space is at a premium.

Cercocarpus montanus var. glaber

Smooth Mountain Mahogany

(Mountain Mahogany, True Mountain Mahogany)

Smooth Mountain Mahogany is the tallest of all the Texas species of *Cercocarpus*. On the steep limestone slopes of the Edwards Plateau in Kimble and Real counties, it reaches heights up to 20 feet and occurs singly or in drifts. It differs from Silver Mountain Mahogany in its smooth, almost hairless leaves, its greater height, and its range, which is the Edwards Plateau and southern Trans-Pecos. There are a number of trees of this species along Green Gulch Road in Big Bend National Park.

Chilopsis (desert willow)

Bignoniaceae (catalpa family)

Desert Willow is the only species in the genus *Chilopsis*. It is a 40-foot tree of the dry washes and gravelly creek beds of northern Mexico and the southwestern United States. Desert Willow is a classic example of a phreatophyte, a tree that will extend its roots either to a water table or to perched water in the soil profile. In Texas, Desert Willow is native to the dry creek beds of the western Edwards Plateau and the Trans-Pecos, and a disjunct population grows in Uvalde and Zavala counties on the Rio Grande Plains.

Chilopsis linearis

Desert Willow

(Flowering Willow, Willowleaf Catalpa, Desert Catalpa, Flor de Mimbre, Mimbre, Bow Willow)

Desert Willow grows in the dry gravel washes of the Edwards Plateau and Trans-Pecos. It resembles a willow because of its long narrow leaves, hence its common name. Unlike the wood of most willows, which tends to be weak, the wood of Desert Willow is so sinewy that Indians used it to make their prize bows. Though Desert Willow occurs in dry washes, it cannot tolerate overwatering when in cultivation.

The simple leaves of Desert Willow are 5 to 12 inches long and ¼ to ½ inch wide. Its flowers occur in showy clusters at the tips of the branches and on new wood. They are trumpet- or bell-shaped, exceedingly sweetly fragrant, and predominantly light pink to light violet. Pure white flowers are rarely found. In the high country of the Trans-Pecos, the flower color deepens and sometimes has shades of red. For many years there have been rumors of Desert Willows with bright yellow flowers in the Dead Horse and Christmas mountains, although these might actually be tall Yellow Bells (*Tecoma stans* var. *angustata*). Desert Willow flowers from late spring to early fall, depending on the rainfall. The fruits are long, narrow capsules typical of the catalpa family.

The first large population of Desert Willows outside of the Austin—San Antonio area is in the vicinity of Juno in Val Verde County where Granger Draw and Johnson Draw form the headwaters of the Devils River. It is a major occupant of every little dry wash and draw.

The most beautiful Desert Willows occur in the high country from Sierra Blanca to the heart of the Davis Mountains. Here, in bracing mountain breezes, the colors seem clearer and of deeper hues. My other favorite places to view Desert Willow are in the shelter belts established by the Civilian Conservation Corps in the mid-1930s. Some of the interesting places to see these shelter belts are Bridle Bits, Wolf Flat, Cee Vee, and Flomont.

Desert Willow is easily cultivated but must not be overwatered. This is usually not a problem in west Texas, but in areas that receive more than 30 inches of rainfall, it must be planted in raised beds and watered carefully, especially in winter. Desert Willow is beautiful when it is 20 to 30 feet high, but it is also attractive when pruned back to form a shrub 3 to 10 feet high, because it blooms only on new wood. The more it is pruned, the more pronounced is its flowering.

Chionanthus (fringe tree)

Oleaceae (olive family)

There are only two species in this genus, one in America and one in China. The American species is found from eastern Texas across the southeast to Virginia and Maryland. It grows in damp woods and is usually an understory tree.

Chionanthus virginicus

Fringe Tree

(White Fringe Tree, Flowering Ash, Old Man's Beard, Snowflower Tree, Grandfather Graybeard, Grancy Graybeard)

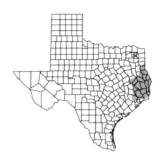

Fringe Tree is a part of the pine-hardwood forest association, where it becomes a small tree of 25 to 30 feet, occupying the well-drained but richer upland sands and sandy loams. It is an understory tree, preferring dappled shade and decidedly acid soils.

In the early spring, travelers along the sandy lanes and rutted logging roads of the Pineywoods and the Gulf Prairies and Marshes will see small trees with white flowers of finest, gossamer lace peeking from the edges of the dark woodland. This ethereal beauty is Fringe Tree, with its 5- to 10-inch-long panicles of delicate white flowers. The flowers have four to six strap-shaped petals that are about 2 inches long. Upon opening, they are wonderfully fragrant and are usually of one sex (the flowers will appear to be perfect but are functionally of one sex). The flowers occur in the axils of the leaves of the previous growing season. The dark blue to purple drupe is covered with a bloom and ripens in late summer. It is eaten by many species of wildlife.

The leaves of Fringe Tree are persistent, almost evergreen, where it occurs in the south, but farther north the leaves turn a clear yellow in late fall before they drop to the forest floor.

Condalia (brasil)

Rhamnaceae (buckthorn family)

Condalia is a genus with approximately eighteen species in tropical and warm temperate America. The species occur from the arid southwestern United States and Mexico to Argentina and Brazil. In the United States, only two species are trees, and only Brasil is found in Texas.

Condalia hookeri var. *hookeri*

Brasil

(Bluewood, Capul Negro, Purple Haw, Logwood, Capulin, Chaparral)

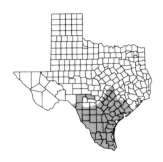

Condalia hookeri var. *hookeri* is a small tree growing to 30 feet and occurring on sandy soils of the Rio Grande Plains, southern Post Oak Savannah, Gulf Prairies and Marshes, and the Edwards Plateau.

Brasil is a small spiny tree that forms thickets and chaparral. It has simple, alternate, often fascicled leaves that are bright and shiny green. The wood is heavy, hard, and much valued for firewood. In its southernmost habitat, Brasil flowers any time of the year and produces purple to black berry-like fruit in the spring, summer, and fall. The sweet and juicy fruits are used to make jellies. They are also avidly eaten by many birds and other wildlife.

Cordia (cordia)

Boraginaceae (borage family)

The genus *Cordia* has approximately 250 species of trees and shrubs worldwide. Almost all are tropical or nearly tropical, with the largest numbers occurring in the New World. The leaves are evergreen or highly persistent. Two tree species of *Cordia* are found in the United States. They are *Cordia boissieri,* which is native to Texas, and *Cordia sebestena,* which was probably introduced and has become naturalized in Florida.

Cordia boissieri

Wild Olive

(Mexican Olive, Anacahuita)

Wild Olive is native to the most southern tier of counties in the Rio Grande Plains. From Sullivan City to McAllen, it is a minor constituent of the chaparral and can be easily observed on the east side of the road. It also occurs by the thousands in the chaparral from Laredo toward Sabinas Hidalgo in Mexico.

Wild Olive is an evergreen and can be planted as far north as the San Antonio area, although it freezes back in cold winters. The trees flower mainly in late spring to early summer, although they will flower in all seasons if they receive enough water. The trumpet-shaped flowers are borne in terminal cymes and are nearly 3 inches wide. They are brilliant white with yellow throats. The white fruit is sweet and relished by wildlife and livestock.

Cornus (dogwood)

Cornaceae (dogwood family)

There are approximately 40 species of dogwood occurring in the temperate regions of North America, Asia, Europe, and Africa, with 1 species in Peru. Eleven species occur in the United States. There are 1 tree and 2 or 3 shrub species in Texas, although the shrub species can at times become small trees. With one exception, *Cornus drummondii,* the Texas species are understory plants that grow best in sandy, slightly acidic soils that receive more than 40 inches of rainfall per year.

Cornus florida

Flowering Dogwood

(Dogwood, Virginia Dogwood, Florida Dogwood, Arrowwood, Boxwood, False Box, White Cornel)

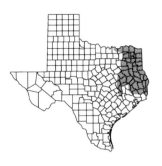

From late March until early May, blossoms of Flowering Dogwood are seen in the woodlands of the Pineywoods and Post Oak Savannah, where they grow on well-drained, sandy, acid soils. They are most numerous as understory trees to 40 feet in height, but they are most beautiful and shorter when in full sun.

Flowering Dogwood is a tree for all seasons. After the trees flower in the spring, the large, simple, opposite leaves, with their dark green upper surfaces and almost silvery under surfaces, take over until fall. Long before the leaves turn to brilliant crimsons and scarlets, the dense clusters of fruit turn a bright, glistening red and are relished by many birds and other wildlife. The fat flower buds are prominent at the ends of the twigs throughout the winter.

Cotinus (smoke tree)

Anacardiaceae (sumac family)

There are probably no more than three species of *Cotinus* in the world. One is strictly American, and the other two are found from southern Europe through the Himalayas to central China.

Cotinus coggygria (European Smoke Tree), from the Old World, is widely cultivated and is difficult to distinguish from the native Texas species, *C. obovatus* (American Smoke Tree). Supposedly the American species has better fall color, but *C. coggygria* has showier flowers. The major difference is the leaves, which in American Smoke Tree are obovate (wider at the tip of the leaf than at the base) and sparsely hairy underneath; those of the European Smoke Tree are generally ovate (widest at the base) and smooth.

Cotinus obovatus

American Smoke Tree

(Smokebush, Wild Smoke Tree, Chittamwood)

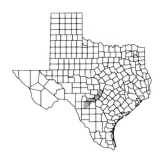

American Smoke Tree occurs on the hard limestone of Bandera, Kendall, Kerr, and Uvalde counties in the Edwards Plateau. This is a relict tree from the Miocene epoch approximately 25 million years ago. At one time, its distribution was probably continuous from northeastern Alabama and Tennessee, through southwestern Missouri, northwestern Arkansas, eastern Oklahoma, and central Texas. The remnant population of American Smoke Tree in the Hill Country of Texas is more than 500 miles from the trees in Cherokee County, Oklahoma, and approximately 900 miles from those in Madison County, Alabama.

American Smoke Tree flowers in midspring, from April to May, and is covered with fleecy clouds or puffs of pink "smoke." This illusion is created by the terminal panicles of flowers, which are pistillate, staminate, or perfect. Each individual tree usually has a few perfect flowers, but the majority are of only one sex.

The alternate leaves are rounded and nearly twice as long as they are broad. They turn shades of old gold, bright scarlet, and orange in autumn. During the winter months, American Smoke Tree continues to grace the limestone slopes with its dark gray to black flaking bark on the older parts of the trunk. In old age, the limbs are gnarled and twisted, giving an appearance of serene antiquity.

Crataegus (hawthorn)

Rosaceae (rose family)

Hawthorns are found primarily in the eastern United States, but they range from Europe and Asia to South America and Mexico. Charles Sprague Sargent, director of the Arnold Arboretum of Harvard University, named and described more than 700 species, which is more than the total number of all other species of trees in the United States, 650 to 680. However, in his last work, Sargent cut that lengthy list to about 153 species and listed only 20 hawthorns for Texas. Vines lists 31 hawthorns for Texas, Correll and Johnston list 33, T. S. Elias lists only 26 hawthorn tree species for the United States and 7 for Texas, and Little lists 35 hawthorns for the United States and 15 species in Texas.

 Crataegus is intolerant of shade, and when large areas of the United States were cleared for planting in the late nineteenth and early twentieth centuries, *Crataegus* began to colonize them. Most species of *Crataegus,* if not all, are apomictic; that is, they can produce seed without fertilization. Many of the seeds become sterile triploids, and the resultant seedlings can be genetically identical to the parent. It is as if they reproduce vegetatively. One tree can produce a colony of plants that are identical, and often a new species will be mistakenly described.

 Thirteen species of hawthorns are listed and described here. *Crataegus uniflora* is a shrub and is omitted. *C. douglasii* (*C. rivularis*) is not believed to be present in Texas and has also been omitted.

The hawthorns of Texas are presented alphabetically by series in Table 8. The synonyms for each taxon are also given. Thus, under series Crusgallianae in the table, *Crataegus berberifolia* (Barberry Hawthorn) is a legitimate species; *C. edita* and *C. engelmannii* are synonyms; and *C. cherokeensis, C. sublobulata,* and *C. warneri* are synonyms of *C. engelmannii* and also of *C. berberifolia.* See plates 1 through 13 for range maps showing *Crataegus* synonyms.

Table 8
The Hawthorns of Texas, Series and Species, With Synonyms and Possible Synonyms

Series Aestivales
    Crataegus opaca   Mayhaw

Series Apiifolia
    Crataegus marshallii   Parsley Hawthorn
        C. apiifolia

Series Brevispinae
    Crataegus brachyacantha   Blueberry Hawthorn

Series Crus-gallianae
    Crataegus berberifolia   Barberry Hawthorn
        C. edita
        C. engelmannii
            *C. cherokeenis**
            *C. sublobulata**
            *C. warneri**
    Crataegus crus-galli   Cockspur Hawthorn
        C. bushii
        *C. cherokeenis**
        C. pyracanthoides
            C. sabineana
            C. uniqua
    Crataegus reverchonii   Reverchon Hawthorn
    *Crataegus tracyi**   Tracy Hawthorn
        *C. montivaga**

Series Macracanthae
    Crataegus calpodendron   Pear Hawthorn

Series Microcarpae
    Crataegus spathulata   Littlehip Hawthorn

Series Molles
    Crataegus greggiana   Gregg Hawthorn
    Crataegus mollis   Downy Hawthorn
        C. berlandieri
        C. brachyphylla
        *C. brazoria**
            *C. dallasiana**
        *C. invisa**
        C. limaria
        *C. viburnifolia**
    *Crataegus texana**   Texas Hawthorn

Series Viridis
    Crataegus viridis   Green Hawthorn
        *C. anamesa**
            *C. antiplasta**
        *C. glabriuscula**
        *C. poliophylla**
        *C. stenosepala**
        *C. sutherlandensis**

*Endemic to Texas

121

Crataegus berberifolia

Barberry Hawthorn

(Bigtree Hawthorn)

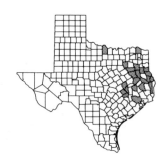

Barberry Hawthorn grows to 40 feet in the more fertile, moist sites of eastern Texas. It occurs from Montague County on the west to Burleson, Harris, and Washington counties and in the southeast. It is a prolific fruit bearer, and the orange-red pomes ripen from September to November. Barberry Hawthorn is a complex species, as can be seen in Table 8, having five synonymous species, three of which are endemic to Texas (*C. cherokeensis, C. sublobulata,* and *C. warneri*) (see plate 1). *C. cherokeensis* is also synonymous to *C. crus-galli* (Little) as well as synonymous to *C. engelmannii* (Correll and Johnston), thus becoming synonymous to *C. berberifolia.*

Crataegus brachyacantha

Blueberry Hawthorn

(Blue Haw, Pommette Bleue, Hog Haw)

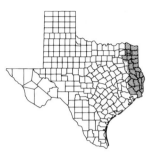

Blueberry Hawthorn is the largest of the Texas hawthorns, approaching 50 feet in height. It grows on rich, wet soils of the Pineywoods, Gulf Prairies and Marshes, and Post Oak Savannah. Generally, the leaves are almost mature by the time the flowers appear. The crowning beauty of this hawthorn is the bright, shiny, almost metallic-blue fruit. It is the only hawthorn in Texas with blue fruit, although one putative western and several imported species bear fruits that are black to purple. The fruit, with its white bloom, ripens in August and does not hang long on the tree.

Blueberry Hawthorn is also called Hog Haw because of the unpleasant taste of the fruit to the human palate. In southern Louisiana it is known as Pommette Bleue.

Crataegus calpodendron

Pear Hawthorn

(Pear Haw, Pear Thorn)

Pear Hawthorn grows to 20 feet in height and is fairly uncommon in the dry open woods in the Pineywoods of east Texas. I have seen it in only one location in Jasper County. It is widespread all across the southeastern United States, north to New York, and west to Wisconsin and Minnesota. The dull yellow to orange-red pear-shaped fruit ripens in October and November.

Crataegus crus-galli

Cockspur Hawthorn

(Hog Apple, Cockspur Thorn, Newcastle Thorn)

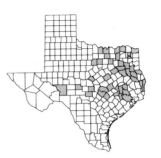

Cockspur Hawthorn is the most widespread of all the Texas hawthorns, occurring over all of eastern Texas to Harris County on the Gulf Coast and on the far western reaches of the Edwards Plateau in Crockett County. It grows on the limestone soils of the Blacklands, Grand Prairie, Lampasas Cut Plains, and Edwards Plateau as well as the acid sands of the Pineywoods and Post Oak Savannah. (See plate 4 for range map showing synonyms.) It is small, up to 25 feet in height, and has dull red to greenish fruit. Its long, fat thorns are 4 to 8 inches in length. The branching of the tree is strongly horizontal.

Crataegus greggiana

Gregg Hawthorn

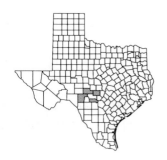

This is probably the rarest of all the hawthorns in Texas. Herbarium specimens from the year 1945 show this species to be 7 miles southwest of Telegraph in Edwards County and 5 to 5½ miles northeast of Utopia on the O'Bryan Ranch in Bandera County.

Gregg Hawthorn is a small tree to almost 20 feet tall, flowering in early April, with the brick-red fruit ripe in October or November. It is easily identified from all other hawthorns of the Edwards Plateau because of the relatively large, somewhat hairy leaves that are reminiscent of Downy Hawthorn (*C. mollis*) in eastern and central Texas.

I have taken specimens of what I consider to be this tree east of Junction in Kimble County and near Harper in Gillespie County. In each case they were single trees.

Most of the land where Gregg Hawthorn was once found has been heavily grazed by goats and deer. Probably the only possible chance of finding new locations for this tree will be in April, when they are in full flower and thus easily seen.

Crataegus marshallii

Parsley Hawthorn

(Parsleyleaf Hawthorn)

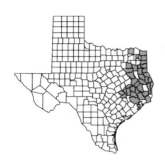

Parsley Hawthorn, a small tree to 25 feet, has an ethereal beauty. From the early spring flowers with their rosy pink stamens and white petals in numerous hanging clusters, from the unfurling of the lacelike, deeply incised fuzzy leaves, to the bright red oblong fruit in September to October, this is a tree of delicate, subdued flamboyancy.

An edge dweller of the Pineywoods, Post Oak Savannah, and Gulf Prairies and Marshes, it will be found in the well-drained, rich, acid sands and sandy loams of these areas. (See plate 6 for range map showing synonyms.)

If brought into cultivation, this species is probably as tolerant of disease and insects as any hawthorn.

Crataegus mollis

Downy Hawthorn

(Red Haw, Downy Thorn)

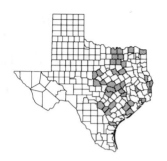

Downy Hawthorn is almost as widely distributed across Texas as Cockspur Hawthorn. It can grow up to 25 feet but is usually not over 12 to 15 feet in height. It is as well adapted on the heavy alkaline clays of the Blacklands as it is on the acid clays of the Gulf Prairies and Marshes and the acid sands and sandy loams of east Texas.

Downy Hawthorn flowers in March to April, and its bright scarlet to crimson fruit ripens from August to October. The large variable leaves are thick with hair on the upper surface and densely fuzzy-white on the undersurface.

Many species have been listed as synonyms for *C. mollis*, such as *C. berlandieri*, *C. brachyphylla*, *C. invisa*, and *C. limaria*. Some authors believe *C. viburnifolia*, *C. texana*, *C. brazoria*, and *C. dallasiana* should be merged with this taxon. (See plate 7 for range map showing synonyms.)

Crataegus opaca

Mayhaw

(May Hawthorn, Western Mayhaw, Apple Haw, Riverflat Hawthorn)

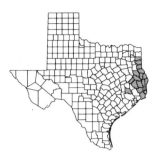

Mayhaw grows to 40 feet in low areas that have standing water most of the year. It occurs in the Pineywoods, with an isolated population west of Interstate Highway 45 just west of Conroe. The five-petaled, fragrant, white flowers are produced from February to March. Mayhaw fruit is quick to mature, and the 1-inch-diameter pomes ripen and fall in May. It is then that entire families go "mayhawing," for some of the best jellies and preserves are made from the fruit. The best way to gather the fruit is to skim the floating haws from the surface of Mayhaw bogs or slashes.

When Mayhaw is grown in cultivation, rather than in standing water, it usually flowers and sets fruit earlier than when it occurs in flooded conditions.

Crataegus reverchonii

Reverchon Hawthorn

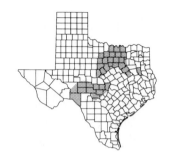

Reverchon Hawthorn is one of the most attractive small trees of north central Texas. Except for a few outlying populations in Cherokee and Freestone counties, this species grows on the limestone soils of the Blacklands, Grand Prairie, and Edwards Plateau and on the neutral to slightly acidic sands and sandy loams of the East and West Cross Timbers. It occurs along the White Rock Escarpment from the Red River through Dallas and the Balcones Escarpment north of Travis County to Uvalde County.

The tree is small, approaching 20 feet in height, and has glistening tan, flaky bark. The fragrant white flowers are borne from April to May, and the reddish orange to red fruit ripens from September to October. Reverchon Hawthorn is the most numerous of all hawthorns in the Dallas—Fort Worth area.

Crataegus spathulata

Littlehip Hawthorn

(Pasture Hawthorn, Small-fruit Hawthorn)

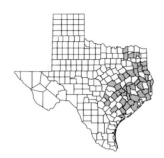

Littlehip Hawthorn is the most numerous hawthorn in east Texas. It grows on almost any soil type and occurs in open pasturelands of the Pineywoods, Post Oak Savannah, and eastern Gulf Prairies and Marshes.

A tall shrub to small tree of about 20 feet in height, it has three- to five-lobed spoon-shaped leaves. It flowers from late March to mid-April, with the bright red fruit ripening in September.

Crataegus texana

Texas Hawthorn

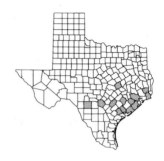

Texas Hawthorn occurs in the rich bottomlands of the Navidad, Brazos, and Guadalupe rivers in the Gulf Prairies and Marshes and in the rich sandy clay loams of the Post Oak Savannah and northern Rio Grande Plains. It flowers in March and April when the leaves are half grown. The large 1-inch fruit ripens in mid-October and is glowing scarlet. Sweet and edible, it is eagerly eaten by wildlife.

Texas Hawthorn and *C. viburnifolia* have been proposed for merger with *C. mollis*.

Crataegus tracyi

Tracy Hawthorn

(Mountain Hawthorn)

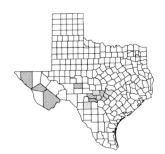

Tracy Hawthorn grows from 12 to 15 feet and occurs on acidic, igneous soils in the Trans-Pecos. The closest I have seen it to growing on limestone soil was on the Caballos Novaculite at Sunshine Springs near Marathon. I have seen this small tree under cultivation on Houston black clay soil with a pH of 7.7 to 8.3, which is typical of the Edwards Plateau, and it became very chlorotic.

Putative Tracy Hawthorn has been collected from limestone soils in Bandera, Hays, Kerr, Comal, Travis, Kendall, Gillespie, Blanco, Uvalde, and Sutton counties on the Edwards Plateau. The tree is closely related to Cockspur Hawthorn, whose western form does grow on strong limestone. Perhaps the Tracy Hawthorn of the Edwards Plateau is more closely related to the western Cockspur Hawthorn than it is to the western Tracy Hawthorn. (See plate 12 for range map showing synonyms.)

Crataegus viridis

Green Hawthorn

(Southern Hawthorn)

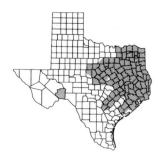

Green Hawthorn is widely distributed over the eastern two thirds of Texas, on clays of the Blacklands and Grand Prairie and on sands, sandy loams, and gravelly clays of the East and West Cross Timbers, Post Oak Savannah, Pineywoods, Gulf Prairies and Marshes, and Edwards Plateau. Average annual rainfall in these areas varies from 11 inches in the west to 55 inches in the east. Soils vary from strong limestone in the west to quite acidic in eastern Texas.

This is a confusing species with several synonyms (see plate 13). Green Hawthorn is usually a shrub in the west and a tree reaching 35 feet in the east. In many cases it is thornless, or it might have small slender thorns. The bark is smooth and light grayish tan.

Cupressus (cypress)

Cupressaceae (cypress family)

There are approximately fifteen species of *Cupressus* in the warm temperate and subtropical areas of the world. The seven species native to the United States are difficult to distinguish from one another. The cypresses are drought resistant, and they are used for erosion control and ornamental purposes wherever rainfall is low and temperatures will permit.

Cupressus arizonica var. *arizonica*

Arizona Cypress

(Arizona Rough Cypress, Cedro, Cedro Blanco, Rough Bark Arizona Cypress)

Arizona Cypress is native to Texas only in the Chisos Mountains of Big Bend National Park in Brewster County. In the protected canyons where they grow, the trees attain heights of almost 90 feet. They constitute a healthy, reproductive population, for the floor of the canyon is replete with small seedlings, 10-foot-tall saplings, and mature trees.

It is unclear why Arizona Cypress occurs only in the Chisos Mountains and not other mountain ranges in the Trans-Pecos.

Almost 60 years ago, orders for seeds of this beautiful evergreen were received from foreign countries that needed a tree for hot, drought conditions. It was then noted that Arizona Cypress was almost a perfect Christmas tree for the arid southwestern states. Today, it is by far the most widely planted tree in west Texas and the southern High Plains, used not only as a specimen tree but also as a dense windbreak on the north, west, and sometimes south sides of farmsteads.

Cyrilla (Leatherwood)

Cyrillaceae (cyrilla family)

Cyrilla is a monotypic genus of the southeastern United States, Central America, and Puerto Rico. Some authors split the species into several varieties and forms.

Cyrilla racemiflora
var. *racemiflora*

Leatherwood

(Black Titi, American Cyrilla, Titi, Swamp Cyrilla, Burnwood Bark, Red Titi, White Titi)

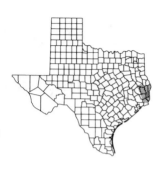

Leatherwood is an attractive small tree that grows to 30 feet in height. The trunk usually divides just above the ground, giving it a symmetrical, round-topped crown. The semievergreen to evergreen leaves are alternate and 2 to 3 inches long. When the leaves color in the fall, they are shades of deep glossy red with patches of green. The fragrant flowers are in dense, white racemes that cover the tree from May through June. The flowers are attractive to bees, and Leatherwood is considered an excellent honey plant.

Leatherwood occurs in wetlands of the Pineywoods and Gulf Prairies and Marshes. It is found where the waters are clear and flowing, in the quiet, pitch-black eddies of the most secluded baygall, or mixed with myrtle and Sweet Bay, as the final natural succession of plants that eventually create new forests from swamps and sphagnum bogs. Yet it might also occur on sandy ridges, for like the Bald Cypress, it does not require an excess of water to survive.

Diospyros (persimmon)

Ebenaceae (ebony family)

Diospyros is chiefly tropical and subtropical in its distribution, although a few species occur in eastern North America, Asia, and the Mediterranean region. There are 175 to 500 species of this genus worldwide. Many of the species are attractive and have edible fruit. Others are prized for their dark, heavy, strong wood, which takes a lustrous polish. The trees have an irregular appearance because there are no terminal buds, so new growth begins each year from buds in the axils of the leaves. The flowers are either male or female and usually occur on separate trees.

Diospyros texana

Texas Persimmon

(Mexican Persimmon, Black Persimmon, Chapote)

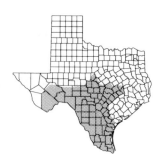

Texas Persimmon occurs in all areas of Texas except the Pineywoods, Rolling Plains, and High Plains. It is a small tree scarcely higher than 10 feet, but reaching 40 feet in favorable situations. In the Edwards Plateau and on the Rio Grande Plains, heavy thickets of Texas Persimmon crowd out all other vegetation and create a serious problem for ranchers.

The trees are dioecious, with the male plants far outnumbering the female plants. The tree is intricately branched, with small, almost stemless leaves that are evergreen in its most southern range and deciduous from San Antonio north. The sweet, edible fruit is small, rarely more than 1 inch in diameter, and turns black when ripe. But it is so crowded with seeds that it is hardly worth eating.

Texas Persimmon has beautiful peeling outer bark and smooth inner bark with shades of gray, white, and pink. Only Texas Madrone has more beautiful bark, yet some individuals of Texas Persimmon match the dark beauty of that fabulous tree. It is one of Texas' premier small trees and is a good tree to use in landscape situations where there is little space. Where space is not a problem, it looks good if used in groves.

It is easily raised from seed or transplanted, although it takes about ten years before the bark starts to peel and slough off when planted from seed. Flowering begins within five or six years after germination.

Diospyros virginiana

Persimmon

(Common Persimmon,
Eastern Persimmon,
Possumwood, Date Plum,
Jove's Fruit, Winter Plum)

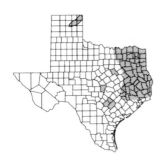

Persimmon can grow to 60 feet in height, although it is usually smaller. The male and female flowers occur on separate trees. The large bright pink fruit is not edible until after sharp freezes. The late Don Correll, who had a passion for the fruit of this tree, had a favorite trick to sweeten the fruit. He would gather the ripened fruit in a plastic bag, leave it overnight in the ice-tray compartment of his refrigerator, and then let it thaw in a crisper drawer, repeating the freezing and thawing if necessary. After a frost, the ripe fruit is eagerly eaten by many species of wildlife.

Persimmon can grow on many soil types, ranging from the acid sands of the east Texas Pineywoods and Post Oak Savannah, the neutral sands and sandy loams of the prairies of the East and West Cross Timbers, and the heavy, alkaline gumbo clays of the Blackland and Grand prairies. However, it is most prolific on the transitional soils on the eastern edge of the Blackland Prairies, where it occurs in great drifts and thickets on the slightly acidic Burleson, Crockett, and Wilson soils.

A large population of Persimmon occurs in the valley of the Canadian River. Here the trees grow in large thickets that predate the settlement of Texas by Europeans. They were probably planted by Indians, who may have brought them out of eastern Kansas or central Oklahoma.

Ehretia (ehretia)

Boraginaceae (borage family)

There are approximately 50 species of *Ehretia* world-wide, with the majority occurring mostly in the Old World. Only one species, *Ehretia anacua,* occurs in northeastern Mexico and southern Texas.

Ehretia anacua

Anacua

(Sugarberry, Knockaway, Knackaway, Anacahuita, Manzanita, Manzanillo)

Anacua is native to the Gulf Prairies and Marshes, Rio Grande Plains, and Edwards Plateau along the Balcones Escarpment in Comal, Hays, and Travis counties. Anacua grows best on alkaline soils with good drainage, although it will grow on neutral to slightly acidic sands and clays. On sandy soils, the tree forms thickets by suckering freely from underground rhizomes. A subtropical tree, it is somewhat cold hardy as far north as Dallas, although it seldom flowers or fruits in that area. It grows to 50 feet in height.

Anacua flowers from late fall, through the winter, and into early spring, depending on rainfall and temperature. The pure white, fragrant flowers cover the tree with densely branched clusters. The bright orange drupes ripen from April to June. They are about the size of the fruit of Hackberry and occur in such numbers as to almost hide the leaves, although they do not remain on the tree long after opening. Anacua fruit is sweet and palatable to many species of wildlife.

Esenbeckia (esenbeckia)

Rutaceae (citrus family)

Esenbeckia is a genus of the New World with approximately 30 tropical and subtropical species. Only one, *Esenbeckia berlandieri,* occurs in Texas and the United States.

Esenbeckia berlandieri

Jopoy

(Berlandier Esenbeckia,
Runyon Esenbeckia)

Jopoy is a small tree of only 15 feet in height. The dark, glossy evergreen or persistent leaves are trifoliate. The perfect white to greenish white fragrant flowers are in terminal clusters. The fruit is a five-part, deeply lobed woody capsule. Jopoy is believed to grow best on well-drained alkaline sands to clays.

For many years, Jopoy was thought to be extinct in Texas. It was last seen as a grove of four small trees on the banks of the Resaca Vieja near Los Fresnos in Cameron County. The land was cleared, and the species was considered extinct until several specimens were found by members of the Native Plant Project, a group of concerned people who are trying to save small acreages of native plant habitat in the Rio Grande Valley. Jopoy is considered the rarest of all trees in Texas.

Fagus (beech)

Fagaceae (beech family)

There are approximately ten species of beech found in the northern temperate regions of the world. One species occurs in North America, and the others occur in Europe, Asia, and Asia Minor. All species have smooth bark and alternate, simple leaves. The sweetly edible fruit is a three-angled nut.

Fagus grandifolia

American Beech

(Beech, White Beech, Red Beech, Ridge Beech, Beech Nut)

American Beech grows in deep, rich, fertile soil in the Piney-woods, preferring well-drained, alluvial, acid sandy loam soils along streams and valleys. The tree will be found with Southern Sugar Maple, Southern Magnolia, Flowering Dogwood, Black Gum, Sweet Gum, Sassafras, Red Oak, White Oak, Wax Myrtle, and other trees that occupy the Loblolly Pine—Sweet Gum association of the pine-hardwood forests throughout southeastern Texas. It attains heights of 130 feet and has beautifully smooth, gray bark. The fruits are easily recognized burs, and the three-angled nuts are sweet and edible.

American Beech is a magnificent tree in all seasons. It has shiny green leaves in the spring that turn a clear, golden yellow in autumn. The leaves then turn a tan brown and remain on the tree well into late February and early March.

Forestiera (forestiera)

Oleaceae (olive family)

The twenty species of *Forestiera* occur in the New World. There are nine species of trees and shrubs in the United States. Five species occur in Texas, of which only one is a tree. The others are large shrubs to small trees. They grow in varying habitats, from swamps to the dry hillsides of the Chihuahuan Desert.

Forestiera acuminata

Swamp Privet

(Texas Privet)

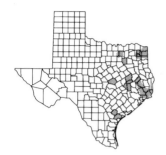

Swamp Privet grows to about 20 feet in height and is found in low swampy areas and wet drainages of northeastern to southeastern Texas. It is also found south to Victoria and Refugio counties and west to Bell County. An uncommon tree in these lowland woods, Swamp Privet is best seen when in flower in early spring. The male and female flowers are without petals and occur on separate trees. The bright yellow male flowers are borne in dense clusters. The fruit is a purple drupe and is eaten by various species of waterfowl.

Fraxinus (ash)

Oleaceae (olive family)

There are about 70 species of *Fraxinus* worldwide, with approximately 50 species in eastern Asia south to Java. Four or 5 species occur in Mexico and Guatemala; of the 16 species found in the United States, 7 also occur in Mexico and 9 occur in Texas. Those in the eastern part of the state may grow in standing water, and those in the west grow in desert washes. They range from more than 100 feet in height to scarcely 20 feet and are evergreen or deciduous.

Fraxinus americana

White Ash

(Biltmore Ash,
Biltmore White Ash,
Cane Ash,
Smallseed White Ash)

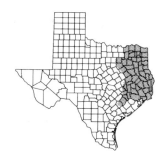

White Ash grows to 100 feet and occurs in the deep, rich moist soils in the eastern third of Texas. The male and female flowers are produced on separate trees in April to May. The male trees flower yearly, but the female trees flower and fruit only every three to five years. The leaves are deciduous and turn to delicate pastel shades of pink, orange, and purple in autumn. They are pinnately compound with five to nine leaflets, although seven is the usual number.

Fraxinus berlandieriana

Mexican Ash

(Berlandier Ash, Plumero, Fresno)

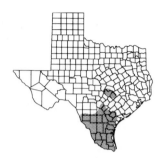

Mexican Ash grows to 30 feet in height in moist canyons, stream banks, and sloughs of the Rio Grande Plains and southern Gulf Prairies and Marshes. Except for a disjunct population in Bastrop and Travis counties in the Edwards Plateau, it is seldom seen east of the Colorado River. The tree's range is mostly west of, but includes, the valleys of the San Antonio River.

Fraxinus caroliniana

Carolina Ash

(Water Ash, Swamp Ash, Pop Ash, Florida Ash, Poppy Ash)

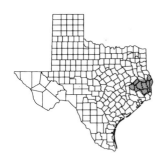

Carolina Ash, usually less than 40 feet tall, occurs in deep river swamps, lagoons, and baygalls that are flooded most of the year. It is part of the Bald Cypress—Water Tupelo swamp and Willow Oak—Water Oak—Black Gum forest association of deep southeast Texas. It is possible that at one time this tree occurred in any of the flooded areas of the Big Thicket. The fruit of Carolina Ash is three-winged and quite different in appearance from the fruit of other ash species. Two places to observe this tree are Big Cow Creek in Newton County and the east side of Dam B in Jasper County.

Fraxinus cuspidata

Fragrant Ash

(Flowering Ash, Fresno)

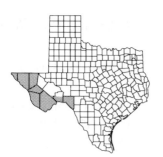

Fragrant Ash differs from the other ash species in having strongly fragrant white-petaled, perfect flowers. The flowers appear as the leaves begin to unfurl and are borne in clusters 3 to 4 inches long. The four white petals have long, narrow lobes, and the trees sometimes seem to be completely covered with a blanket of white.

Fragrant Ash is only 12 to 20 feet tall, growing in side canyons of the Devils and Pecos rivers and the Rio Grande in Val Verde County on the western Edwards Plateau. It also occurs in the Trans-Pecos on rocky, gravelly hillsides at altitudes of 4,000 feet or more in the Chisos, Santiago, Davis, Vieja, Diablo, Quitman, and Hueco mountains. It seems to grow equally well in slightly acidic igneous or slightly alkaline limestone soils. It grows in cultivation on heavy blackland clay soils with a pH of 7.5.

Fraxinus greggii

Gregg Ash

(Littleleaf Ash, Dogleg Ash, Escobilla, Barreta China, Fresno)

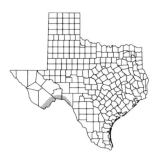

Gregg Ash is an outstanding large shrub or small tree, reaching heights of 20 feet. It occurs on harsh limestone hillsides but more often in dry creek beds and desert washes in Val Verde County on the western Edwards Plateau, Terrell County, and the southern part of Brewster County west of the Pecos River. It attains its greatest size just west of the Pecos on the road from Ozona to Langtry and is most numerous in the dry wash of Blue Creek Canyon in Big Bend National Park.

The flowers of Gregg Ash are perfect, male, or female, and all can occur on different trees, the same tree, or even in the same cluster. The evergreen leaves are usually trifoliate, but sometimes they are pinnately compound, with five to seven small leaflets.

Fraxinus papillosa

Chihuahua Ash

Chihuahua Ash ranges from 12 to 20 feet in height and has pinnately compound leaves with seven to nine leaflets. The leaflets are somewhat leathery, with microscopic papillae on the underside, and are more or less sessile (no stalk).

Chihuahua Ash occurs in the Chinati Mountains in Presidio County and is also thought to occur in the Bofecillos Mountain range to the east and the Sierra Vieja range just north of Chinati Peak. Several botanists believe it is part of the *Fraxinus velutina* complex on Big Bend Ranch, especially around Madera Falls.

Fraxinus pennsylvanica

Green Ash

(Red Ash, Darlington Ash, Swamp Ash, River Ash, Water Ash)

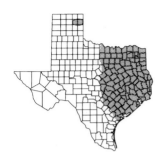

The most wide-ranging of all ashes in Texas is Green Ash. This species grows to 80 feet in height and occurs in the Pineywoods, Gulf Prairies and Marshes, Post Oak Savannah, Blackland Prairies, Cross Timbers and Prairies, Rio Grande Plains, and Rolling Plains. It ranges as far west and north as Hemphill and Roberts counties in the Texas Panhandle along the banks of the Canadian River. Green Ash grows equally well on heavy limestone clays and acid sands and sandy loams. However, it requires quite a bit of moisture, so it grows along rivers and streams, in alluvial woods, swamps, and floodplains, and in swales and depressions in prairies. Although Green Ash is widely planted in shelter belts and cultivated landscapes on the Northern Plains, it does not do well in areas below 3,000 feet in the central and southern parts of Texas.

Fraxinus texensis

Texas Ash

(Mountain Ash)

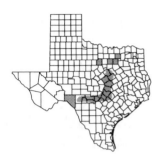

Texas Ash is a small tree less than 50 feet in height. It grows on high limestone bluffs in Dallas and Tarrant counties north to the limestone Arbuckle Mountains in Oklahoma, west to Palo Pinto County, and then down the Balcones Escarpment of the Edwards Plateau, through Real to Val Verde County on the far west. In these vegetative areas, rainfall barely totals 15 to 32 inches per year, and effective rainfall on these steeply sloped, thin-soiled hills is less. This tree is useful for landscaping because of its low water requirements.

In the fall of the year, these small trees turn pastel hues of red, gold, orange, and purple that compete favorably with the brisk reds of Texas Red Oak and Prairie Flameleaf Sumac.

Fraxinus velutina

Velvet Ash

(Arizona Ash, Modesto Ash, Desert Ash, Leatherleaf Ash, Smooth Ash, Toumey Ash, Fresno, Standley Ash)

Velvet Ash grows to 85 feet in height and occurs in the high mountains and cool, narrow canyons of the Trans-Pecos. It grows along streams, rivers, moist washes, dry streambeds, narrow canyons, on the north sides of mountains and hills, and at altitudes of 2,500 to 6,000 feet. It grows on either limestone or igneous soils in the Chisos, Chinati, Bofecillos, Vieja, Davis, and Guadalupe mountains in the Trans-Pecos.

Because it is easily raised from seed and grows off rapidly in nursery situations, it has been planted in almost every landscape. Every summer across Texas, borers decimate the millions of Arizona and Modesto ashes planted in the landscapes of various homes, institutions, and businesses.

Gleditsia (honey locust)

Leguminosae (legume family)

There are approximately fourteen species of *Gleditsia* in Africa, Asia, North America, and South America. There are two species native to the United States. Both are trees and both occur in Texas.

Gleditsia aquatica

Water Locust

(Swamp Locust)

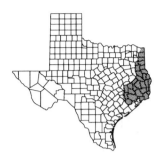

One of the most interesting causeways florally in Texas is U.S. Highway 190 as it crosses B. A. Steinhagen Lake on the Neches River at the Jasper-Tyler county line. Here are the best examples of Two-wing Silverbells in Texas, along with the most accessible Water Locust.

Water Locust grows to a height of 60 feet, although it is a 10-foot-tall shrub on the Dam B causeway. It grows along rivers and swamps or in standing water of lagoons and sloughs. It sometimes forms large thickets in rather deep water. Water Locust is limited to the Pineywoods, the Gulf Prairies and Marshes, and the river bottoms and drainageways of the Post Oak Savannah. Flowering occurs from May to June after the tree has leafed out. The fruit is a small legume with usually one seed per pod, but sometimes up to three seeds per pod, that ripens in August. The tree is sharply spined.

Gleditsia triacanthos

Honey Locust

(Sweet Locust, Thorny Locust Sweet Bean Tree, Sweet Locust, Honey Shucks Locust)

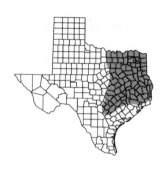

Honey Locust is a viciously thorned tree that grows to 100 feet in height. It occurs on rich soils in the eastern third of Texas. It was recorded many years ago in Palo Duro Canyon, although that specimen might have been planted.

The tree flowers late, as do almost all leguminous trees in Texas, but they are never caught by frosts. The 12- to 18-inch-long fruit pods form in late summer and early autumn and are eagerly eaten by cattle, deer, and other animals.

The three-pronged thorns of Honey Locust can sometimes be 12 inches long, although some trees are thornless. The thorns grow from buds deep within the tree.

Honey Locust is relatively tolerant of salt and drought, although it will sometimes throw off limbs to survive long dry periods. It is widely used in landscapes on the High Plains and other areas of west Texas.

Halesia (silverbell)

Styracaceae (storax family)

There are three species of *Halesia* in the United States and one in China, for a total of four worldwide. *Halesia carolina* is listed by many authors as occurring in Texas, although I have never seen the tree in Texas or any herbarium specimen from Texas. I have never conversed with anyone who has firsthand knowledge of this plant in Texas. It might be expected to grow in Bowie and Red River counties because it occurs just across the state line in McCurtain County, Oklahoma. The fruit has four wings instead of two, and the plant is larger than *Halesia diptera* (Two-winged Silverbell).

Halesia diptera

Two-winged Silverbell

(Silverbell, Snowdrop Tree, Snowbell, Cowlicks)

Two-winged Silverbell is a small understory tree of the southern Pineywoods and the eastern Gulf Prairies and Marshes. It grows on rather moist acid soils, usually on stream banks. The alternate leaves are deciduous and range from 3 to 7 inches long. The beauty of Two-winged Silverbell is its annual spring show in March and April, when its waxy white, four-petaled, 1-inch flowers bloom on wood formed the previous year. The tight little clusters of stamens sometimes turn upright and resemble bright candles at Christmastime. The lovely flowers are soon followed by the 2-inch-long fruit with its two corky wings.

Helietta (helietta)

Rutaceae (citrus family)

There are approximately eight species of *Helietta* in the subtropics of the New World. Only one species, *Helietta parvifolia,* occurs in the United States, where it grows on the limestone soils in the Rio Grande Valley of Texas.

Helietta parvifolia

Baretta

Baretta is a slender evergreen tree that grows to between 12 and 20 feet in height. In Texas it is confined to several small gravelly hills just east of Rio Grande City in Starr County and the chaparral for quite a few miles north of Rio Grande City. It apparently was rather common in those areas before 1940 but is less common now. The plant is widespread south of the Rio Grande in Mexico.

Tiny, greenish white, perfect flowers are borne in terminal clusters from March to May, with the small, dry, winged fruit ripening from September to October. The bark breaks into large brown patches and flakes off, leaving lighter tan wood underneath. The resinous evergreen leaves are trifoliate and emit a pungent, though not unpleasant, odor when crushed.

Ilex (holly)

Aquifoliaceae (holly family)

The genus *Ilex* has 300 to 380 species worldwide in the tropical, subtropical, and temperate regions of Africa, America, Asia, and Europe. Most of the species are tropical, occurring in China and Brazil. The United States has 11 to 13 treelike and 1 shrub species of holly. Many of the treelike species are also large shrubs. Hollies occur in the eastern to south-central and southeastern regions of the United States. *Ilex vomitoria* and *I. decidua* occur farther west in Texas (Kerr County) than in any other area of the United States. *I. opaca* ranges to the eastern shores of Massachusetts and is the most northern of all hollies. There are 7 treelike and 1 shrub species of holly in Texas. Three additional species are of questionable occurrence in the state (*I. cassine, I. montana,* and *I. myrtifolia*). The male and female flowers of holly usually occur on different trees, although sometimes they occur on the same tree, and most species will produce a few perfect flowers.

Ilex ambigua

Carolina Holly

(Sand Holly, Possum Holly)

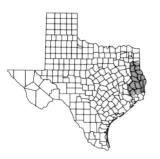

Carolina Holly is extremely rare in Texas. It grows in moist uplands, sandy woods, and along streams in Hardin County, in the Big Thicket west to Montgomery County, and north to Smith and Upshur counties. This appears to be a wide range, but there are usually only a few plants at each location, and they tend to be shrubs more often than trees.

This holly is difficult to identify, as the specific epithet suggests. One of the problems in finding this small tree is that the bright red, translucent drupe ripens in August or September and falls quickly. However, the fruit is without a stem (sessile), which should be a helpful identifying characteristic.

Ilex coriacea

Baygall Bush

(Large Gallberry, Gallberry, Inkberry, Shining Inkberry, Tall Inkberry Holly)

This little evergreen tree grows only 12 to 15 feet tall and probably should not be included with the large hollies. It is one of the few hollies with black fruit. Baygall Bush occurs in swamps and along sluggish streams as part of the Willow Oak—Water Oak—Black Gum association, and the Bald Cypress—Water Tupelo swamp association, and the young forest—grassland association. This holly is abundant in the forests and swamps north of Sour Lake in Hardin County in the Big Thicket and ranges as far west as Montgomery County north of Houston.

Ilex decidua

Possum Haw

(Bearberry, Deciduous Holly, Meadow Holly, Prairie Holly, Swamp Holly, Welk Holly, Winterberry)

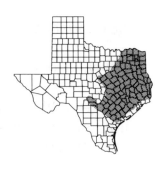

Possum Haw grows 10 to 15 feet tall but can attain heights of 20 to 25 feet. However, it is often a shrub of less than 8 feet tall. The widest ranging of any of the Texas hollies, it occurs as far south as Aransas County, as far west as Kerr County on the Edwards Plateau and Comanche County on the West Cross Timbers, as far north as the Red River Valley, and northwest to Grayson County. Possum Haw ranges from the extremely acidic sands and 55-inch rainfall belt of Newton County, the heavy, rich alkaline clay soils of the Blackland Prairies in the 32-inch rainfall belt, to the slightly acidic sands and 28-inch rainfall belt of Comanche County. Male plants outnumber female plants almost ten to one. The female trees, with their crimson, scarlet, orange, or almost yellow fruit, are easily spotted from November to February. The drupes are eaten by many birds, but only reluctantly, after many freezing and thawing cycles.

Ilex longipes

Georgia Holly

(Chapman Holly)

Georgia Holly can grow to 25 feet in height but is usually a shrub of 6 to 12 feet. It is closely related to *Ilex decidua,* and some authors consider it a variety of Possum Haw. The red, persistent fruits are borne on 1½-inch stalks and are usually solitary. The leaves are tardily deciduous in Texas. In Jasper, Newton, San Jacinto, Trinity, Polk, Harris, Montgomery, Madison, and Walker counties, Georgia Holly is an understory plant that grows on acid sands and sandy loams along stream banks. It probably also occurs in Tyler, Hardin, Liberty, Angelina, San Augustine, and Sabine counties.

Ilex opaca var. *opaca*

American Holly

(Yule Holly, White Holly, Christmas Holly, Prickly Holly, Evergreen Holly)

American Holly, one of Texas' premier broad-leaved evergreens, grows in the Pineywoods, Gulf Prairies and Marshes, and Post Oak Savannah. The trees attain their largest size, almost 60 feet, in moist, rich soils but also grow well on dry hillsides. In all cases, the soils are acidic.

The male and female flowers are borne on separate trees, with the males outnumbering the females ten to one. To most people, the female trees are the prettiest because they bear the bright red holly berries.

Many specimens of American Holly can be easily seen along Interstate Highway 45. These trees grow on both sides of the highway beginning just southeast of Corsicana, on the acid sands of the Post Oak Savannah.

Ilex verticillata

Winterberry

(Common Winterberry, Black Alder)

Winterberry was discovered in Texas in 1959 and is still not listed by many authors. It grows to heights of 15 feet and is part of the Bald Cypress—Water Tupelo swamp association and the Willow Oak—Water Oak—Black Gum forest association of the lower Sabine River floodplains in Orange and Newton counties. The best way to see it is by boat on the Sabine River, or walk up the river from the Interstate Highway 10 bridge at Orange. The first trees occur within 100 feet of the bridge. The best time to see these trees is from early November on through the winter when the bright red fruit covers the limbs. The fruit, at least farther north, persists all through the winter, hence the name "Winterberry."

Ilex vomitoria

Yaupon

(Cassine, Evergreen Cassena, Emetic Holly, Evergreen Holly, Indian Blackdrink, Cassio Berry Bush Tea)

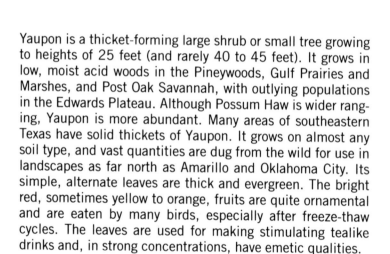

Yaupon is a thicket-forming large shrub or small tree growing to heights of 25 feet (and rarely 40 to 45 feet). It grows in low, moist acid woods in the Pineywoods, Gulf Prairies and Marshes, and Post Oak Savannah, with outlying populations in the Edwards Plateau. Although Possum Haw is wider ranging, Yaupon is more abundant. Many areas of southeastern Texas have solid thickets of Yaupon. It grows on almost any soil type, and vast quantities are dug from the wild for use in landscapes as far north as Amarillo and Oklahoma City. Its simple, alternate leaves are thick and evergreen. The bright red, sometimes yellow to orange, fruits are quite ornamental and are eaten by many birds, especially after freeze-thaw cycles. The leaves are used for making stimulating tealike drinks and, in strong concentrations, have emetic qualities.

Juglans (walnut)

Juglandaceae (walnut family)

There are approximately twenty species of *Juglans* in temperate and tropical areas of the world. Eurasia has five and the West Indies has one species. There are five species in the Andes of South America, three in Mexico and Central America, and six in the United States, with three of them in Texas. The species are all medium-to-large trees with deep taproots. Their edible nuts are valued by many species of wildlife. Some of the world's finest cabinet wood comes from walnut.

Juglans major

Arizona Walnut

(Nogal, Nogal Silvestre, Arizona Black Walnut, River Walnut, Mountain Walnut)

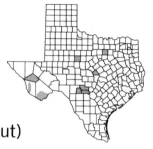

Arizona Walnut grows to 50 feet high in the dry waterways, canyons, and streambeds of Kerr, Bandera, and Real counties of the Edwards Plateau and the Chisos, Davis, and Chinati Mountains of the Trans-Pecos. It is closely related to *Juglans microcarpa* (Nogalito) but is larger, has fewer leaflets, and bears a nut that is only 5 millimeters larger. The putative stands of Arizona Walnut near Fort Worth in Tarrant County and in Taylor and Lampasas counties may actually be *J. microcarpa*. Nogalito does exist in Fort Richardson State Park at Jacksboro in Jack County, and in Palo Pinto County.

Juglans microcarpa

Nogalito

(Little Walnut, Texas Walnut, Texas Black Walnut, River Walnut, Nogal, Namboca)

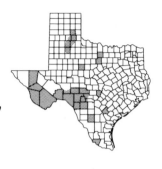

Nogalito is a many-trunked shrub or small tree growing 30 feet tall in valleys, rocky streambeds, and the first terraces of dry riverbeds in Karnes, LaSalle, Starr, and Uvalde counties on the Rio Grande Plains; Blanco, Edwards, Kerr, Kimble, Sutton, and Val Verde counties on the Edwards Plateau; Jack and Palo Pinto counties in the West Cross Timbers; Crosby, Donley, Floyd, Motley, and Taylor counties in the Red Rolling Plains; and Brewster, Culberson, Jeff Davis, Presidio, and Terrell counties in the Trans-Pecos. It occurs in other areas where it can obtain water from stream sides or flash floods. Nogalito is also a phreatophyte: its long taproot can extract shallow water from below, whether from running, table, or perched sources.

This species produces small nuts that are only ½ to ¾ inch in diameter. The high-quality meat has an excellent taste and is eaten by rock squirrels and other rodents. It is closely related to Arizona Walnut; the two species are difficult to distinguish when they occur together.

Juglans nigra

Black Walnut

(American Black Walnut, Eastern Black Walnut)

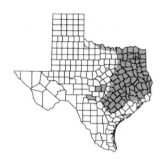

Black Walnut has probably been "high-graded" several times during the 1800s, and it has certainly been picked over a time or two since 1900, because the tallest trees are less than 80 feet high. It occurs in all areas of Texas except the Rio Grande Plains, High Plains, and Trans-Pecos. It requires deep, rich limestone soils and, therefore, is not especially abundant in the Pineywoods. When found in east Texas, it is usually on deep alluvial soils that are rich in calcium.

Black Walnut requires a fairly constant source of moisture. It occurs in the valley and on the banks of the Red River westward into Wilbarger County on the Red Rolling Plains. On the Blackland Prairies, which normally receive 35 inches of rain annually, Black Walnut suffers massive die-offs of limbs in long, dry summers.

Some botanists believe that the absence of vast thickets of Black Walnut is due to allelopathy (the action of one plant against another). Roots and leaves exude a chemical called juglone (a tannic acid) that prevents the growth of seedlings, even other walnuts, around the parent tree.

Juniperus (juniper)

Cupressaceae (cypress family)

Junipers total about 50 species worldwide. All are native to the Northern Hemisphere, with 25 species occurring in the New World and 25 species in the Old World. There are 13 species of *Juniperus* in the United States, with Texas having 9 species. Junipers are evergreen and resinous, with separate male and female cones that usually occur on different trees. The fruits are fleshy or leathery berrylike cones. Except for *Juniperus virginiana,* which grows in relatively fertile soil and fair moisture conditions, and *J. silicicola,* which must grow under high-moisture regimes, the Texas species of *Juniperus* grow best on well-drained soils in low-rainfall areas. Some species are found in highly alkaline soil, and a few grow in igneous soils.

Juniperus ashei

Ashe Juniper

(Mountain Cedar, Rock Cedar, Post Cedar, Mexican Juniper, Break Cedar, Texas Cedar, Sabino)

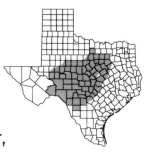

Ashe Juniper occurs on limestone soils that were part of an ancient reef more than 60 million years old. The juniper ranges from the southern Ozarks in Arkansas and Missouri, down through the Arbuckle Mountains in Oklahoma, and into Texas, where it approximately marks the eastern edge of the Balcones Escarpment fault line. It then crosses the Pecos River into Terrell County and northern Mexico. Here it forms great thickets and drifts. When the Edwards Plateau was first settled, Ashe Juniper occupied only the stoniest, steepest hillsides and the heads of canyons, places where they were not destroyed by fires. After the settlers stopped the fires, Ashe Juniper began to colonize the lands.

Ashe Juniper is a small, many-stemmed tree growing to 38 feet in height. The bark comes off in long, narrow strips that are used for nest material by the golden-cheeked warbler. The leaves are minutely saw-toothed and smell like cedar. Male and female flowers are borne on separate trees, and the large blue berrylike cones are eagerly eaten by wildlife. The heartwood of this species makes excellent fence posts. Ashe Juniper is closely related to *Juniperus monosperma* in west Texas, but they do not overlap in distribution. Some authors believe that Ashe Juniper hybridizes with *J. virginiana,* but generally *J. virginiana* flowers later.

Crataegus berberifolia
Barberry Hawthorn

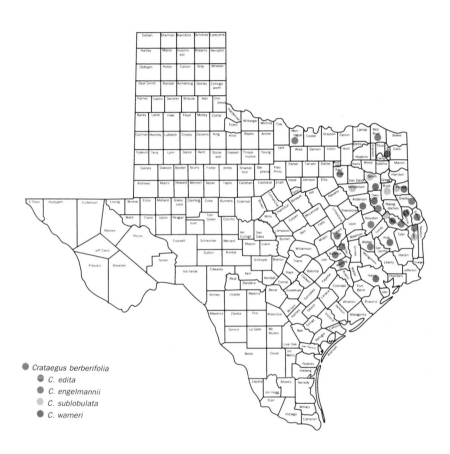

Crataegus berberifolia
- C. edita
- C. engelmannii
- C. sublobulata
- C. warneri

Plate 1

Crataegus brachyacantha
Blueberry Hawthorn

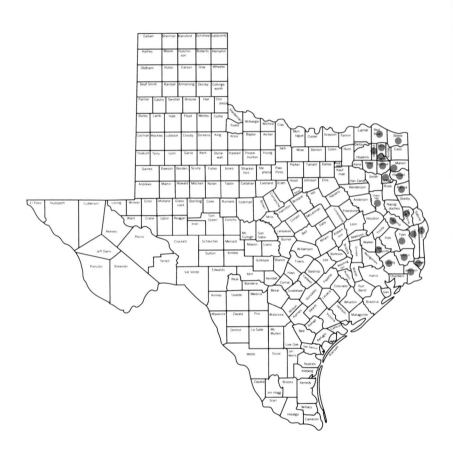

Plate 2

Crataegus calpodendron
Pear Hawthorn

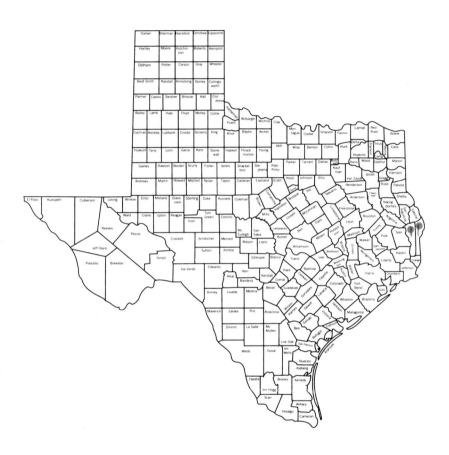

Plate 3

Crataegus crus-galli
Cockspur Hawthorn

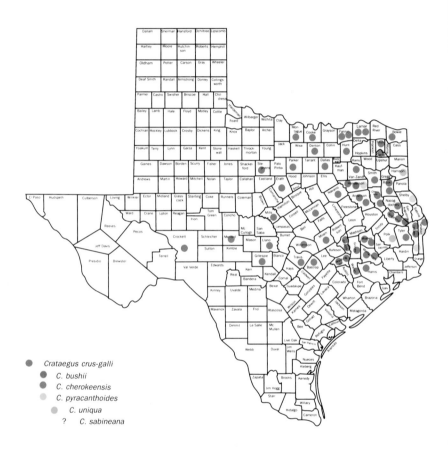

- ● *Crataegus crus-galli*
  - ● *C. bushii*
  - ● *C. cherokeensis*
  - ○ *C. pyracanthoides*
  - ● *C. uniqua*
  - ? *C. sabineana*

Plate 4

Crataegus greggiana
Gregg Hawthorn

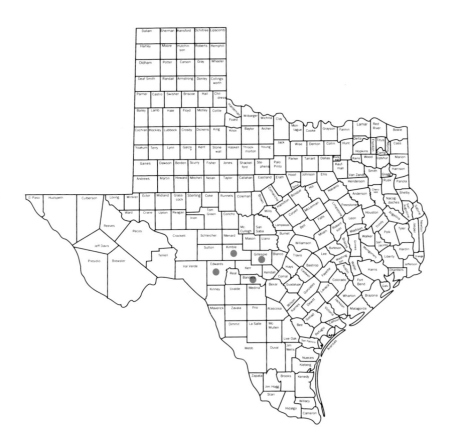

Plate 5

Crataegus marshallii
Parsley Hawthorn

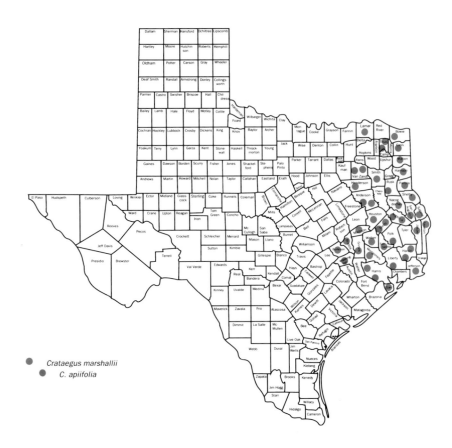

● *Crataegus marshallii*
● *C. apiifolia*

Plate 6

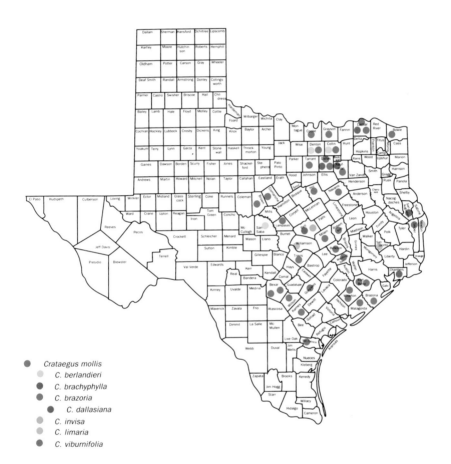

Crataegus mollis
Downy Hawthorn

- *Crataegus mollis*
- *C. berlandieri*
- *C. brachyphylla*
- *C. brazoria*
- *C. dallasiana*
- *C. invisa*
- *C. limaria*
- *C. viburnifolia*

Plate 7

Crataegus opaca
Mayhaw

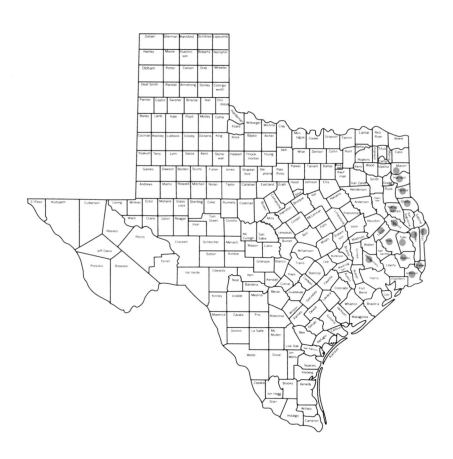

Plate 8

Crataegus reverchonii
Reverchon Hawthorn

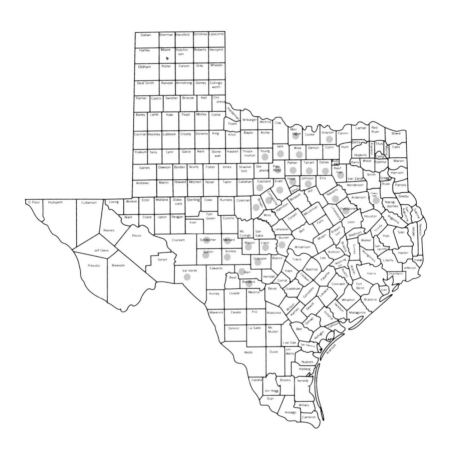

Plate 9

Crataegus spathulata
Littlehip Hawthorn

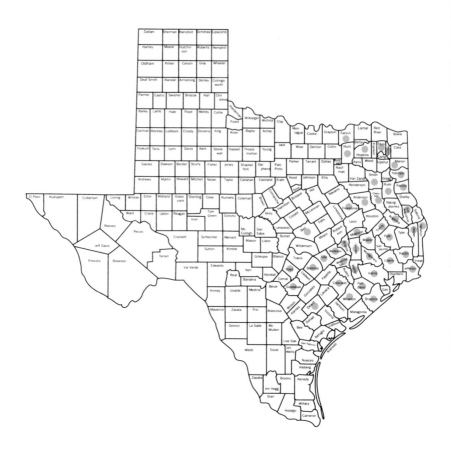

Plate 10

Crataegus texana
Texas Hawthorn

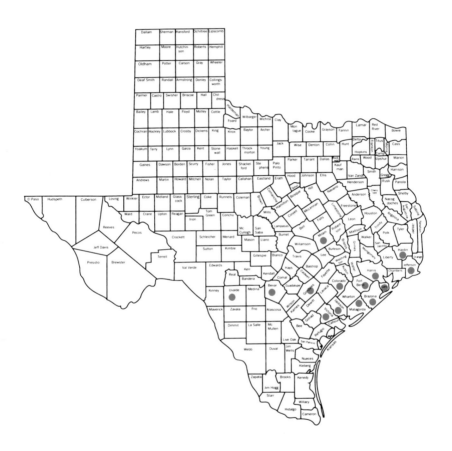

Plate 11

Crataegus tracyi
Tracy Hawthorn

● *Crataegus tracyi*
  ○ *C. montivaga*

Plate 12

Crataegus viridis
Green Hawthorn

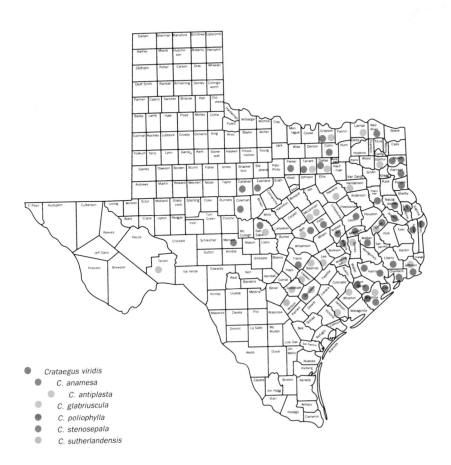

- ● Crataegus viridis
  - ● C. anamesa
    - ● C. antiplasta
  - ● C. glabriuscula
  - ● C. poliophylla
  - ● C. stenosepala
  - ● C. sutherlandensis

Plate 13

Red Oak Complex

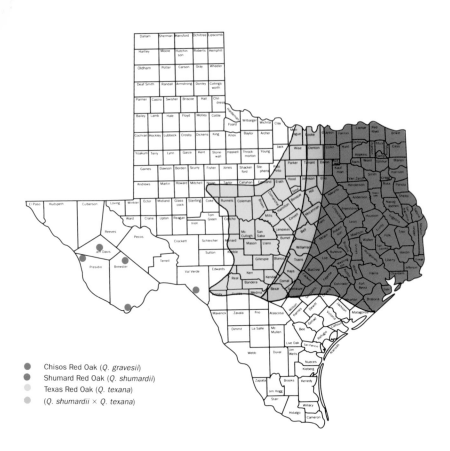

● Chisos Red Oak (*Q. gravesii*)
● Shumard Red Oak (*Q. shumardii*)
○ Texas Red Oak (*Q. texana*)
○ (*Q. shumardii* × *Q. texana*)

Plate 14

Live Oak Complex

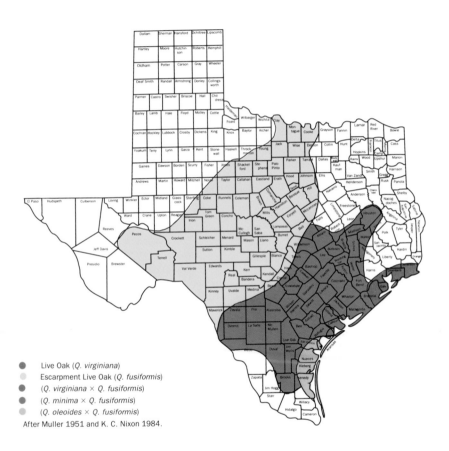

- Live Oak (*Q. virginiana*)
- Escarpment Live Oak (*Q. fusiformis*)
- (*Q. virginiana* × *Q. fusiformis*)
- (*Q. minima* × *Q. fusiformis*)
- (*Q. oleoides* × *Q. fusiformis*)

After Muller 1951 and K. C. Nixon 1984.

Plate 15

Acacia farnesiana
(*Acacia smalii*)
Huisache

Acacia greggii
Gregg Acacia

Plate 16

Acacia roemeriana
Roemer Acacia

Acacia tortuosa
(*A. schaffneri* var. *bravoensis*)
Huisachillo

Acacia wrightii
Wright Acacia

Plate 17

Acer barbatum
Southern Sugar Maple

Acer grandidentatum
Bigtooth Maple

Plate 18

Acer leucoderme
Chalk Maple

Acer negundo
Box Elder

Plate 19

Acer rubrum
Red Maple

Aesculus glabra
var. *arguta*
Texas buckeye

Aesculus pavia
var. *flavescens*

Plate 20

Aesculus pavia
var. *pavia*
Red Buckeye

Alnus serrulata
Smooth Alder

Plate 21

Amelanchier utahensis
Utah Serviceberry

Aralia spinosa
Devil's Walking Stick

Plate 22

Arbutus texana
(*Arbutus xalapensis*)
Texas Madrone

Arbutus texana
(*Arbutus xalapensis*)
Texas Madrone

Arbutus texana
(*Arbutus xalapensis*)
Texas Madrone

Plate 23

Asimina triloba
Pawpaw

Betula nigra
River Birch

Plate 24

Bumelia celastrina
Saffron Plum

Bumelia lanuginosa
Gum Bumelia

Bumelia lycioides
Buckthorn Bumelia

Plate 25

Caesalpinia mexicana
Mexican Caesalpinia

Carpinus caroliniana
American Hornbeam

Plate 26

Carya aquatica
Water Hickory

Carya cordiformis
Bitternut Hickory

Carya glabra var. *glabra*
Pignut Hickory

Plate 27

Carya illinoensis
Pecan

Carya myristiciformis
Nutmeg Hickory

Carya ovata var. *ovata*
Shagbark Hickory

Plate 28

Carya texana
Black Hickory

Carya tomentosa
Mockernut Hickory

Castanea pumila
Allegheny Chinquapin

Plate 29

Celtis laevigata
Sugarberry

Celtis lindheimeri
Lindheimer Hackberry
Vernon L. Wesby

Plate 30

Celtis occidentalis
Hackberry

Celtis reticulata
Netleaf Hackberry

Celtis tenuifolia
Dwarf Hackberry

Cercidium texanum
Texas Paloverde

Plate 31

Cercis canadensis
var. *canadensis*
Eastern Redbud

Cercis canadensis
var. *mexicana*
Mexican Redbud

Cercis canadensis
var. *texensis*
Texas Redbud

Plate 32

Cercocarpus breviflorus
(*Cercocarpus montanus*
var. *paucidentatus*)
Hairy Cercocarpus

Cercocarpus montanus
var. *argenteus*
Silver Mountain Mahogany

Cercocarpus montanus
var. *glaber*
Smooth Mountain Mahogany

Plate 33

Chilopsis linearis
Desert Willow

Chionanthus virginicus
Fringe Tree

Condalia hookeri
var. *hookeri*
Brasil

Cordia boissieri
Wild Olive

Plate 34

Cornus florida
Flowering Dogwood

Cornus florida
Flowering Dogwood

Cornus florida
Flowering Dogwood

Plate 35

Cotinus obovatus
American Smoke Tree

Crataegus berberifolia
Barberry Hawthorn

Crataegus brachyacantha
Blueberry Hawthorn

Plate 36

Crataegus calpodendron
Pear Hawthorn

Crataegus crus-galli
Cockspur Hawthorn

Crataegus greggiana
Gregg Hawthorn

Plate 37

Crataegus marshallii
Parsley Hawthorn

Crataegus mollis
Downy Hawthorn

Plate 38

Crataegus opaca
Mayhaw

Crataegus reverchonii
Reverchon Hawthorn

Plate 39

Crataegus spathulata
Littlehip Hawthorn

Crataegus texana
Texas Hawthorn

Crataegus tracyi
Tracy Hawthorn

Plate 40

Crataegus viridis
Green Hawthorn

Crataegus viridis
Green Hawthorn

Plate 41

Cupressus arizonica
var. *arizonica*
Arizona Cypress

Cyrilla racemiflora
var. *racemiflora*
Leatherwood

Plate 42

Diospyros texana
Texas Persimmon

Diospyros virginiana
Persimmon

Plate 43

Ehretia anacua
Anacua

Esenbeckia berlandieri
Jopoy

Plate 44

Fagus grandifolia
American Beech

Forestiera acuminata
Swamp Privet
J. H. Gardenhire

Plate 45

Fraxinus americana
White Ash

Fraxinus berlandieriana
Mexican Ash

Fraxinus caroliniana
Carolina Ash

Plate 46

Fraxinus cuspidata
Fragrant Ash
Barton H. Warnock

Fraxinus greggii
Gregg Ash

Plate 47

Fraxinus papillosa
Chihuahua Ash

Fraxinus pennsylvanica
Green Ash

Fraxinus texensis
Texas Ash

Plate 48

Fraxinus velutina
Arizona Ash

Gleditsia aquatica
Water Locust

Gleditsia triacanthos
Honey Locust

Plate 49

Halesia diptera
Two-winged Silverbell

Helietta parvifolia
Baretta

Ilex ambigua
Carolina Holly

Ilex coriacea
Baygall Bush

Plate 50

Ilex decidua
Possum Haw

Ilex longipes
Georgia Holly

Plate 51

Ilex opaca var. *opaca*
American Holly

Ilex verticillata
Winterberry

Ilex vomitoria
Yaupon

Plate 52

Juglans major
Arizona Walnut
Vernon L. Wesby

Juglans microcarpa
Nogalito

Plate 53

Juglans nigra
Black Walnut

Juniperus ashei
Ashe Juniper

Plate 54

Juniperus deppeana
Alligator Juniper

Juniperus erythrocarpa
Redberry Juniper

Plate 55

Juniperus flaccida
Weeping Juniper

Juniperus monosperma
One-seed Juniper

Plate 56

Juniperus pinchotii
Pinchot Juniper

Juniperus scopulorum
Rocky Mountain Juniper

Juniperus silicicola
Southern Red Cedar

Plate 57

Juniperus virginiana
Eastern Red Cedar

Leucaena pulverulenta
Great Leadtree

Plate 58

Leucaena retusa
Goldenball Leadtree

Liquidambar styraciflua
Sweet Gum

Plate 59

Maclura pomifera
Bois d'Arc

Magnolia grandiflora
Southern Magnolia

Plate 60

Magnolia pyramidata
Pyramid Magnolia

Magnolia virginiana
Sweet Bay

Plate 61

Malus angustifolia
Southern Crabapple

Malus ioensis
Prairie Crabapple

Plate 62

Morus microphylla
Texas Mulberry

Morus rubra
Red Mulberry

Myrica cerifera
Southern Wax Myrtle

Plate 63

Nyssa aquatica
Water Tupelo

Nyssa sylvatica var. *biflora*
Swamp Tupelo

Nyssa sylvatica var. *sylvatica*
Black Gum

Plate 64

Ostrya chisosensis
Chisos Hop Hornbeam

Ostrya knowltonii
Knowlton Hop Hornbeam

Ostrya virginiana
Eastern Hop Hornbeam

Plate 65

Parkinsonia aculeata
Retama

Persea borbonia
var. *borbonia*
Red Bay

Plate 66

Persea borbonia
var. *pubescens*
Swamp Bay

Pinus cembroides
Mexican Pinyon

Pinus echinata
Shortleaf Pine

Pinus edulis
Pinyon

Plate 67

Pinus palustris
Longleaf Pine

Pinus ponderosa
var. *scopulorum*
Rocky Mountain Ponderosa Pine

Plate 68

Pinus strobiformis
Southwestern White Pine

Pinus taeda
Loblolly Pine

Plate 69

Pistacia texana
Texas Pistache

Pithecellobium flexicaule
Texas Ebony

Plate 70

Planera aquatica
Water Elm

Platanus occidentalis
Sycamore

Plate 71

Populus deltoides
var. *deltoides*
Eastern Cottonwood

Populus deltoides
var. *occidentalis*
Plains Cottonwood

Populus fremontii
var. *mesetae*
Meseta Cottonwood

Plate 72

Populus fremontii
var. *wislizenii*
Rio Grande Cottonwood

Populus tremuloides
Quaking Aspen

Plate 73

Prosopis glandulosa
var. *glandulosa*
Mesquite

Prosopis glandulosa
var. *glandulosa*
Mesquite

Prosopis glandulosa
var. *glandulosa*
Mesquite

Plate 74

Prosopis glandulosa
var. *glandulosa*
Mesquite

Prosopis glandulosa
var. *glandulosa*
Mesquite

Plate 75

Prosopis glandulosa
var. *torreyana*
Western Mesquite

Prosopis pubescens
Screwbean

Plate 76

Prunus caroliniana
Cherry Laurel

Prunus mexicana
Mexican Plum

Plate 77

Prunus munsoniana
Munson Plum

Prunus murrayana
Murray Plum
Barton H. Warnock

Prunus serotina var. *eximia*
(*Prunus serotina*
subsp. *eximia*)
Escarpment Black Cherry

Plate 78

Prunus serotina var. *rufula*
(*Prunus serotina* subsp. *virens*)
Southwestern Black Cherry

Prunus serotina var. *serotina*
(*Prunus serotina* subsp. *serotina*)
Black Cherry

Plate 79

Prunus umbellata
Flatwoods Plum

Pseudotsuga menziesii
var. *glauca*
Blue Douglas Fir

Plate 80

Quercus alba
(white oak group)
White Oak

Quercus arizonica
(white oak group)
Arizona White Oak

Plate 81

Quercus drummondii
(white oak group)
Drummond Post Oak

Quercus emoryi
(black oak group)
Emory Oak

Plate 82

Quercus falcata
(black oak group)
Southern Red Oak

Quercus falcata
(black oak group)
Cherrybark Oak

Quercus falcata
(black oak group)
Three-lobe Red Oak

Plate 83

Quercus fusiformis
(white oak group)
Escarpment Live Oak

Quercus gambelii
(white oak group)
Gambel Oak

Plate 84

Quercus glaucoides
(white oak group)
Lacey Oak

Quercus graciliformis
(black oak group)
Graceful Oak

Plate 85

Quercus gravesii
(black oak group)
Chisos Red Oak

Quercus grisea
(white oak group)
Gray Oak

Quercus hemisphaerica
(black oak group)
Coast Laurel Oak

Plate 86

Quercus hypoleucoides
(black oak group)
Silverleaf Oak

Quercus incana
(black oak group)
Bluejack Oak

Quercus laurifolia
(black oak group)
Laurel Oak

Plate 87

Quercus lyrata
(white oak group)
Overcup Oak

Quercus macrocarpa
(white oak group)
Bur Oak

Quercus margaretta
(white oak group)
Sand Post Oak

Plate 88

Quercus marilandica
(black oak group)
Blackjack Oak

Quercus michauxii
(white oak group)
Swamp Chestnut Oak

Quercus mohriana
(white oak group)
Mohr Oak

Plate 89

Quercus muehlenbergii
(white oak group)
Chinkapin Oak

Quercus nigra
(black oak group)
Water Oak

Quercus nuttallii
(black oak group)
Nuttall Oak

Plate 90

Quercus oblongifolia
(white oak group)
Mexican Blue Oak

Quercus phellos
(black oak group)
Willow Oak

Quercus pungens
var. *pungens*
(white oak group)
Sandpaper Oak

Plate 91

Quercus pungens
var. *vaseyana*
(white oak group)
Vasey Oak

Quercus rugosa
(white oak group)
Netleaf Oak

Quercus shumardii
(black oak group)
Shumard Red Oak

Plate 92

Quercus similis
(white oak group)
Bottomland Post Oak

Quercus sinuata
var. *breviloba*
(white oak group)
Bigelow Oak

Quercus sinuata
var. *sinuata*
(white oak group)
Durand White Oak

Plate 93

Quercus stellata
(white oak group)
Post Oak

Quercus texana
(black oak group)
Texas Red Oak

Quercus turbinella
(white oak group)
Shrub Live Oak

Plate 94

Quercus velutina
(black oak group)
Black Oak

Quercus virginiana
(white oak group)
Live Oak

Plate 95

Rhamnus caroliniana
Carolina Buckthorn

Rhus copallina var. *copallina*
Shining Sumac

Plate 96

Rhus lanceolata
Prairie Flameleaf Sumac

Robinia neomexicana
New Mexico Locust

Plate 97

Sabal mexicana
Texas Palmetto

Salix amygdaloides
Peachleaf Willow

Plate 98

Salix nigra
Black Willow

Salix taxifolia
Yewleaf Willow

Sambucus caerulea
(*S. glauca*)
Blue Elder

Plate 99

Sapindus drummondii
Western Soapberry

Sassafras albidum
Sassafras

Sophora affinis
Eve's Necklace

Plate 100

Styrax grandifolius
Bigleaf Snowbell

Symplocos tinctoria
Sweetleaf

Taxodium distichum
var. *distichum*
Bald Cypress

Plate 101

Taxodium mucronatum
Montezuma Bald Cypress

Tilia caroliniana
Carolina Basswood

Ulmus alata
Winged Elm

Plate 102

Ulmus americana
American Elm

Ulmus crassifolia
Cedar Elm

Ulmus rubra
Slippery Elm

Plate 103

Vaccinium arboreum
Farkleberry

Vauquelinia angustifolia
Chisos Rosewood

Viburnum rufidulum
Southern Blackhaw

Plate 104

Yucca carnerosana
Carneros Yucca

Yucca elata
Soaptree Yucca

Yucca faxoniana
Faxon Yucca

Plate 105

Yucca rostrata
Beaked Yucca

Yucca torreyi
Torrey Yucca

Yucca treculeana
Trecul Yucca

Plate 106

Zanthoxylum clava-herculis
Hercules'-club

East Texas
Maples near Rusk

Plate 107

Coast Prairies
Dwarf Palmetto
Brazoria County

Post Oak Savannah
Sumac and Grass
Lamar County

Plate 108

Blackland Prairies
Tallgrass Prairie
Dallas County

Cross Timbers
Wise County

Rio Grande Plains
Huisache-Mesquite
Atascosa County

Plate 109

Edwards Plateau
Fall Scenery
Kerr County

Rolling Plains
Plains Cottonwood
Motley County

Plate 110

High Plains
Sand Bluestem
Winkler County

Trans-Pecos
Calamity Creek and Cathedral Mountain
Brewster County

Plate 111

Sophora secundiflora (Texas Mountain Laurel or Mescal Bean)
Usually a shrub of 4 to 8 feet but sometimes a tree to over 20 feet.

Leucaena greggii (Gregg Leadtree)
  Perhaps not now or ever in Texas; to be expected in the western Edwards Plateau (upper Devils River).

Plate 112

Crataegus viburnifolia (Viburnum-leaf Hawthorn)
Probably an asexual apomictic triploid (a clone of hybrid origin). Certainly *C. mollis* would be one of the parents, the seed being formed vegetatively without fertilization from the male and with 1-1/2 times the normal number of chromosomes.

Sabal louisiana (Louisiana Palmetto)
Probably not a form of *Sabal minor* but instead a possible introgressed (back-cross) hybrid of *S. palmetto* × *S. minor*.

Plate 113

Nyssa sylvatica
var. *sylvatica*
Blackgum

Juniperus pinchotii
Pinchot Juniper

Plate 114

Juniperus erythrocarpa
Redberry Juniper

Cordia boissieri
Wild Olive

Plate 115

Quercus buckleyi
(Quercus texana)
Texas Red Oak

Chilopsis linearis
"Dark Storm" Desert Willow

Plate 116

Juniperus deppeana

Alligator Juniper

(Checkerbark Juniper,
Western Juniper,
Oakbark Cedar, Thickbark Cedar,
Mountain Cedar, Tascate)

Alligator Juniper is a small tree, up to 25 feet tall, with green to blue-green leaves. It occurs at moderate elevations of 4,500 to 7,000 feet in the Chinati, Chisos, Davis, Eagle, Guadalupe, and Vieja mountains in the Trans-Pecos. All these mountain ranges are of igneous origin, except for the Guadalupe Mountains, which are of the Capitan Reef formation of limestone. The trees apparently do equally well on both soil types, although they seem to do better on the slightly acidic igneous soils. That might explain why Alligator Juniper is not found in the Glass and Del Norte mountains, which are limestone. In Dallas, Alligator Juniper is growing on alkaline Houston black clay and is doing well.

The most attractive specimens of Alligator Juniper are in the Davis Mountains above 1 mile in elevation. Many of the trees are quite silvery gray in the fall and winter.

The fruit does not mature until the second year, beginning to ripen in September and continuing through December. The blue-green female cones are berrylike and have a blush the first year; they become brown and leathery as they ripen.

The vernacular name refers to the bark, which becomes checkered and resembles the skin of an alligator.

For many years a variety of Alligator Juniper called the Sperry Juniper (*J. deppeana* var. *sperryi*) was recognized by many botanists. Gas-liquid chromatograms of the terpenoids of this taxon show that the tree is similar to Alligator Juniper.

Juniperus erythrocarpa

Redberry Juniper

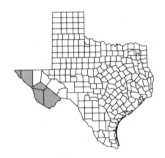

For many years, Redberry Juniper was confused with One-seed Juniper until Cory, in 1936, proposed a new taxon, *Juniperus erythrocarpa,* a rosy-red-fruited juniper. The type specimen for this new species is a juniper at the west base of the summit of Mount Emory in the Chisos Mountains of Big Bend National Park.

Redberry Juniper attains heights of 12 to 15 feet and has spreading and ascending branches that form an open, irregular crown. The one-seeded female cones are rosy red and fleshy when ripe. One half to three quarters of each seed is covered with a dark-colored band.

Redberry Juniper occurs at relatively high elevations, above 4,000 feet, on igneous soils in the mountain ranges of the Trans-Pecos: the Chisos, Davis, Chinati, Vieja, Eagle, Quitman, Blanca, and Hueco mountains. It also occurs on the hills alongside Interstate Highway 10 west of Sierra Blanca, where it mingles with Faxon Yucca. And it is the only juniper in Hueco Tanks State Park; it grows on the eastern to southeastern side of the low hills just south of park headquarters.

Juniperus flaccida

Weeping Juniper

(Drooping Juniper, Mexican Drooping Juniper, Weeping Cedar, Drooping Cedar, Tascate, Cedro)

Weeping Juniper occurs only in Big Bend National Park in Brewster County. It grows at elevations of 5,000 feet or more in dry, rocky, igneous soils on the sides and valleys of the Chisos Mountains. It is more common in the mountains of northern Mexico.

Weeping Juniper usually grows to 25 or 30 feet in height but can get as tall as 55 feet. It has pendent, or weeping, branchlets, hence its common name. The fruit is dull black and leathery and requires two years to ripen.

Many years ago the trees of the western mountains were high-graded, or top-cruised, just as the eastern forests were. Pines and junipers were hauled from the Chisos Mountains to be used in the mines at Boquillas.

Cold temperatures do not play a major role in the ecology of this tree. The loveliest Weeping Junipers that I know of are many hundreds of miles to the northeast of the Chisos Mountains. On the outer limits of Woodward, Oklahoma, stands the Southern Great Plains Field Station of the U.S. Department of Agriculture. Two Weeping Junipers grow here among the needle evergreens planted over the years by E. W. Johnson.

Juniperus monosperma

One-seed Juniper

(Cherrystone Juniper, West Texas Juniper, New Mexico Juniper, Enebro)

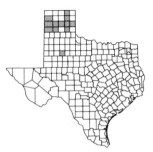

One-seed Juniper is usually less than 20 feet tall in most situations, although there are individual trees of 30 feet or more. This species is much more prevalent in New Mexico and Arizona than in Texas. It grows on steep slopes, eroded hillsides, and the rimrock and breaks of plateaus and escarpments. It occurs on the Canadian River breaks of Oldham County, Palo Duro Creek in Deaf Smith County, and the rocky banks of Rita Blanca Creek in Hartley County. It is accessible in Palo Duro Canyon in Armstrong County. Here, One-seed Junipers can be seen hanging from the east-facing walls of the canyon along Texas Highway 207. In the canyon proper and south of the Prairie Dog Town Fork of the Red River are two female Rocky Mountain Junipers. All along the canyon floor, and especially on the flatlands north of the Prairie Dog Town Fork, are Pinchot Junipers with their tan, pink, or red fruits. Then, coming out of the canyon on the north side, all of the hillsides are crowded with gnarled, twisted One-seed Juniper. The trees are scarcely 6 to 12 feet tall, and in a good year, the female trees are loaded with bloom-covered purplish-blue to black cones.

Juniperus pinchotii

Pinchot Juniper

(Redberry Juniper, Texas Juniper, Christmas Berry Juniper)

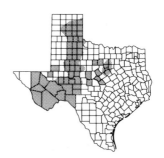

The specimen from which Pinchot Juniper was described in 1905 came from the valley of Palo Duro Canyon in Randall County. The small, 20-foot-tall tree is cradled in the foothills of the Caprock of the Llano Estacado, and although Pinchot Juniper is found from the mountains of the Trans-Pecos almost to the Fort Worth city limits, this redland country is its proper home. Pinchot Juniper grows on open flats in sand, clay, or mixed soils, arroyos and canyons, caprocked mesas, and talus slopes, usually in limestone or gypsum soils, from Hemphill County in the north to Val Verde County in the south. It occurs in many mountain ranges of the Trans-Pecos and extends east from the Caprock Escarpment in an almost unbroken wave to the 100th meridian, where it grows on the redbeds and gypsum beds of the Permian formation of 250 million years ago. On the redbeds, Pinchot Juniper forms a dense clumpy tree of 15 to 20 feet in height, but on gypsum the plants form thickets of hundreds of acres and are essentially a 3-foot-tall groundcover.

Pinchot Juniper readily sprouts from the stump after the tops have been killed by fires. Most trees have either male or female flowers, although some trees have both.

Juniperus scopulorum

Rocky Mountain Juniper

(Rocky Mountain Red Cedar,
Mountain Red Cedar,
Colorado Red Cedar,
Western Red Cedar, River Juniper,
Western Juniper, Cedro Rojo)

Rocky Mountain Juniper grows on limestone hillsides at elevations of 6,000 feet in the Guadalupe Mountains in Culberson County, but it is also found at lower elevations of 2,000 to 3,000 feet in Armstrong, Brisco, Potter, Randall, Lubbock, and Garza counties and will occupy moist pockets of soil.

Two female trees can be easily observed on Texas Highway 207 on the south side of the Prairie Dog Town Fork of the Red River—one is growing in a buffalo wallow and the other is in a dry creekbed.

A 20- to 30-acre grove of Rocky Mountain Juniper occurs in Palo Duro Canyon. Dozens of these trees are more than 100 feet tall and were most likely saplings when Francisco Vásquez de Coronado visited the area in 1541. Many of them are dead or dying, probably from old age. Some botanists think they are a hybrid of *Juniperus virginiana* and *J. scopulorum*.

Juniperus silicicola

Southern Red Cedar

(Sand Cedar, Coast Juniper)

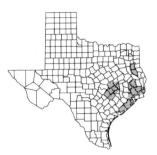

Southern Red Cedar seems far removed from the many species of juniper in central, western, and Panhandle Texas. It usually grows to 30 feet, although the state champion tree, at the Robert A. Vines Environmental Science Center in Houston, is 75 feet tall.

This species occurs in the Gulf Prairies and Marshes in Matagorda, Brazoria, and Galveston counties, and inland in Brazos, Milam, Bastrop, Washington, Fayette, Rusk, Nacogdoches, San Jacinto, Polk, and other counties. It almost always grows near water or in areas with a very shallow water table.

Although the specific epithet *silicicola* implies that Southern Red Cedar grows on sand, this is not true for those trees in the Gulf Prairies. Here they grow on acidic Lake Charles—Beaumont clay soils and Moreland-Pledger-Norwood clays of Brazoria County.

Southern Red Cedar has slender, pendulous branches and usually a single trunk. The bright blue cones are much smaller than those of Eastern Red Cedar, its close relative. It is a handsome tree in a cultivated situation.

Juniperus virginiana

Eastern Red Cedar

(Pencil Cedar, Virginia Juniper, Red Juniper, Carolina Cedar, Baton Rouge, Red Savin)

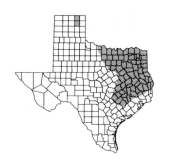

Eastern Red Cedar grows to approximately 70 feet and occurs in the Pineywoods, Post Oak Savannah, Blacklands, Cross Timbers and Prairies, Rolling Plains, and High Plains. It grows in almost any soil type, whether alkaline or acidic, sand or clay. However, it reaches its greatest size on rich, deep soils east of the 35-inch rainfall belt.

With rare exceptions, the trees are either male or female. The female is more showy when loaded with dark blue fruit in late fall and early winter. The fruit is eaten by many birds and other wildlife. This species is an alternate host for cedar apple rust. The heartwood is a beautiful shade of red, and the sapwood is white. The wood is wonderfully aromatic. Almost every home has a cedar chest or a cedar-lined closet, because the odor supposedly repels clothes moths and other insects. Fence posts have been made from the branches of this tree from the day the first settlers found it. Although the wood is extremely light and easy to work, it is also quite resistant to decay when in contact with the soil.

Leucaena (leucaena)

Leguminosae (legume family)

There are approximately 10 to 50 species of *Leucaena* in tropical and subtropical regions of North America, South America, and Polynesia. In the tropical areas, some species are becoming quite valuable for livestock fodder and green-manuring. In Texas they are heavily browsed by grazing animals and are of economic importance as landscape plants. *Leucaena greggii* is not considered here because it is probably not native to Texas.

Leucaena pulverulenta

Great Leadtree

(Mexican Leadtree,
Great Leucaena, Tepeguaje)

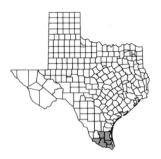

Great Leadtree grows to 55 feet and occurs on rich soils in Cameron, Hidalgo, Willacy, and Starr counties in the Rio Grande Valley. It is possibly native to Kenedy and Brooks counties as well. The white and sweet-scented flowers bloom in dense balls throughout the spring and summer. The leaves are twice-pinnately compound and range from 4 to 10 inches long. The wood is hard and heavy.

Great Leadtree is widely used in the lower Valley for landscape purposes. It is susceptible to cold and is not adapted outside this limited area.

Leucaena retusa

Goldenball Leadtree

(Wahootree,
Littleleaf Leadtree,
Lemonball,
Little Leucaena)

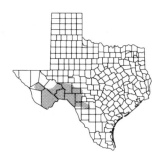

Goldenball Leadtree grows to 25 feet in height, with bright green, twice-pinnately compound leaves and bright brown young branchlets. It begins to flower in midspring and will flower after every rain throughout the summer and fall months. The bright golden balls of flowers, the small blue-green rounded leaves, and the flaking, cinnamon-colored bark make this tree a suitable candidate for use as a landscape plant. The wood, however, is extremely brittle, and high winds and ice storms cause it to break up easily.

The leaves and young branches are palatable and readily eaten by livestock, so it can exist only in hard-to-get-at areas, such as in the borrow ditches of fenced roads, in craggy, inaccessible niches of limestone in the Edwards Plateau and Trans-Pecos, and in the mountain ranges of the southern Trans-Pecos. It is found on both igneous and limestone soils.

Liquidambar (sweet gum)

Hamamelidaceae
(witch hazel family)

There are three to five species of sweet gum, all of which are highly ornamental trees with excellent fall color. One species is native to North and Central America, and the others are from Asia. *Liquidambar formosana* (Formosa Sweet Gum) has been introduced to the United States, and although its fall color surpasses that of the native tree, it lacks cold tolerance and must be kept in southern areas.

Liquidambar styraciflua

Sweet Gum

(Red Gum, White Gum, Star-leaved Gum, Liquidambar, Alligator Tree, Bilsted, Satin Walnut)

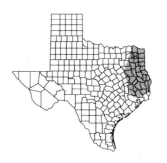

Sweet Gum grows to 110 feet and occurs in low wet areas on the acid sands of the Pineywoods, Gulf Prairies and Marshes, and Post Oak Savannah. It is a part of the east Texas pine-hardwood forest association (Longleaf Pine—Sandjack Oak, Loblolly Pine—Sweet Gum, Shortleaf Pine—Post Oak—Southern Red Oak), the young forest/grassland association, and the Willow Oak—Water Oak—Black Gum forest association. On the extreme eastern edge of the Post Oak Savannah, it can be a part of the Post Oak woods/forest and grassland mosaic association, and will be a minor part of the Bald Cypress—Water Tupelo swamp association in the Gulf Prairies and Marshes. It also occurs on the drier upland soils, although in fewer numbers. Sweet Gum is easily distinguished from all other trees in any season of the year. It has large star-shaped leaves with five to seven lobes, ranging from light yellow, golden yellow, bright scarlet, and dark crimson to the more subtle purples and dark mahoganies in autumn. The large, corky wings of the branchlets and the persistent, spiny fruit balls are evident in winter.

Maclura (Bois d'Arc)

Moraceae (mulberry family)

Maclura is a monotypic genus native to the rich bottomlands of the Red River Valley between Texas and Oklahoma. There is a closely related genus in tropical America and Africa that may someday be merged with *Maclura*. The tree has been widely planted as a hedge fence, making it impossible to fully determine its native range.

Maclura pomifera

Bois d'Arc

(Osage Orange, Bodark, Bow Wood, Hedge Apple, Horse Apple, Hedge, Naranjo Chino, Yellow Wood)

This small tree, to 40 feet, with a short trunk and shallow root system, is clearly native to the Great Blackland Prairies of Texas. It comes right down the spine of the Blackland Prairies and feathers off into the Post Oak Savannah, where it runs out of the transitional soils (Wilson, Crockett, Burleson) on the eastern edge. It is unsuited to the Grand Prairie (too shallow and droughty), and so it misses Denton County and Tarrant County and stays in Hill and McLennan and Bell. It reaches its largest size in the Red River and Trinity River valleys in northern Texas.

The tree has now been planted in so many areas that it is hard to tell where it was really native. It does seem to appreciate rich clay soils, high in limestone, and 32 to 35 inches of rainfall. The successful hedge plantings have always been to the north and the east, where there is more moisture and the moisture is used more efficiently. Hedges in Motley County (20 inches average annual rainfall) died from the drought of the 1930s. Bois d'Arc shows up in many places in the Trans-Pecos—always at Indian campgrounds or caves, which of course were always by water (seeps, springs, creeks). Today, great thickets of Bois d'Arc are found in these areas, seeded from the horse apples carried by these tribes. No one is sure why they had the fruit. Was it just an accessory, picked up when bow wood was cut, or did they use the seed in some way?

Magnolia (magnolia)

Magnoliaceae (magnolia family)

Magnolia is an ancient genus inhabiting the earth as far back as the lower Cretaceous, 130 million years ago. There are approximately 80 species worldwide, with 50 species occurring in eastern Asia. North America has 8 species, 3 of which occur in Texas. Magnolias occur in somewhat acidic, moist, sandy soils. *Magnolia grandiflora* (Southern Magnolia), native to North America, is grown worldwide where climatic and soil conditions permit. The native range of magnolias in Texas is in the southeastern Pineywoods, with the population centered in the Big Thicket.

Magnolia grandiflora

Southern Magnolia

(Bull Bay, Big Laurel, Evergreen Magnolia, Loblolly Magnolia, Great Laurel Magnolia)

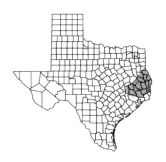

Southern Magnolia, to 110 feet in height, is one of Texas' most regal trees. It is easily identified by its bright green, glossy evergreen leaves that are 5 to 8 inches wide. This species grows in moist but well-drained soils of the rich bottomlands and gentle hills of the southeastern Piney-woods. Southern Magnolia grows interspersed with Sweet Gum, Flowering Dogwood, and other hardwoods of the Lob-lolly Pine—Sweet Gum association, the American Beech—Magnolia-Loblolly slopes association, and the deeper-soiled areas of the Longleaf Pine—Sandjack Oak association.

Southern Magnolia has a fleshy root structure, and larger trees are difficult to dig from the wild. The terminal buds produce musty-scented flowers from April to July. The six to twelve petals are waxy and pure white. Each flower opens by midmorning of the first day and closes at night. The next day it opens much wider and generally starts shedding petals. The seed pods are tan to rusty-colored, and the bright red seeds hang by thin threads from the pod. The seeds are eaten by several species of birds and other wildlife. It is widely planted and can tolerate most soil types as long as they are well drained. It can be planted as far north as Lubbock and Amarillo.

Magnolia pyramidata

Pyramid Magnolia

Pyramid Magnolia is both rare and local, occurring only on deeply wooded sandy ridges in Jasper and Newton counties in the Pineywoods. It is closely related to *Magnolia fraseri* (Mountain Magnolia). Some botanists think that it grows side by side with Mountain Magnolia in this area, but others think that all of the trees are Pyramid Magnolia, with some having larger leaves, flowers, and seed pods.

Pyramid Magnolia grows to 30 feet and is easily distinguished from Southern Magnolia and Sweet Bay by its leaves. The deciduous leaves are about 9 inches long and 4 inches wide, with earlike lobes at the base and whorls around the stem. It flowers when only a few feet tall. The terminal flowers are white and fragrant. The rosy-red seed pod is 2½ inches long.

Pyramid Magnolia has not been cultivated much in Texas, although it has been grown in the warmer parts of Europe for many years. It requires a lot of shade, along with acidic, sandy, moist soils.

Magnolia virginiana

Sweet Bay

(Swamp Bay, Southern Sweet Bay, Laurel Magnolia, Swamp Magnolia, Sweet Magnolia, White Bay, White Laurel, Swamp Laurel)

Sweet Bay grows to 80 feet in the acid swamps, sphagnum bogs, and baygalls of the southeastern Pineywoods and eastern tip of the Gulf Prairies and Marshes; it is a part of the Bay—Gallberry Holly bogs association. It can survive on drier sites but does not grow as well on high limestone clays as Southern Magnolia.

The leaves of Sweet Bay are bright, glossy green above with a glittering, silky white underside. They are only slightly smaller than those of Southern Magnolia. The trees are tardily deciduous to evergreen. From April to July they produce fragrant, velvety flowers 3 inches across. The flowers open in midafternoon on the first day and close before midnight, then open widely the second day and remain open. The small seed pod, or follicle, turns cherry red in the fall.

Malus (apple)

Rosaceae (rose family)

This genus is called either *Malus* (apple) or *Pyrus* (pear), although newer terminology leans toward *Pyrus*. The main differences are that pears have typical pear-shaped fruit with more or less gritty stone cells, and apples have rounded fruits and no stone cells. The flowers and leaves are essentially the same in both groups.

There are between 30 and 55 species of *Malus* worldwide. Absolute numbers are difficult to determine because of intergrading and hybridization. There are 4 species in the United States and 2 species in Texas.

Malus angustifolia

Southern Crabapple

(Narrowleaf Crabapple)

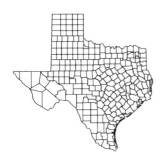

Southern Crabapple occurs on upland sandy loam soils in Newton County. It grows to 30 feet tall, although it usually is not over 10 feet in height. I have seen this tree within the city limits of Burkeville and on Texas Highway 87 just south of Burkeville. It is rumored that a grove of these trees occurs in Montgomery County just north of Houston. Possibly they are introduced around the city of Conroe.

Although Southern Crabapple occurs on acid soils in the Burkeville area, its distribution is limited by rainfall.

By the time Prairie Crabapple begins to bloom in April, Southern Crabapple has already shed its flowers and is loaded with fruit. The flowers are most attractive in the bud stage, for they are a deep glowing pink, opening to shell pink and fading to almost white. The leaves of Southern Crabapple turn many shades of red, orange, and gold in autumn.

Malus ioensis

Prairie Crabapple

(Prairie Crab, Iowa Crab, Western Crabapple)

Prairie Crabapple occurs on limestone soils only on the Edwards Plateau in Blanco, Comal, Gillespie, Kendall, and Bexar counties. It is most numerous in shaded canyons around Blanco. There should be groves of Prairie Crabapple on the Blackland and Grand prairies and the West Cross Timbers, for this is a true prairie plant. In all probability it is a relict tree on the Edwards Plateau, which indicates that it should be even more abundant north toward the Red River.

Prairie Crabapple grows to 30 feet, creating broad thickets from underground rhizomes. It flowers from April to early May. The buds are a glowing pink, opening to sweet, fragrant soft-pink flowers that fade to pure white. The little crabapples mature in early fall and are green to greenish yellow.

Morus (mulberry)

Moraceae (mulberry family)

The genus *Morus* is not extensive, having approximately ten species worldwide. The United States has two native and one naturalized mulberries. The same three taxa are also found in Texas. Probably the most famous is *Morus alba,* the White Mulberry from China. Its leaves are used to feed silkworms. A silkworm industry was started in the United States, but it was abandoned when labor costs became prohibitive. Mulberries bear male and female flowers on separate trees. The fruit is a syncarp (an aggregate fruit).

Morus microphylla

Texas Mulberry

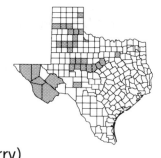

(Mountain Mulberry,
Mexican Mulberry,
Littleleaf Mulberry,
Wild Mulberry, Dwarf Mulberry)

Texas Mulberry is a small tree averaging 25 feet in height and growing in the western two thirds of Texas. It is distinguished from Red Mulberry by its dwarf size and much smaller fruit. Its leaves are also smaller and are exceedingly rough on both surfaces. Texas Mulberry occurs in dry, well-drained habitats, as opposed to Red Mulberry, which occurs in deep, rich soils and river bottoms.

Texas Mulberry is usually found on thin limestone soils. In the mountains of western Texas, however, it grows equally well on igneous, rocky soils. It is most prevalent west of the Colorado River, although it is quite common on the hard limestone of the White Rock Escarpment in Dallas County, where it is perhaps best considered a shrub of 6 to 12 feet in height. In the drainage basin of the Little Red River in Hall County, it forms a narrow tree of about 20 feet. It can be found throughout the Hill Country on hard limestone soils of the Balcones Fault Zone of the Edwards Plateau. This species grows equally well on the slightly acid sands of Erath and Comanche counties before switching to the limestone clays and redlands of Brown, Coleman, Runnels, Coke, Tom Green, and Sterling counties. In the Trans-Pecos, it is found on igneous soils in the Chisos, Chinati, Vieja, Davis, and Hueco mountains and on the Capitan Reef formation in the Guadalupe and Glass mountains.

Morus rubra

Red Mulberry

(Moral, Lampasas Mulberry)

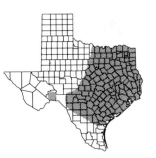

Red Mulberry occurs in the eastern two thirds of Texas, where it inhabits river bottoms and deep, rich soils, reaching almost 50 feet in height. It extends from the eastern border with Arkansas and Louisiana as far west as Clay County on the Red River, down through the central-western part of the Edwards Plateau to Terrell County, and then back to the southeast to the Corpus Christi area. It is absent south of this line in the Rio Grande Valley.

Red Mulberry grows on a broad spectrum of soils and pH ranges, such as clays, sands, and loams that are fairly moist but well drained. This tree requires a fair amount of sunlight, although it can occasionally be found in dappled to rather heavy shade. Of particular interest is the so-called Lampasas Mulberry of the Lampasas Cut Plains area, a handsome tree with large leaves that are glossy above and very white with dense fuzz below. The fruit of this geographical strain can be quite large.

Myrica (wax myrtle)

Myricaceae (wax myrtle family)

Depending on various interpretations, the genus *Myrica* has between 35 and 50 species worldwide. The species occur in temperate as well as tropical and subtropical areas of the Old and New Worlds. The United States has 5 tree and 2 shrub species. Except for the Odorless Bayberry of the central U.S. Gulf Coast, all wax myrtles have more or less resinous aromatic leaves. Of great interest is the ability of this genus to fix atmospheric nitrogen through root nodules containing the nitrogen-fixing bacterium *Actinomycetes*. Texas has 1 tree (*M. cerifera*) and 2 shrub species (*M. heterophylla,* which is treelike in some areas outside Texas, and *M. pusilla,* which many authors consider synonymous with *M. cerifera*).

Myrica cerifera

Southern Wax Myrtle

(Bayberry, Southern Bayberry, Candleberry, Wax Myrtle, Tallow Shrub)

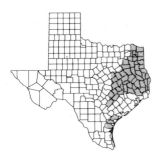

Southern Wax Myrtle is found in sandy swamps and moist woodlands, on the shores of streams and lakes, and in wet grasslands of the Pineywoods and Post Oak Savannah areas of eastern and eastcentral Texas. It is less common in Bowie and Red River counties. Farther west, almost to the Balcones Escarpment of central Texas, it grows on moderately acid soil.

A disjunct population of Southern Wax Myrtle, along the Gulf Coast from Aransas County south to San Patricio and Nueces counties and Flour Bluff at Corpus Christi, grows on coastal sands in oak woodlands that are neutral to slightly saline or even alkaline. Annual rainfall in this area is less than 29 inches, and the leaves on these small trees are narrower than those in eastern Texas.

Nyssa (tupelo)

Cornaceae (dogwood family)

Texas has two species and one variety of Tupelo, out of the three in America and five worldwide. Some authors put the tupelos, or black gums, in their own family, the Nyssaceae. The Texas trees grow to about 100 feet in height, have widely spaced horizontal branching, and occur in low wet areas.

Nyssa aquatica

Water Tupelo

(Cotton Gum, Sour Gum, Tupelo, Swamp Tupelo, Tupelo Gum, Water Gum)

Water Tupelo is a relatively fast-growing, long-lived tree that reaches 100 feet in height. It occurs in swamps, baygalls, and other wet areas in deep southeast Texas. It is found in the Bald Cypress—Water Tupelo swamp association on rich inundated, swampy flats with silty clay to clay bottom soils. Associates of Water Tupelo are Bald Cypress, Swamp Tupelo (Nyssa sylvatica var. biflora), Overcup Oak, Water Oak, Swamp Chestnut Oak, Water Hickory, Carolina Ash, Red Maple, Swamp Privet, Buttonbush, Winterberry, Dwarf Palmetto, various duckweeds, water ferns, and Water Hyacinth.

The root system of Water Tupelo is wide-spreading and shallow. Early in its life, the base of the tree starts flaring and becomes much wider than those of Bald Cypress or Swamp Tupelo. The flaring base and wide root system give the tree great stability in its watery habitat. City planners are finding that plants from wet areas, such as Water Tupelo, are good choices for road medians and other developed areas because they tolerate compacted, low-oxygen soils much better than trees from well-drained sites.

Nyssa sylvatica var. *biflora*

Swamp Tupelo

(Black Gum, Swamp Black Gum)

Swamp Tupelo is a 120-foot tree of the Bald Cypress—Water Tupelo association and the Bay—Gallberry Holly association in southeast Texas.

Many people confuse Swamp Tupelo with Black Gum and prefer to see the two varieties combined into a single species. Although the two varieties grade into each other, definite differences distinguish them from each other. The seeds of Swamp Tupelo are strongly ribbed, the leaves are narrow and approximately three times as long as they are broad, and the trunk is buttressed or flared. In contrast, the seeds of Black Gum are only slightly ribbed, the leaves are shorter and narrower, and the trunk is not buttressed.

Nyssa sylvatica var. *sylvatica*

Black Gum

(Sour Gum, Pepperidge, Tupelo, Black Tupelo, Tupelo Gum)

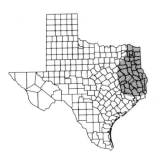

Black Gum is a large tree reaching heights of 140 feet. It occurs on wet and poorly drained sites in the Pineywoods, Gulf Prairies and Marshes, and Post Oak Savannah where it is a part of the Shortleaf Pine–Post Oak–Southern Red Oak association, the Loblolly Pine–Sweet Gum association, the Water Oak–elm-hackberry forest association, the Willow Oak–Water Oak–Black Gum forest association, and the Sweet Gum–Oak floodplains association. The tree is strongly tap-rooted and relatively slow-growing. Its branches are horizontal and rather widely spaced along the trunk of the tree.

The glory of the Black Gum is its fall coloration. It is the first tree to show color, with a few leaves already turning in August. By late September, Black Gum is flaming like an Olympic torch in every swag and hollow in the east Texas woods. The show is brief, for by the time the Sweet Gum and Red Maple turn color, Black Gum is leafless. However, its beauty is carried on into the winter by its clusters of shiny blue to black fruit that are readily eaten by many species of wildlife.

Ostrya (hop hornbeam)

Betulaceae (birch family)

Ostrya is a small genus with not more than eight species, all of which occur in the Northern Hemisphere. The three species in the United States also occur in Texas. One species grows on acid soils in east Texas, and the other two are found west of the Pecos River in the mountains of west Texas. They are small birch-like trees reaching heights of 60 feet in the east and 30 feet in the west. The fruit of all species consists of a seed (nutlet) enclosed in a bladderlike sac (the inflated bracts). The seeds and bracts are clustered and resemble true hops. Care must be taken when breaking these fruit clusters apart, for the base of each bract is clothed in stinging hairs that can be rather painful.

Ostrya chisosensis

Chisos Hop Hornbeam

Chisos Hop Hornbeam is an extremely rare and local tree found only in the Chisos Mountains of Big Bend National Park in southern Brewster County. It is a fair-sized tree, reaching heights of 46 feet.

Before 1965, Chisos Hop Hornbeam was thought to be *Ostrya knowltonii* (Knowlton Hop Hornbeam), and Robert Vines listed it as also occurring in the Davis and Guadalupe mountains. So far as is known, hop hornbeam does not occur in the Davis Mountains. Chisos Hop Hornbeam is found around the summit of Mount Emory at 6,500 to 6,800 feet in altitude. The male flowers are enclosed in bracts or scales that have a sharp, rigid point.

Ostrya knowltonii

Knowlton Hop Hornbeam

(Western Hop Hornbeam, Wooly Hop Hornbeam, Ironwood)

Knowlton Hop Hornbeam is almost as rare as Chisos Hop Hornbeam. It is found in southeastern Utah, northern Arizona, southeastern New Mexico in Eddy County (Lincoln National Forest), and northern Trans-Pecos Texas. It is not a common tree in those areas but is rather local at elevations of 5,000 to 7,500 feet. In Texas it is a component of the Gray Oak—Pinyon Pine—Alligator Juniper parks/woods association at 5,000 to 7,000 feet and the Ponderosa Pine—Douglas Fir parks/forest association at 6,000 to 7,500 feet in the Capitan Reef limestone in Culberson County.

Although this small, 25-foot-tall tree is quite prevalent in the south fork of McKittrick Canyon in the Guadalupe Mountains, Knowlton Hop Hornbeam is hardly noticed amid the Texas Madrone, Pinyon, Southwestern White Pine, Ponderosa Pine, Douglas Fir, Chinkapin Oak, and Bigtooth Maple. The tree covers the canyon floor from the grotto at the old J. K. Hunter lodge at the south end and west to the head of the canyon. In the north fork of McKittrick and in Dog and Bear Spring canyons, Knowlton Hop Hornbeam occurs merely in small groves.

Ostrya virginiana

Eastern Hop Hornbeam

(American Hop Hornbeam, Wooly Hop Hornbeam, Eastern Ironwood, Roughbark Ironwood, Deerwood, Leverwood)

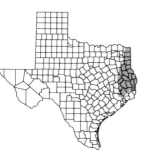

Eastern Hop Hornbeam is usually a single-trunked tree. It can reach heights of 60 feet, although it more commonly grows to 20 or 30 feet. It occurs on gravelly, sandy ridges and deep flatlands of rich sandy loam. Although it is found almost exclusively on acid soils, it will grow with no apparent problems on limestone or alkaline soils in home landscapes. It is a tree of the Pineywoods but is occasionally found in the Post Oak Savannah. Specifically, it is an understory tree of the pine-hardwood forest (Loblolly Pine—Sweet Gum, Shortleaf Pine—Post Oak—Southern Red Oak, Longleaf Pine—Sandjack Oak) association in eastern Texas, often found in the same grove with American Hornbeam (*Carpinus caroliniana*).

This tree is extremely slow-growing and relatively free of insects and disease. It has no terminal buds and begins new growth each year from lateral buds, causing an irregular system of branching. The small nuts of this tree are eaten by several species of birds.

Parkinsonia (parkinsonia)

Leguminosae (legume family)

Parkinsonia is a small genus with only two species, one in the New World and one in Africa. It has been suggested that *Parkinsonia* should be merged with the genus *Cercidium,* the true paloverdes. There is no doubt that the two genera are closely related, as intergeneric (interspecific?) crosses have been known to occur in the wild.

Parkinsonia aculeata

Retama

(Jerusalem Thorn, Horse Bean, Mexican Paloverde, Paloverde)

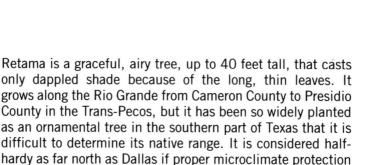

Retama is a graceful, airy tree, up to 40 feet tall, that casts only dappled shade because of the long, thin leaves. It grows along the Rio Grande from Cameron County to Presidio County in the Trans-Pecos, but it has been so widely planted as an ornamental tree in the southern part of Texas that it is difficult to determine its native range. It is considered half-hardy as far north as Dallas if proper microclimate protection is provided, such as planting it against a south wall and allowing for good cold-air drainage.

Retama is almost always on soils of limestone or limestone origin in low flats with good moisture. It can also withstand saline conditions. It occurs in the Mesquite-Granjeno woods association, the Live Oak woods/parks association, and the Cenizo-Blackbrush-Creosote brush association.

Although it grows best in the moister lowlands, Retama is strongly drought-tolerant. In times of severe drought, the small leaflets (1/16 to 1/8 inch long) are shed, leaving only the midrib. But since the midrib, along with the branches and bark, is green and photosynthetic, the tree can manufacture the necessary sugars for survival.

Parkinsonia aculeata hybridizes readily with *Cercidium texanum,* and *C. microphyllum,* the Yellow Paloverde of Arizona, was once called *Parkinsonia microphyllum.* The two genera are so closely related that it has been proposed to merge *Cercidium* into *Parkinsonia.*

217

Persea (persea)

Lauraceae (laurel family)

The genus *Persea* consists of approximately 150 species occurring mostly in the tropics of the New World. The United States has 1 or 2 species, depending on the author cited. The two varieties of *Persea borbonia* are native to temperate coastal and eastern Texas.

Persea borbonia
var. *borbonia*

Red Bay

(Sweet Bay, Silk Bay,
Red Bay Persea, Laurel Tree)

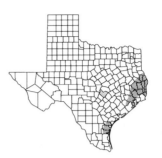

Red Bay is an evergreen or persistent-leaved tree that attains average heights of 15 to 25 feet, although it may get as tall as 60 feet. It occurs in the southeastern Pineywoods and the Gulf Prairies and Marshes, with a disjunct population in the Coastal Bend ranging from near Lavaca Bay in Calhoun County to Baffin Bay in Kleberg and Kenedy counties, and small stands in Travis county, which may be a part of the relictual flora of that area. In east Texas, Red Bay is an understory tree of woods and swamps and on shorelines and stream banks. It is part of the Sweet Gum—oak floodplains association, the Willow Oak—Water Oak—Black Gum forest association, and the Loblolly Pine—Sweet Gum subtype of the pine-hardwood forest association in the Pineywoods of southeast Texas.

In the Coastal Bend area, Red Bay occurs on sandy to sandy loam in the Live Oak—Red Bay—Southern Wax Myrtle association, where it grows in full sun and attains heights of 10 to 15 feet. It grows above the tidal line.

Persea borbonia
var. *pubescens*

Swamp Bay

(Swamp Red Bay,
Swamp Sweet Bay)

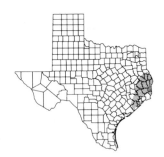

Swamp Bay is often confusing to most hunters of Texas trees. It is smaller than Red Bay, growing no taller than 28 or 30 feet, and the lower surfaces of the leaves, fruit stalks, and young branchlets are more hairy. It has been called both *Persea pubescens* and *P. palustris.* Some authors distinguish it as a variety of *P. borbonia,* but others consider it synonymous with *P. borbonia.* Here it is treated as a variety of *P. borbonia.*

It is found in the Bay—Gallberry Holly bogs association, the Palmetto—oak flats association, the Sweet Gum—oak floodplains association, the Willow Oak—Water Oak—Black Gum forest association, the Loblolly Pine—Sweet Gum subtype of the pine-hardwood forest association, and the Bald Cypress—Water Tupelo swamp association of southeast Texas.

Pinus (pine)

Pinaceae (pine family)

This genus is valuable worldwide for lumber, pulp, and naval stores. There are about 100 species, of which 36 occur in the United States, with Texas having 7 species. Four of the Texas pines occur west of the Pecos River, although *Pinus edulis* (Pinyon) may also be found in the upper reaches of Palo Duro Canyon in Deaf Smith County on the High Plains, and *P. cembroides* grows east out of the Pecos in the southwestern Edwards Plateau.

The pines of eastern Texas are found in 59 counties that occur east of a line running from Lamar through Franklin, Henderson, and Brazoria counties. *Pinus taeda* (Loblolly Pine) grows in a sliver of east Texas soil that lies west of this line to Fayette and Bastrop counties. It is the final western extension of the great southeastern pine belt.

Pinus cembroides

Mexican Pinyon

(Pinyon, Nut Pine, Mexican Pinyon Pine)

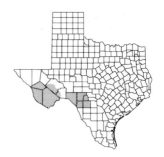

Mexican Pinyon is an attractive pine with a more or less pyramidal shape and a maximum height of 70 feet, although 20 to 30 feet is more common. The flexible blue-green needles are ¾ to 1¾ inch long and grow in bundles of two or three. This tree is part of the Gray Oak–Pinyon Pine–Alligator Juniper parks/woods association, occurring at altitudes of 4,000 to 6,000 feet in the southern mountains of the Trans-Pecos. It grows on igneous soils in the Chinati, Chisos, Davis, and Vieja mountains. On Santiago Peak, the Glass and Del Norte mountains in Brewster County, and Madera Mountain in Pecos County, it grows on limestone soils. Several peaks in the Del Norte Mountains have limestone on the upper reaches and igneous soils at the base. Mexican Pinyon grows only on the upper limestone soils, but Pinchot and putative Redberry Juniper grow on the igneous.

East of the Pecos River, Mexican Pinyon grows on hot, dry, sloping limestone hills at isolated stations in Edwards, Kinney, Real, Uvalde, and Val Verde counties in a Live Oak–Mesquite–Ashe Juniper–Pinyon Pine–Mescal Bean association.

Those trees of the Del Norte and Glass mountains and on Madera Mountain west of the Pecos River and all Mexican Pinyons east of the Pecos usually have only two needles per bundle, and their nuts have the thinnest shells of all pinyons; those from the other ranges listed above probably have the thickest-shelled nuts of all pinyons. The trees with the thin shells are sometimes called *Pinus cembroides* var. *remota* or even *P. remota* (Remote Pinyon).

Pinus echinata

Shortleaf Pine

(Shortleaf Yellow Pine, Longtag Pine, Shortstraw Pine, Arkansas Pine, Southern Yellow Pine)

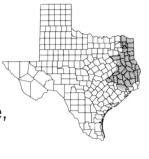

Shortleaf Pine grows on well-drained slopes, hills, and flat woodland in the Pineywoods of eastern Texas. It grows more than 100 feet tall and has short cones 1 to 2½ inches long. Its bluish green needles are in bundles of two or three and are 2 to 5 inches long.

Shortleaf Pine is most prevalent in north and northeast Texas, where it is part of the Shortleaf Pine—Post Oak—Southern Red Oak association, although it is found in mixed stands of Loblolly and Longleaf Pine in the Loblolly Pine—Sweet Gum association and the Longleaf Pine—Sandjack Oak association. It also extends into the southeastern areas of higher moisture along deep sand ridges. Shortleaf Pine is by far the most cold hardy of all southern pines. It prefers well-drained, acid, sandy soils. On the heavier, wetter soils of the east Texas lowlands, Loblolly Pine simply takes over and crowds out Shortleaf Pine. The same situation occurs on the deep sands of southeast Texas; under the higher rainfall of this area Shortleaf Pine cannot successfully compete with Longleaf Pine.

Shortleaf Pine will be found to the west in Burleson, Henderson, and eastern Lamar counties.

Pinus edulis

Pinyon

(Nut Pine, Colorado Pinyon Pine, Pinyon Pine, Two-leaf Pinyon, Two-needle Pinyon)

Pinyon is much smaller than Mexican Pinyon, usually topping out at 40 feet. It generally has only two yellowish green needles but can sometimes be found with three or even one. Its nuts are edible and were once much sought after by the native Americans. The shells of *Pinus edulis* are much thinner than those of *P. cembroides* found in the Davis Mountains and south of the Del Norte Mountains, but they are much thicker than those of Mexican Pinyon (Remote Pinyon?) found in the Glass and Del Norte mountains and on Madera Mountain west of the Pecos, and in the Edwards Plateau east of the Pecos.

Pinyon grows on limestone soils and is found in Texas only in the Guadalupe Mountains in Culberson County and the Sierra Diablo in Hudspeth County. In the Guadalupe Mountains, Pinyon is part of the Ponderosa Pine—Douglas Fir parks/forest association found mostly above 6,000 feet in elevation. In Victoria Canyon and other areas of the Sierra Diablo, it is either a relict tree or part of the Gray Oak—Pinyon Pine—Alligator Juniper parks association.

There are rumors that Pinyon occurs in the Franklin Mountains of El Paso County and at the headwaters of the Prairie Dog Town Fork of the Red River in Deaf Smith County. Both situations are possible although improbable. The Franklin Mountains have been little botanized, and Pinyon occurs in New Mexico just west of Deaf Smith County, in Quay and perhaps Curry counties within 25 miles of the Texas state line.

Pinus palustris

Longleaf Pine

(Longleaf Yellow Pine, Southern Yellow Pine, Longstraw Pine, Hill Pine, Pitch Pine, Hard Pine, Heart Pine)

Longleaf Pine reaches heights of 125 feet and grows on late tertiary sands and gravels. It once occurred in large numbers in Hardin, Jasper, Newton, Sabine, San Augustine, and Tyler counties and parts of Angelina, Chambers, Jefferson, Liberty, Nacogdoches, Orange, Polk, Shelby, and Trinity counties. It is probable that no virgin stands of Longleaf Pine exist, because it has been extensively lumbered in the past. Today this aristocrat of southern pines is found only in remnants and scattered groves of the Longleaf Pine—Sandjack Oak association of the pine-hardwood forest complex. Typical associates of Longleaf Pine are Blackjack Oak, Sand Post Oak, Bluejack (Sandjack) Oak, Sassafras, Southern Red Oak, Wax Myrtle, Yellow Jessamine, and other plants that require high rainfall but excellent drainage.

Longleaf Pine is intolerant of shade, and if the areas where it grows are not burned periodically, the hardwoods invade and shade the pine seedlings out. Longleaf Pine is able to survive fires because the seedlings spend the first part of their lives in a grass stage, remaining only a few inches high while sending down a huge taproot. This stage can last 3 to 25 years, depending on the availability of nutrients and other conditions. The seedlings are so small that most fires pass quickly over them. If fires burn too frequently, the seedlings do not have a chance to grow, but if they are too infrequent, the hardwoods take over.

Pinus ponderosa var. *scopulorum*

Rocky Mountain Ponderosa Pine

(Interior Ponderosa Pine, Black Hills Ponderosa Pine, Ponderosa Pine)

Rocky Mountain Ponderosa Pine must have been high-graded several times for telegraph and telephone poles, mine shoring poles, and lumber. Today this 100-foot pine is a relict tree in Pine Canyon in the Chisos Mountains, a part of the Ponderosa Pine—Douglas Fir parks association in the Guadalupe Mountains in Culberson County, and a member of the Ponderosa Pine—Southwestern White Pine—Gambel Oak association in the Davis Mountains. Other associated plants are Netleaf Oak, Silverleaf Oak, and Quaking Aspen. In the Chisos and Davis mountains it grows in igneous soil; in the Guadalupes it is on hard limestone. At all three locations it is probably in a 16-to-20-inch rainfall belt.

Rocky Mountain Ponderosa Pine can be observed most easily at the Madera Canyon Roadside Park off Texas Highway 118 in the Davis Mountains, or at Pine Springs or on the McKittrick Canyon trail in Guadalupe Mountains National Park in Culberson County.

Pinus strobiformis

Southwestern White Pine

(Limber Pine,
Border Limber Pine,
Border White Pine,
Mexican White Pine)

Southwestern White Pine, one of the most graceful, loveliest, and rarest of the Texas pines, grows to 90 feet tall on the high, north-facing slopes of Mount Livermore in the Davis Mountains, where it is associated with Ponderosa Pine and Gambel, Silverleaf, and Netleaf oaks. In McKittrick and other hidden canyons as well as the Bowl of the Guadalupe Mountains, it is part of the Ponderosa Pine–Douglas Fir forest association.

For many years, Southwestern White Pine was called Limber Pine by laypeople and *Pinus flexilis, P. flexilis* var. *reflexa,* and *P. reflexa* by botanists. Later, taxonomists distinguished it from true Limber Pine, *P. flexilis,* which occurs in the northern highlands of New Mexico.

227

Pinus taeda

Loblolly Pine

(Oldfield Pine)

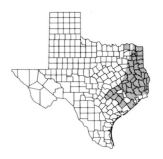

Loblolly Pine is without question the most numerous pine in Texas. It is found in the Pineywoods, Gulf Prairies and Marshes, and Post Oak Savannah. Because it grows in low wet areas and has thick bark, it is more or less resistant to fire. It is the fastest-growing of all southern pines, outstripping even Slash Pine after about twenty years of age. Because of its rapid growth, it is also the most widely planted pine in Texas for timber purposes.

Loblolly Pine is most prevalent in the southeastern part of the Pineywoods, growing to about 140 feet. It is part of the Loblolly Pine—Sweet Gum forest association of the east Texas Pineywoods, with a disjunct population in northern Lamar County. It is also part of the Loblolly Pine—Post Oak forest association in the Lost Pines area of Bastrop, Colorado, Lee, Fayette, Caldwell, and Austin counties west of the true Pineywoods.

The Lost Pines of Bastrop, 35 miles southeast of Austin, are an interesting extension of the Loblolly Pine belt because they are more than 100 miles west of the east Texas pine forest. Many years ago, Bastrop was an important lumbering center that furnished much of the timber for western Texas. The Loblolly Pines in this area seem different from those of the Pineywoods—shorter and highly drought tolerant. They are found on light sandy, gravelly soils on east-west undulating ridges that can be traced by intermittent pine groves back to Montgomery County and the eastern pines.

Pistacia (pistache)

Anacardiaceae (sumac family)

Members of the genus *Pistacia* are trees and shrubs and are either evergreen or deciduous. Trees of this genus total about ten worldwide, with one or two species recognized in North America. Texas Pistache is the only species occurring in the United States. It is found in Texas in Terrell and Val Verde counties in secluded canyons off the Rio Grande.

Pistacia texana

Texas Pistache

(American Pistachio, Wild Pistachio, Lentisco)

Until recently, it was thought that the only population of Texas Pistache occurred in the area that was to become a reservoir named Lake Amistad in the 1960s. As the waters steadily rose, the few depauperate shrublike trees at Good-Enough (Hinojose) Spring disappeared, and the isolated clumps clinging to the limestone cliffs of the Rio Grande were not far behind. Many people feared that Texas Pistache was on its way to extinction. However, other populations were discovered, and since then nurserymen have reproduced the trees and are now selling them to the public.

Texas Pistache occurs in the Edwards Plateau, on hard limestone in the header canyons of the Rio Grande in Val Verde and Terrell counties. In steep, narrow canyons it is tree-like and reaches 40 feet in height. In shallow, wide-bottomed canyons, it often is less than 10 feet tall. Other plant associates are *Quercus pungens* var. *vaseyana* (Vasey Oak), *Q. gravesii* (Chisos Red Oak), and various shrubs. Upland plant associations are Creosote-Lechuguilla shrub and Cenizo-Blackbrush-Creosote brush.

Pithecellobium (blackbead)

Leguminosae (legume family)

The genus *Pithecellobium* has 90 to 150 species of trees occurring in the tropics and subtropics of the New World, Asia, Malaysia, and Australia. Five species occur in the United States, 3 or 4 of which are trees. Of the 2 species in Texas, *Pithecellobium pallens* (Tenaza) is considered a shrub, and *P. flexicaule* (Texas Ebony) is more treelike.

Pithecellobium flexicaule

Texas Ebony

(Ebony Blackbead, Ebano, Ebony Apes-earring)

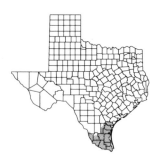

Texas Ebony, reaching heights of 50 feet, grows in the Rio Grande Plains and southern Gulf Prairies and Marshes, on sandy to clay loams, clays, and thin hard limestone soils. It is rather frequent in low woods along the coast as far east as Corpus Christi and San Patricio County near Sinton. To the north and northwest it is found just south of Laredo in Webb County. It is part of several plant associations, such as Mesquite-Blackbrush brush association, Mesquite-Granjeno parks association, Live Oak woods association, and the marsh—barrier island association. In the marsh—barrier island association, Texas Ebony grows on limestone hillocks well above the flood stage. One of the best locations to observe Texas Ebony is in the vicinity of Palmito Hill on Texas Highway 4 heading to Boca Chica Island. Here, the trees are on small hills with Palmito (*Yucca treculeana*), Coma (*Bumelia celastrina*), Colima (*Zanthoxylum fagara*), Berlandier Fiddlewood (*Citharexylum berlandieri*), and several species of cacti and grasses.

Texas Ebony is an attractive tree and is used in landscapes in this area as well as worldwide where temperatures permit.

Planera (Water Elm)

Ulmaceae (elm family)

Planera is a monotypic genus of the southeastern United States and the Mississippi River drainage to lower Illinois. This genus is closely related to *Ulmus* (elm) and *Celtis* (hackberry). *Planera* grows in wet areas, usually in standing or running water.

Planera aquatica

Water Elm

(Planer Tree)

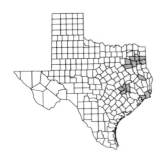

Water Elm is a small tree, reaching heights of 40 feet, though it is usually much smaller. It is most common in rich sediment soils of rivers and creeks in the Post Oak Savannah and extreme southeastern Gulf Prairies and Marshes but only incidentally in the east Texas Pineywoods. It is prevalent in great thickets along the Sabine, Navasota, Angelina, and Caddo Lake watersheds.

This tree is at home in standing water and is found as a component of the Bald Cypress—Water Tupelo swamp association, Water Oak—elm-hackberry forest association, Sweet Gum—oak floodplains association, and Willow Oak—Water Oak—Black Gum association. It may or may not be a part of the Bay—Gallberry Holly bogs association.

Water Elm primarily has perfect flowers but can also have male and female flowers on the same tree. It usually flowers in mid- to late February, with the curious, warty fruit maturing in four to six weeks. This is a favorite food of wood ducks and other waterfowl.

Platanus (sycamore)

Platanaceae (sycamore family)

Platanus is the only genus in the Platanaceae, of which there are only nine or ten species in the North Temperate Zone. Three species occur in the United States, one eastern and two western. Four species occur in Mexico and Central America, and three species in Eurasia. All are large trees easily recognized by their flaking bark and hanging balls of multiple fruits. They are found in deep canyons and wet areas but are misused in ornamental landscaping where they stress easily in dry, hot summers.

Platanus occidentalis

Sycamore

(American Sycamore, Eastern Sycamore, Buttonwood, Plane Tree, American Plane Tree, Buttonball Tree)

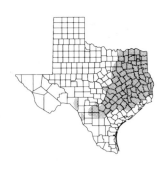

Sycamore is a lofty, majestic tree growing in the river and creek bottoms of the eastern two thirds of Texas. It occurs as far west as the Devils River watershed in Val Verde County and in most of the river and creek bottoms of the Edwards Plateau. Sycamore is present in all vegetational areas of Texas except for the Rolling Plains, High Plains, and Trans-Pecos.

In the Mississippi River basin, Sycamore reaches 120 to 170 feet, but in Texas it rarely attains 100 feet in height.

Sycamore grows in most soils as long as they are deep, rich, and moist. In eastern Texas, Sycamore grows on acidic to highly acidic soils and is part of the Willow Oak—Water Oak—Black Gum forest association, the Loblolly Pine—Sweet Gum and Shortleaf Pine—Post Oak—Southern Red Oak types of the pine-hardwood forest association of the east Texas Pineywoods, and the Pecan-elm forest association of the Gulf Prairies and Marshes. It also occurs in the Bois d'Arc—Shumard Oak—elm—Honey Locust woods association of the Blackland Prairies and Cross Timbers and Prairies, the Water Oak—elm-hackberry forest association of the Post Oak Savannah, and the Sycamore-willow-Buttonbush association of the Edwards Plateau, where it grows on limestone soils.

Populus (cottonwood, poplar)

Salicaceae (willow family)

Cottonwoods are large, fast-growing trees occurring on stream banks and dry riverbeds or wherever a little more moisture may be obtained by their wide-ranging, rather shallow root system. There are 35 to 40 species in the Northern Hemisphere in Asia, Europe, and North America. The United States has 8 species, and Texas has 5 taxa.

Cottonwood is present in every vegetational area of Texas. The Pineywoods, Gulf Prairies and Marshes, Post Oak Savannah, and Rio Grande Plains have only one species, *Populus deltoides* var. *deltoides* (Eastern Cottonwood). The High Plains also has only one species, *P. deltoides* var. *occidentalis* (Plains Cottonwood). The Blackland and Grand prairies, West Cross Timbers, Edwards Plateau, and Rolling Plains have confusing populations of Eastern Cottonwood, Plains Cottonwood, and their hybrids.

Two species (one species with two varieties) of poplar occur in the Trans-Pecos. *Populus fremontii* var. *mesetae* (Meseta Cottonwood) grows in the floodplain of the Rio Grande from Big Bend National Park to above the confluence of the Rio Conchos. Here it is replaced by *P. fremontii* var. *wislizenii* (Rio Grande Cottonwood), which is the most common cottonwood as far north as El Paso. *P. tremuloides* (Quaking Aspen) is found in limited numbers in some of the higher mountain ranges.

Populus deltoides var. *deltoides*

Eastern Cottonwood

(Cottonwood, Southern Cottonwood, Carolina Poplar, Eastern Poplar, Necklace Poplar, Alamo)

Eastern Cottonwood is a fast-growing tree that reaches more than 100 feet. It occurs from Wichita County in the west to the Sabine River in the east and from the Red River in the north to the Gulf Prairies and Marshes on the Gulf Coast and the floodplain of the Rio Grande in the south. It extends through the Edwards Plateau to Uvalde County and Webb County on the southwest. Along the Red River in Montague, Wise, Cooke, and Clay counties, it readily hybridizes with *P. deltoides* var. *occidentalis* (Plains Cottonwood), making identification difficult.

Eastern Cottonwood grows in almost any soil type but does best in the sands and sandy loams at the edges of streams, lakes, and rivers. In eastern Texas, it grows anywhere there is available moisture, though it doesn't do well in areas with constant flooding, such as the Water Tupelo—Bald Cypress swamp or Bay—Gallberry Holly bog associations. In central Texas, Eastern Cottonwood is part of the Pecan-elm forest, Bois d'Arc—Shumard Oak—elm—Honey Locust woods, Sycamore-willow-Buttonbush parks, and cottonwood-hackberry-elm—Salt Cedar parks associations.

Populus deltoides var. *occidentalis*

Plains Cottonwood

(Cottonwood, Texas Cottonwood, Northern Cottonwood)

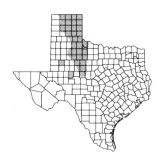

Plains Cottonwood is, in essence, a smaller version of Eastern Cottonwood. It occupies a drier, harsher climate and is shorter lived. In Cook and Montague counties, Plains Cottonwood forms a hybrid swarm with *Populus deltoides* var. *deltoides*. It is distinguished with greater certainty where it occurs to the west and north of Wichita County. Plains Cottonwood is part of the Mesquite—Salt Cedar brush/woods association in the Rolling Plains and the cottonwood-hackberry—Salt Cedar brush/woods association in the Red River and Canadian River basins.

Cottonwood is not recommended as a landscape plant for typical city lots. The root system is invasive of sewage pipes and causes sidewalks to buckle. The wood is brittle, and the tree simply becomes too massive for the size of the building sites.

Populus fremontii var. *mesetae*

Meseta Cottonwood

(Arizona Cottonwood)

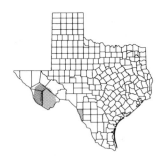

Meseta Cottonwood is small, with the state champion tree being only 60 feet tall. It is common in the Trans-Pecos along the Rio Grande to the east of Big Bend National Park. It follows the Rio Grande to the confluence of the Rio Conchos at Presidio. Above that point, it is replaced by *Populus fremontii* var. *wislizenii* (Rio Grande Cottonwood). Meseta is by far the most common cottonwood in Brewster and Presidio counties and, to a lesser degree, in Jeff Davis County, where great care is needed in separating the two varieties.

Populus fremontii
var. wislizenii

Rio Grande Cottonwood

(Valley Cottonwood, Wislizenus Cottonwood, Alamo)

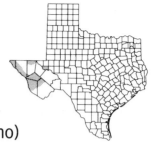

Rio Grande Cottonwood reaches 110 feet in height, occurring in the northern and western portions of the Trans-Pecos as far east as Ward County near Barstow. Some botanists believe it is closely related to *Populus deltoides* var. *occidentalis* (Plains Cottonwood) in the High Plains. Collections in Deaf Smith and Hutchinson counties indicate a hybrid designation of *P. fremontii* var. *wislizenii* and *P. deltoides* var. *occidentalis.*

Rio Grande Cottonwood is part of the Mesquite—Salt Cedar brush/woods association of the Rio Grande from above Presidio to Fort Quitman, where it then is a tree of the irrigation canals and drainage ditches all the way to El Paso. Local and spotty along the Guadalupe Mountain streams, it is easily observed on the grounds of old Fort Davis, in the city of Fort Davis, and along Limpia Creek, where it is part of the cottonwood-willow—Desert Willow association. It is also abundant on the upper reaches of Alamito Creek out of Marfa and in San Estaban Canyon just below San Estaban Lake in Presidio County.

Populus tremuloides

Quaking Aspen

(Aspen, Golden Aspen,
Trembling Aspen,
Mountain Aspen,
Quaking Asp,
Trembling Poplar,
Alamo Blanco)

The only Texas populations of Quaking Aspen are found high on the northwest and southwest flanks of Mount Emory in the Chisos Mountains, on the northern slope of Mount Livermore in the Davis Mountains, and in the Bowl of the Guadalupe Mountains. It is slender and scarcely reaches 40 feet in height. Its bark is smooth and white, reminding one of a beech back in east Texas. The rather small, rounded leaves are on long stems flattened at a right angle to the plane of the leaves, so that at the slightest breeze, the entire canopy of the tree trembles with a delightfully gentle rustling of the leaves. The leaves turn to brilliant, sparkling golden orbs on the tree in autumn.

Quaking Aspen is always found above 7,000 feet in elevation. In the Chisos Mountains, it can be observed on the southwest slope of Mount Emory just past the Laguna on the trail to the South Rim. The little colony of trees is on the wrong side of the mountain, but giant igneous boulders are a mulch to the suckering roots. The best stand is on the north side of Mount Livermore in the Davis Mountains, where it is surrounded by the Ponderosa Pine—Southwestern White Pine—Gambel Oak parks association. In the Bowl of the Guadalupe Mountains there are scattered, small colonies of Quaking Aspen in the Ponderosa Pine—Douglas Fir parks/forest association.

Prosopis (mesquite)

Leguminosae (legume family)

There are 35 to 40 species of *Prosopis* occurring primarily in the warmer areas of Argentina and other South American countries, with a few species found in Africa and southwestern Asia. There are 5 species in North America and 3 in Texas: 1 shrub and 2 tree species, with one tree species having 2 varieties. They occur in almost every county in the state. All are valuable forage plants for many species of livestock and have great value for landscaping purposes. They are prized as honey plants and for their wood, which burns with a white-hot heat, and all except Screwbean are highly drought tolerant.

Southeast of Calallen in Nueces County is a small, adventive colony of *Prosopis laevigata,* native to Mexico. It is possible that plants from this colony might someday spread and become naturalized.

Prosopis glandulosa var. *glandulosa*

Mesquite

(Honey Mesquite, Glandular Mesquite, Algaroba)

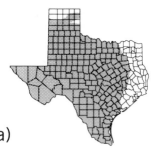

Mesquite is a tree to 30 feet with twice-pinnately compound leaves, giving it a light, airy appearance and providing dappled shade. Because of this, grass will grow right to the base of the tree, which makes it nice for landscaping purposes. In late spring and early summer, and after heavy rains, Mesquite is covered with 2-inch, sweetly fragrant blossoms. It is a superlative bee tree, for the honey is light and clear, comparable to the fabulous Uvalde honey made earlier in the spring from blossoms of related legume species. The sweet Mesquite beans, once widely used by Indian tribes, are avidly consumed by all livestock. Many a rancher has been able to weather droughts because of the abundance of Mesquite beans.

When the settlers fenced the land, controlled the fires, and severely overgrazed the rangeland, Mesquite quickly spread from the well-drained hillsides and fertile valleys and exploded across the land. Mesquite now infests more than 60,000,000 acres of Texas rangeland. It occurs in all areas of the state, although only sparingly in the Pineywoods. Mesquite resembles a classical nonnative plant, being rather ubiquitous in its habitat requirements, but it is native and was described by the early Texas explorers. Cabeza de Vaca tells of the flour of the *"mesquiquez"* in his bitter odyssey through Texas more than 400 years ago. In 1845, Lt. James W. Abert remarks on the "musquit," as does Captain Randolph Marcy in 1849, when he found it on the Llano Estacado. In 1854, west of the Cross Timbers, he stated that

Mesquite was in great abundance but the trees were spaced widely apart, much as the trees in an orchard.

Mesquite is almost impossible to eradicate. The seeds are covered by a hard seedcoat and can remain dormant for many decades until conditions become just right for germination. When plants are cut down to the soil level, latent buds below the soil vigorously sprout, forming a multitrunked tree in place of the original single-trunked tree. Mesquite has a deep and wide-spreading root system that saps the soil of all its moisture, leaving the rangeland barren of other vegetation. It forms dense, thorny, impenetrable thickets that can cause wounds in livestock, making them susceptible to the dreaded screwworm.

The most beautiful Mesquites seen today are those in J. Frank Dobie country; in Live Oak, Jim Wells, and Nueces counties are the grand, gnarled patriarchs whose ancestors were here when Texas was first settled.

Prosopis glandulosa var. *torreyana*

Western Mesquite

(Western Honey Mesquite, Torrey Mesquite)

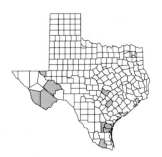

Western Mesquite is quite common west of the Pecos River. Some botanists put this variety in the Rio Grande Plains, southern Gulf Prairies and Marshes, and the southern Blackland Prairies in Gonzales and Travis counties. Even in Brewster and Presidio counties, where this tree is fairly common, it is often hopelessly mixed in groves and hybridized with *P. glandulosa* var. *glandulosa* and *P. velutina* (Velvet Mesquite), which is usually thought of as occurring only west of the Continental Divide, primarily in Arizona and with outlying populations in New Mexico and California.

This variety occupies the same types of terrain and soil as Mesquite. The leaflets of Mesquite are smoother and at least twice but usually three times as long as those of Western Mesquite.

Prosopis pubescens

Screwbean

(Screwbean Mesquite,
Tornillo, Screwpod Mesquite,
Twisted Bean,
Fremont Screwbean)

Screwbean is a small, dainty, and graceful tree barely reaching 30 feet in height. It is almost always found in river bottoms, creek beds, and irrigation ditches and in alluvial, limestone, or igneous soils in swags and depressions that are periodically flooded. Although it can survive in the desert, it does best where there is available moisture or the chance for moisture to accumulate from the next flash flood. The best place to observe Screwbean in Texas is along the River Road between Big Bend National Park and Presidio, especially where Alamito Creek flows by on its way to the Rio Grande. Here there are several good-sized trees along the west bank of the creek. Another area to view these plants is around Tornillo in El Paso County. This town was named after the Screwbean, or Tornillo, which in this area is more shrub than tree.

Several hundred miles to the southeast, in the Rio Grande Plains, is a close relative of this western tree, *Prosopis reptans,* the Dwarf Screwbean, which is usually only 2 feet in height. It is a miniature Screwbean in every aspect and prefers the same moist habitats.

Prunus (plum, cherry, peach)

Rosaceae (rose family)

Prunus contains 125 to 400 species of both trees and shrubs. These plants are native to temperate areas of the Northern Hemisphere and are rather abundant in North America, Europe, and Asia. A few species occur in tropical America and eastern Asia. Species of *Prunus* in the United States number approximately 18 trees and 15 shrubs. There are 6 Texas trees, with 3 varieties, and 7 shrubs. Several species are valuable for their edible fruit, which is eaten by both humans and livestock. Almost all species are highly ornamental and widely planted in landscapes. Some species are valuable timber trees, highly prized for their decorative wood, which is used in furniture.

Prunus caroliniana

Cherry Laurel

(Laurel Cherry, Carolina Cherry Laurel, Mock Orange, Carolina Cherry, Wild Peach)

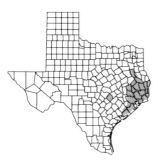

Cherry Laurel requires deep, moist, but well-drained bottomlands. It occurs in small numbers in the Pineywoods in the Loblolly Pine—Sweet Gum forest association, the Willow Oak—Water Oak—Black Gum forest association, and the outer, drier perimeter of the Bald Cypress—Water Tupelo swamp association. A small tree reaching heights of 35 to 40 feet, it has glistening black inedible fruits. The leaves are evergreen or persistent and contain high amounts of prussic acid (hydrocyanic acid), which can be especially dangerous if the leaves are wilted from drought or after a sharp frost.

Thirty years ago, Cherry Laurel was the most widely planted broad-leaved evergreen in Texas. Every yard had one or two specimen trees, and large estates had tall hedges made from dozens of the trees. After the drought of the 1950s weakened the Cherry Laurels, borers took over and decimated them. By the time the rains returned in 1957, most Cherry Laurels had turned chlorotic or had been destroyed by borers. They were never replaced, so today a few large, old Cherry Laurels can be seen in older landscapes, but they are not present in newer landscapes.

Prunus mexicana

Mexican Plum

(Big Tree Plum, Inch Plum)

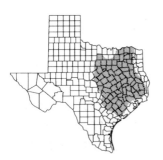

Mexican Plum is a single-trunked, irregularly shaped tree reaching 25 feet in height. It grows everywhere in Texas except the Rio Grande Plains, Rolling Plains, High Plains, and Trans-Pecos, with a wide distribution in the eastern half of Texas. But it usually occurs singly in fencerows and deep, rich soils of river bottoms, lake shores, open forested slopes, and well-drained prairies. Mexican Plum is rather drought tolerant and has been widely used for grafting stock.

Long before the Flowering Dogwood heralds the coming of spring in hills and coves of east Texas, the Mexican Plum foretells the demise of winter in the northcentral part of the state by flaunting billowing clouds of white, fragrant flowers.

Its leaves are large for a plum, being 2 to 3 inches wide and up to 4 inches long. They are simple, alternate, thick, and sometimes folded over like the keel of a boat. The flowers are five-petaled, white, fragrant, and borne in rather loose umbels. The dark red to purple fruit ripens quite late, sometimes not falling until September. Though the fruits are not exceptionally tasty from the tree, they are prized for making tart, colorful jams and jellies. Sharp exfoliating bark on the older portions of the trunk and limbs completes the portrait of this resplendent Texas tree.

Prunus munsoniana

Munson Plum

(Wildgoose Plum)

Munson Plum is a thicket-forming tree growing to 25 feet in height. It occurs in Calhoun County on the Gulf Prairies, Clay County in the West Cross Timbers, Collin, Fannin, Grayson, Hunt, Lamar, and Rockwall counties in the Blackland Prairies, and Burnet, Lampasas, and Travis counties in the Edwards Plateau.

Munson Plum is extremely rare; it is even questionable that the species actually occurs in Texas. It is closely related to and possibly the same as *P. rivularis* (Hog Plum). Hog Plum forms thickets, generally grows on hard limestone soils, and has small, deep red, tart, almost inedible plums.

The two known Munson Plums that occur in Collin County grow in a roadside thicket of Hog Plum. These two trees stand taller than the others and have large, succulent, extremely tasty yellow fruit.

Wildgoose Plum, by legend, is only a selection of Munson Plum and should be considered the vernacular name of a clone, not a species.

Prunus murrayana

Murray Plum

Murray Plum is one of the rarest and least known trees in Texas. Certainly it is the rarest of all the plums. It is also of interest because, since its discovery more than half a century ago (April 21, 1928), no one has seen this plant with fruit.

Murray Plums usually occur as shrubs, but in a small grove of 30 or 40 plants in Jail Canyon in the Glass Mountains they are single-trunked and 12 to 15 feet tall. These trees are spaced 6 to 20 feet apart and give the impression that they were once a dense thicket that has been browsed out, probably by mule deer. I have also seen this plant as a thicket-forming shrub of 3 to 6 feet tall near Altuda Mountain in the Del Norte Mountains. Murray Plum was discovered in the Davis Mountains, and it is thought to be present on Eagle Mountain. In both places, the soil is igneous in origin. It also appears to be growing on igneous soil in the Del Nortes, but it is on the Capitan Reef limestone formation in the Glass Mountains. The plant could possibly be found in the Guadalupe, Apache, Delaware, and Santiago mountains if these were searched thoroughly.

Prunus serotina

Black Cherry

(Wild Black Cherry, Rum Cherry, Wild Cherry)

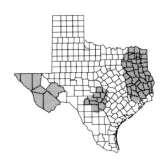

Black Cherry is native to all areas of Texas except the West Cross Timbers, Rolling Plains, and High Plains. It grows to almost 110 feet tall in eastern Texas and 50 feet tall in the canyons of the Trans-Pecos, perhaps averaging 25 to 30 feet.

Black Cherry flowers when the leaves have just emerged, usually in March in the eastern part of the state and April in the western mountains. Each individual cherry ripens at its own pace, so there will be ripe black cherries, all shades of ripening red cherries, and green cherries on the same tree, sometimes within the same cluster. The leaves turn shades of yellow in the fall. Wilted twigs and leaves contain lethal doses of prussic acid and are to be avoided by humans and animals. Black Cherry wood is second only to Black Walnut for use in furniture.

In Texas, Black Cherry has three varieties. They are *Prunus serotina* var. *eximia* (Escarpment Black Cherry), *P. s.* var. *rufula* (Southwestern Black Cherry), and *P. s.* var. *serotina* (Black Cherry).

Prunus serotina var. *eximia* (*Prunus serotina* subsp. *eximia*)

Escarpment Black Cherry

(Edwards Plateau Black Cherry, Escarpment Cherry)

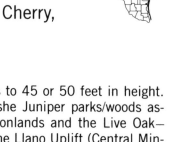

Escarpment Black Cherry grows to 45 or 50 feet in height. It is found in the Live Oak—Ashe Juniper parks/woods association of the Balcones canyonlands and the Live Oak—Mesquite parks association of the Llano Uplift (Central Mineral Region) of the Edwards Plateau. It follows some of the streambeds into the Post Oak woods/forest association of the Rio Grande Plains.

Prunus serotina var. *rufula* (*Prunus serotina* subsp. *virens*)

Southwestern Black Cherry

(Chisos Wild Cherry, Capulin)

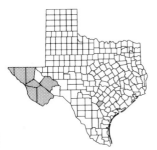

Southwestern Black Cherry grows to a height of 30 feet, although it is usually much smaller. It occurs in the deep canyons and protected bottomlands of the Chinati, Chisos, Davis, Del Norte, Diablo, Glass, Guadalupe, Quitman, and Vieja mountains of the Trans-Pecos. Many miles to the east in the Rio Grande Plains is an isolated colony growing on the Bexar-Wilson county line in deep Carrizo sands.

Southwestern Black Cherry is very adaptable in its soil requirements. The soils in the Del Norte, Diablo, Glass, and Guadalupe mountains are limestone and can be quite alkaline, with a pH of 8.3. The other mountain ranges are igneous, and their soils can be neutral to somewhat acidic, with a pH of 5.8.

Southwestern Black Cherry is readily accessible on the scenic drive around the Davis Mountains. It can be seen in Wild Cherry Canyon on Texas Highway 118 on the northwest side of the mountains and at Bloys Campground at Skillman Grove on Texas Highway 166 on the south side of the mountains. The mountain tree has proved poorly adapted when grown in the Dallas and San Antonio areas.

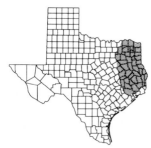

Prunus serotina
var. *serotina*
(*Prunus serotina*
subsp. *serotina*)

Black Cherry

(Wild Black Cherry, Wild Cherry, Rum Cherry)

Black Cherry is widely distributed across eastern Texas, where it grows to almost 110 feet in height. It occurs in the Pineywoods, the Post Oak Savannah, the southeastern tip of the Gulf Prairies, and the transitional soils of the Blackland Prairies.

This variety grows on almost any of the east Texas soils as long as they are neutral to acidic. It does best on rich sands and sandy loams that are moist but well drained. The tree is highly intolerant of shade and is found in forest openings and roadsides where the sunlight is brightest. Railroad rights-of-way are places to gather Black Cherries. The Texas and Pacific tracks along U.S. Highway 82 between Clarksville in Red River County and New Boston in Bowie County are especially rich in Black Cherry.

Prunus umbellata

Flatwoods Plum

(Black Sloe, Sloe, Hog Plum)

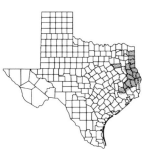

Flatwoods Plum is not rare in east Texas, although it is uncommon and is little known by the public. Perhaps it is confused with the more common, larger Mexican Plum, which grows in the same area. This is a lovely small tree of scarcely 15 feet in height, although the state champion specimen is almost 40 feet tall. It grows only in the true Pineywoods, from Cass County in the northeast to Jasper and Newton counties in the southeast, Harris and Montgomery counties in the southwest, and Cherokee County on the west, with an isolated population in Henderson County.

It is highly intolerant of shade and is usually found in fencerows and the edges of woods and forest groves where it receives more sunlight. The tree is found in acid sands to sandy loams that are moist but well drained. Sometimes the plant will come up quite thickly in cutover land, and it is extensive in the young forest/grassland association.

Flatwoods Plum is the last plum to flower in east Texas. Heavy crops of plums occur only every three to four years. The plums are late in maturing, sometimes not ripening until late August to early October.

Pseudotsuga (Douglas fir)

Pinaceae (pine family)

There are only five to seven species of Douglas fir worldwide. Three to five occur in eastern Asia and two in the United States. Texas has one species of this valuable timber tree, and it occurs in limited numbers.

Pseudotsuga menziesii var. *glauca*

Blue Douglas Fir

(Rocky Mountain Douglas Fir, Inland Douglas Fir, Interior Douglas Fir, Colorado Douglas Fir, Pino Real Colorado)

Blue Douglas Fir attains its largest size, more than 80 feet in height, in the Ponderosa Pine—Douglas Fir parks/woods association in the Bowl and steep-sided canyons above 6,000 feet in the Guadaupe Mountains. In the Chisos Mountains 200 miles to the south, Blue Douglas Fir grows at 6,000 to 7,000 feet in elevation but is not as robust as it is in the Guadalupe Mountains. This species does not occur in the Davis Mountains. In the Guadalupes it grows on limestone, whereas in the Chisos it grows on igneous soils. The Davis Mountains presumably have suitable habitat for Blue Douglas Fir, so its absence from the range is a mystery.

Compared with *Pseudotsuga menziesii* var. *menziesii* of the Pacific Coastal ranges, Blue Douglas Fir is a pallid tree, for it does not receive the same amount of rainfall where it occurs in the sheltered canyons and slopes of the Chisos and Guadalupe mountains.

In 1883, Valery Havard collected a specimen of Blue Douglas Fir that he found in the Vieja Mountains. Since that day, all plant distribution maps show this species in that hostile country. L. C. Hinckley spent four years in the wildly beautiful range, mapping its botanical entities, without seeing Blue Douglas Fir.

Quercus (oak)

Fagaceae (beech family)

It is difficult to determine how many species of oak exist worldwide because of varying taxonomic opinion. It has been estimated that there are 500 species worldwide, 250 in the New World, with 150 or more in Mexico alone, probably 58 species in the United States, and 43 species with 2 varieties in Texas. Based on those numbers, Texas has about 8 percent of the total species of oak, 17 percent of the species in the New World, and 74 percent of all the species in the United States.

Of the Texas oaks, 38 are considered trees. Of those, 23 are in the white oak group, which produces acorns annually. The inside of the white oak acorn cup is smooth, the leaves are without bristle tips, and the bark is generally white and scaly. The red or black oak group has 15 species. They produce acorns that usually require two years to mature, the inside of their acorn cup has dense hairs or fuzz, the leaves are bristle-tipped, and the bark is black, hard, and furrowed. Fifteen of the 38 tree species have evergreen or persistent leaves.

Every area of Texas has at least one species of oak (including shrubs), and with the exception of the High Plains, each area has at least one tree species.

Quercus undulata and *Q. tardifolia* (*Q. hypoxantha* x *Q. gravesii*) are considered hybrids and are not treated here. *Q. undulata* in Texas is thought to be a hybrid of *Q. gambelii with Q. arizonica, Q. grisea, Q. havardii, Q. mohriana, Q. muehlenbergii, Q. turbinella,* or *Q. toumeyi.*

Quercus alba
(white oak group)

White Oak

(Stave Oak, Ridge White Oak, Forked-leaf White Oak)

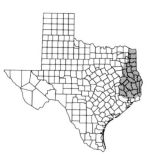

White Oak usually occurs in small groups or as a single tree on the rich, deep, well-drained acid sands, loams, and loamy clays of the Pineywoods. To a lesser degree, it is part of the creek and river banks in the eastern portions of the Post Oak Savannah and the better-drained soils of the southeastern Gulf Coast Prairies.

White Oak grows to more than 100 feet and is part of the Water Oak—elm-hackberry forest association of northeastern Texas, the Shortleaf Pine—Post Oak—Southern Red Oak association, and the Loblolly Pine—Sweet Gum association in the Pineywoods.

In other areas of the United States, White Oak is timbered for its lumber, which is widely used in cooperage. It is a desirable tree for landscape situations where a large tree is required. White Oak is one of east Texas' most regal and colorful trees in the fall of the year.

Quercus arizonica
(white oak group)

Arizona White Oak

(Arizona Oak)

Arizona White Oak is present in several of the mountain ranges of Trans-Pecos Texas but never in large numbers. It often hybridizes with other species, including *Quercus grisea* (Gray Oak), *Q. mohriana* (Mohr Oak), and *Q. toumeyi* (Toumey Oak), and is not common in its pure form.

Arizona White Oak is small to moderate sized, reaching 20 to 30 feet in height. It has hybridized extensively with Gray Oak in the Chisos Mountains in Brewster County. Several fairly representative specimens occur in Hudspeth County on Eagle Mountain and in the Sierra Blanca and Quitman mountains. In Culberson County, this species is found in the Guadalupe and Diablo mountains. The largest numbers of trees are in the Hueco Mountains of El Paso and Hudspeth counties and the Franklin Mountains of El Paso County. Pack rat middens indicate that *Q. toumeyi* was at one time the dominant oak in the Huecos. It has now been replaced by Arizona White Oak, which has in turn hybridized extensively with *Q. mohriana*. Introgression (back-crossing) with Toumey Oak is suspected in the Huecos and in those populations in the Sierra Blanca, Quitman, and Eagle mountains.

Quercus drummondii (white oak group)

Drummond Post Oak

Drummond Post Oak is considered either a true species that occupies a special ecological niche in the deep Tertiary sands of southcentral Texas or a variant population of Post Oak. It occurs just south of Seguin in the Sarita-Wilco soil association in Guadalupe County, a deep sand belt that runs, along with other soil associations, several counties to the east. These windblown and water-deposited sands and sandy clay loams hold little available water and can form dunes. These soil formations and resident oak populations occur in Medina, Bexar, Wilson, Guadalupe, Caldwell, Gonzales, Bastrop, Austin, and Robertson counties. Drummond Post Oak intergrades with *Quercus stellata* and *Q. margaretta* and can be expected to occur in Fayette, Lee, Burleson, Washington, Brazos, Milam, Leon, and Madison counties.

In this area, remnant stands of *Q. margaretta* occur on the deepest sand and *Q. stellata* is found on sandy gravel and clay beds. Drummond Post Oak grows on intermediate sands between those two areas and is considered a stabilized hybrid between the two species. If it is indeed stabilized, then Drummond Post Oak should be considered a viable species.

Quercus emoryi
(black oak group)

Emory Oak

(Black Oak, Bellota, Roble Negro, Holly Oak, Apache Oak, Desert Live Oak, Western Black Oak)

Emory Oak grows in deep, well-watered canyons of the Trans-Pecos, where it can attain heights of 60 to 70 feet, although it usually averages 15 to 25 feet. Its greatest populations are in the Chisos, Davis, Chinati, and Vieja mountains at 4,500 feet and higher—the middle to southern ranges of that area of Texas. Emory Oak requires acid soils of igneous origins and will not grow on alkaline soils. In the Glass Mountains, which are primarily limestone, it occurs on Iron Mountain and other igneous intrusions.

Emory Oak is evergreen, or at least persistent-leaved. Most oaks in the black oak group have acorns that take two years to mature and are quite bitter, requiring prolonged leaching with water to rid them of their bitter principle. Emory Oak's acorns, however, are sweet and can be eaten out of hand without parboiling or leaching. They are also produced annually and ripen by late August.

Quercus falcata
(black oak group)

Southern Red Oak

(Spanish Oak, Swamp Red Oak, Swamp Spanish Oak, Cherrybark Oak, Bottomland Red Oak, Three-lobe Red Oak)

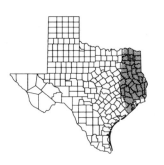

Southern Red Oak grows to heights of more than 125 feet in the Pineywoods, Post Oak Savannah, and eastern Gulf Prairies and Marshes. It is by far the dominant oak in the Pineywoods and will compete with the Post Oak and Escarpment Live Oak for the highest numbers in Texas.

Southern Red Oak is exceedingly polymorphic; that is, it has many forms. This is especially true of its leaves, which can have only three lobes right at the tip or as many as thirteen lobes along the leaf length. The leaves are 4 to 10 inches long and 2½ to 7 inches wide. The upper and lower leaf surfaces are either hairy or hairless. All of these leaf types can sometimes be found on the same tree.

Many authors divide the Southern Red Oak complex into the following four varieties: *Quercus falcata* var. *falcata* (Southern Red Oak), *Q. falcata* var. *leucophylla* (True Cherrybark Red Oak), *Q. falcata* var. *pagodifolia* (Swamp Red Oak), and *Q. falcata* var. *triloba* (Three-lobe Red Oak). Several authors recognize only Southern Red Oak. They consider Cherrybark Red Oak and Swamp Red Oak to be the same tree and ignore the Three-lobe Red Oak. Part of the problem is that Southern Red Oak occupies many different sites and habitats. The Cherrybark and Swamp phases are found mostly east of a 45-inch rainfall line ranging from Bowie County in the northeast to Walker and Montgomery counties, then southeast to Chambers and Jefferson counties. Much research is necessary to determine the taxonomic status of Southern Red Oak.

This confusing oak, or group of oaks, grows on almost any of the acidified soils of eastern Texas as part of the Shortleaf Pine—Post Oak—Southern Red Oak forest association, the Loblolly Pine—Sweet Gum forest association, the Water Oak—elm-hackberry forest association, the Willow Oak—Water Oak—Black Gum forest association, the Post Oak woods/forest association, and the fringes of the Bald Cypress—Water Tupelo swamp association.

Cherrybark Red Oak usually occurs as a single tree, not in groves. One hypothesis holds that it is allelopathic—salicylic acid leached from the leaves suppresses surrounding seedlings.

Quercus fusiformis (white oak group)

Escarpment Live Oak

(Plateau Live Oak, Scrub Live Oak, West Texas Live Oak, Live Oak)

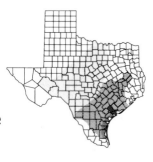

Escarpment Live Oak grows in mottes, attaining heights of 50 feet, on almost any alkaline to slightly acid, well-drained soil. It is rather rare on the true Blackland Prairies, possibly because of the poor internal drainage of those soils, but it does occur in the West Cross Timbers and Grand Prairie, west and north of the Balcones Escarpment on the Edwards Plateau, and, to a lesser degree, east of the Balcones Fault Line on the Blackland Prairies. It grows in hybrid swarms of *Quercus virginiana* x *Q. fusiformis* from the Balcones Escarpment to the coastal area and then eastward to the Brazos River, where, on the east side, more or less pure forms of *Q. virginiana* are encountered. (See plate 15 for range map.)

A rhizomatous, dwarf, evergreen oak covers many square miles of the sandy prairie lands in Calhoun and Victoria counties. Most authors concede that it is a juvenile form of *Q. virginiana* x *Q. fusiformis*. The plants are 3 to 10 feet high, yet they fruit heavily and remain at that height almost indefinitely. Others think it is a cross between *Q. minima* and *Q. fusiformis*. *Q. minima* is a dwarf live oak of the southeastern United States no longer present in Texas.

Similar dwarf trees occur farther south along the coast, yet they appear to be an introgressed hybrid of *Q. oleoides* x *Q. fusiformis*. These plants occupy the deep sands through Aransas, San Patricio, Nueces, Kleberg, Kenedy, and Brooks counties. *Q. oleoides* is an oak of Mexico no longer present in Texas.

Quercus gambelii
(white oak group)

Gambel Oak

(White Oak, Rocky Mountain
White Oak, Utah White Oak)

Gambel Oak is a small tree 15 to 25 feet in height, growing at elevations of 7,500 to 8,000 feet in the Chinati, Chisos, Davis, and Guadalupe mountains in the Trans-Pecos. It does equally well on alkaline and acid soils but is never found at low elevations.

Gambel Oak is a remarkable look-alike of *Quercus alba* (White Oak). Because it requires acid soils, the White Oak will not grow in the alkaline Blackland soils around Dallas. Gambel Oak, however, grows without a hint of iron chlorosis (one of the first red flags of a plant growing on soil that is too alkaline) and otherwise does well until the hot days of July and August. Then the trees stress badly and become susceptible to debilitating leaf spot diseases.

269

Quercus glaucoides
(white oak group)

Lacey Oak

(Smoky Oak, Canyon Oak, Rock Oak)

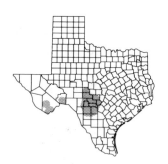

Lacey Oak is one of the most attractive of the Texas oaks and should be more widely used in amenity plantings in western and central Texas. It is a moderate-sized tree, growing to approximately 35 feet, with dusky blue to blue-gray deciduous leaves that sometimes have good fall color of golds or golds and grays.

Extremely drought tolerant, Lacey Oak grows on the thin, hard limestone rock of the central Edwards Plateau. It can be observed on farm-to-market road 337 from Medina in Bandera County through Vanderpool to Leakey and Camp Wood in Real County. Along this scenic drive, Lacey Oak dots the steep hills and crests of each peak.

It also occurs in isolated populations west of the Pecos River in Terrell County, in the Left-hand Shutup of the Solitario, and in Mouse Canyon in the Chisos Mountains of Big Bend National Park.

Quercus graciliformis
(black oak group)

Graceful Oak

(Slender Oak, Chisos Oak)

Graceful Oak occurs only in the Chisos Mountains in Brewster County and just a few miles to the southeast in the Sierra del Carmens in the Mexican state of Coahuila.

It grows to 25 or 30 feet in height, although the state champion is 66 feet tall. It is closely related to *Quercus canbyi* from Mexico; some botanists believe Graceful Oak is only a variation of that species.

Graceful Oak is difficult to find in the Chisos Mountains. It generally won't grow below 5,000 feet, and it is most prevalent on canyon floors, presumably always growing over a high water table. Blue Creek Canyon is one of the more attractive and easily reached habitats of Graceful Oak. Here, and in Oak Canyon to the north, it hybridizes with Emory Oak, creating Tharp Oak (*Q.* x *tharpii*). Chisos Red Oak, Robust Oak (*Q.* x *robusta*), an Emory—Chisos Red Oak cross, and Tharp Oak strongly resemble Graceful Oak in this area.

271

Quercus gravesii (black oak group)

Chisos Red Oak

(Graves Oak, Mountain Red Oak, Rock Oak)

Chisos Red Oak was first discovered by Wright, Parry, Bigelow, and Schott in the 1850s while they were with the United States–Mexican Boundary Survey. The trees they found have become known as the Lost Oaks of the Pecos because no one has been able to relocate them. The site was originally described as "a rocky ravine near the mouth of the Pecos and on the Limpio," but the meaning of "Limpio" is uncertain. It is possible that a small watered canyon still shelters these magnificent oaks.

Chisos Red Oak is more properly at home west of the Pecos River in the high country of the Chisos, Davis, Del Norte, and Glass mountains and in the mountains of Coahuila in Mexico. The best place to observe it is in the Basin of the Chisos, where, in late November to December, it will spectacularly clothe the north-facing mountainsides with shades of old gold and carmine. (See plate 14 for range map showing Shumard Red Oak–Texas Red Oak–Chisos Red Oak group.)

The species appears to grow equally well in igneous soils (Chisos, Davis Mountains) or limestone (Del Norte and Glass mountains and Val Verde County—the Lost Oaks of the Pecos—east of the Pecos River). It grows exceptionally well in the Dallas area (on limestone soils) but will *not* give fall color, acting instead like a typical southern tree that doesn't have time to initiate the color mechanism of the leaves before a hard freeze hits. It colors well in all mountain ranges to the west but does not occur any farther north (that is, in the Apache, Delaware, Diablo, or Guadalupe mountains). The Val

Verde County tree, from acorns, is an evergreen oak in Dallas, losing its leaves only at the start of spring growth.

Chisos Red Oak is closely related to Texas Red Oak and Shumard Red Oak, although neither occurs west of the Pecos.

This is the only oak west of the Pecos River and in Mexico that gives such brilliant fall coloration. It is true that the Rocky Mountain White Oak and a few others do give some coloration, but only the Chisos Red Oak can compete with the Texas, Shumard, and White oaks of lands east of the Pecos.

Quercus grisea
(white oak group)

Gray Oak

(Encino Prieta)

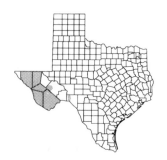

Gray Oak, as far as this author is aware, does not occur east of the Pecos River, although most distribution maps show it in Crockett and Val Verde counties. An isolated population probably does occur in Val Verde County on Fielder Draw, but the drainageway comes into the Pecos River from the west side. I know of no Gray Oak colonies in Crockett County. It just may be that both stands are, in reality, specimens of Mohr Oak, which is closely related and strongly favors the Gray Oak in appearance. Also, they could be hybrid swarms of introgressed (by Mohr Oak) Gray Oak x Mohr Oak.

Gray Oak prefers igneous soils, but it does grow on limestone. It is generally a small tree of 20 feet or under, although the reputed state champion tree from Big Bend National Park is said to be 50 feet tall. Gray Oak is found in the Chinati, Chisos, Davis, Del Norte, Glass, Guadalupe, Hueco, and Vieja mountains on acid, igneous soils in most cases. It grows on limestone in the Guadalupes and Huecos (in the mountains proper, not the state park), occupies the igneous masses of the Del Nortes, and in the Glass Mountains occurs on the flanks of Iron Mountain and on an igneous intrusion in Hess Canyon with Emory Oak.

The only Gray Oak—Mohr Oak hybrid that I have seen is in Hess Canyon. Gray Oak also hybridizes with Arizona White Oak, Gambel Oak, Netleaf Oak, and probably other white oaks.

Quercus hemisphaerica (black oak group)

Coast Laurel Oak

Coast Laurel Oak belongs to one of the most confusing of all the oak complexes. Most taxonomists do not even consider it a variety, much less a species. It is very closely related to *Quercus laurifolia* (Laurel Oak) of the Pineywoods in eastern Texas. Perhaps Coast Laurel Oak is better thought of as a geographical or climatic species.

Coast Laurel Oak, a small tree of 30 feet or less in height, has small, thick, toothed leaves that are evergreen or at least persistent. It is a prolific producer of small acorns. It grows on the sandy hummocks and prairies of the Coastal Bend in Aransas, Calhoun, Nueces, Refugio, San Patricio, and Victoria counties. Unlike Laurel Oak to the east, this much smaller tree forms extensive mottes.

Quercus hypoleucoides
(black oak group)

Silverleaf Oak

(Whiteleaf Oak)

Silverleaf Oak is a regal and striking tree with its lance-shaped leaves of silvery white below and dark green above. It averages 20 to 30 feet tall and is found only in the higher reaches of the Davis Mountains in Jeff Davis County. It is not rare in these mountains, but it is highly local.

The species generally grows at altitudes above 6,000 feet, exhibiting two characteristic growth habits in the canyons running north and south at elevations of 6,000 to 8,000 feet. On the east-facing (west) side of the canyon, Silverleaf Oak grows 20 to 40 feet tall with 3- to 4-inch-long leaves that can be almost 2 inches wide. On the west-facing (east) wall, it scarcely grows to 10 or 15 feet and has very narrow leaves. So critical is the moisture supply that just a few more hours of sunlight, a few more degrees of heat, and consequently a higher evaporation-transpiration rate causes these trees to appear completely different. On the northern side of the Davis Mountains, coming out of Balmorhea, Silverleaf Oak forms dense 3- to 4-foot thickets that cover several acres of land.

As a black oak, Silverleaf Oak would be expected to have acorns that require two years to mature, yet its acorns will mature in either one or two years.

Quercus incana
(black oak group)

Bluejack Oak

(Sandjack Oak,
Upland Willow Oak, Cinnamon Oak,
Shin Oak, Turkey Oak)

Bluejack Oak, found on the deep sands of the Pineywoods, Gulf Prairies and Marshes, and Post Oak Savannah, grows to 50 feet in height, although it is usually much smaller, even shrublike.

In the Post Oak Savannah, Bluejack Oak is part of the Post Oak woods/forest association and the Post Oak woods/forest and grassland mosaic association. Some of the associated plants are Blackjack Oak, Black Hickory, Mesquite, Escarpment Live Oak, Post Oak, Drummond Post Oak, Sand Post Oak, Sand Love Grass, and Three-awn Grass. In the northeast Pineywoods, Bluejack Oak occurs in the Shortleaf Pine—Post Oak—Southern Red Oak affiliation of the pine-hardwood forest association, and in southeast Texas it grows along well-drained ridges and is also an integral part of the Longleaf Pine—Bluejack Oak grouping of the pine-hardwood forest association. Some of the same associates are always present in these several associations, namely Black Hickory, Sand Post Oak, Post Oak, Flowering Dogwood, and hackberry.

Bluejack Oak is a most decorative and striking oak. The white, hoary undersides of its leaves are intriguing because they are an attribute of plants growing in drought-prone environments. It is possible that Bluejack Oak experiences a shortage of moisture where it occurs on the deep sugar sands, and the leaf is an adaptation for conserving moisture.

Quercus laurifolia
(black oak group)

Laurel Oak

(Darlington Oak, Diamondleaf Oak, Swamp Laurel Oak, Laurel Leaf Oak, Obtusa Oak)

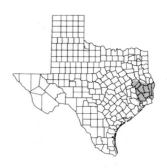

Laurel Oak belongs to a series of oaks that are very difficult to identify in the field. Along with Willow Oak and Water Oak, it constitutes a perplexing complex of oaks. It is evergreen and grows to 125 feet in height.

For the most part, Laurel Oak grows on soils that are better drained than those where Water and Willow oaks occur. Its diamondleaf form, however, grows in absolute wet sites. Laurel Oak is limited in range, occurring in southeast Texas in the Big Thicket area and north to Anderson, Cherokee, Nacogdoches, and Shelby counties. It is found from the uplands of the Shortleaf Pine—Post Oak—Southern Red Oak association to the more mesic Loblolly Pine—Sweet Gum association, in the still wetter Willow Oak—Water Oak—Black Gum forest association, and finally in the Bald Cypress—Water Tupelo swamp association. Laurel Oak is associated with Nuttall Oak, Water Locust, Water Hickory, Southern Red Oak, Sweet Gum, Black Gum, Overcup Oak, Loblolly Pine, Shortleaf Pine, Longleaf Pine, Red Maple, Mockernut Hickory, and Southern Wax Myrtle.

Quercus lyrata
(white oak group)

Overcup Oak

(Swamp Post Oak, Swamp White Oak, Water White Oak)

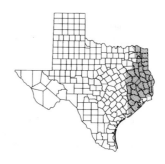

Overcup Oak is sometimes confused with Bur Oak, but they are hardly look-alikes, even though they are closely related. Their areas of growth, their soil types and soil reactions, are so far apart that there should be no question about their identities, unless of course they are growing side by side in a cultivated state in an arboretum or other unnatural grouping. Bur Oak quite simply is a prairie oak of calcareous soils, and although it does prefer some moisture, it also needs fair drainage or at least not continuously wet soils.

Overcup Oak, nearly 90 feet tall, grows in acid sands, sandy loams, and clays in oxygen-deficient, wet soils in the Pineywoods, Post Oak Savannah, and Gulf Prairies and Marshes in the eastern part of the state. It is almost always confined to swamps, otherwise standing water, or the banks and edges of flowing streams. It will be found in the Bald Cypress—Water Tupelo swamp association, the Pecan—elm forest association, the Water Oak—elm-hackberry forest association, the Willow Oak—Water Oak—Black Gum forest association, the Palmetto—oak flats association, and the Bay—Gallberry Holly bogs of the Big Thicket area of southeast Texas.

Quercus macrocarpa
(white oak group)

Bur Oak

(Mossycup Oak,
Mossy Overcup Oak, Prairie Oak)

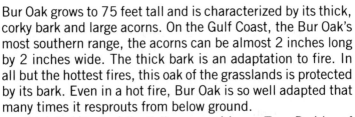

Bur Oak grows to 75 feet tall and is characterized by its thick, corky bark and large acorns. On the Gulf Coast, the Bur Oak's most southern range, the acorns can be almost 2 inches long by 2 inches wide. The thick bark is an adaptation to fire. In all but the hottest fires, this oak of the grasslands is protected by its bark. Even in a hot fire, Bur Oak is so well adapted that many times it resprouts from below ground.

An inhabitant of the tallgrass prairie, or True Prairie, of central North America, Bur Oak occurs in lesser numbers in New York, Maine, and Pennsylvania, down through West Virginia, Kentucky, and Tennessee, and into the Ozarks in Arkansas. It grows best on limestone soils of riverbanks and valleys in the Blackland Prairies, the Cross Timbers and Prairies, the western edges of the Post Oak Savannah, the central portion of the Gulf Prairies and Marshes, the Lampasas Cut Plains, the Central Mineral Region, and the northern part of the Edwards Plateau as far west as Menard County. There is a broad band of Bur Oak in Atascosa and Live Oak counties on the Rio Grande Plains, which are on the Atascosa River and Nueces River watersheds, respectively.

Bur Oak is probably the easiest to grow of all oaks because it requires only a little extra water. Schoolchildren in Menard County use pecan shakers and sweepers to harvest the acorns of Bur Oak. Those particular acorns are valuable because they produce probably the most drought-tolerant Bur Oaks found in Texas.

Quercus margaretta
(white oak group)

Sand Post Oak

(Dwarf Post Oak, Post Oak, Runner Oak, Scrubby Post Oak)

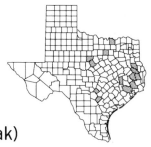

Sand Post Oak grows to only 20 feet in height. At times, it forms thickets, but at other times it is single-trunked. This oak grows on deep, fine, almost sterile sand. Where gravel and clays are mixed with the sand, broad belts of Post Oak and small pockets of Drummond Post Oak will grow, but if it is almost pure sand the post oak complex will be either entirely Sand Post Oak or a Post Oak hybrid swarm with Sand Post Oak being a major part.

Sand Post Oak grows in the eastern half of Texas wherever deep sands occur. This usually limits the species to small enclaves in the Post Oak Savannah and Pineywoods, with a few stands in the Cross Timbers. It is part of the Longleaf Pine—Sandjack Oak, the Shortleaf Pine—Post Oak—Southern Red Oak, and the Post Oak parks associations. Generally, however, even in these sandyland associations, Sand Post Oak grows in sand so deep and fine that it is a small association of its own. There is a rather extensive population west of Garrison in Nacogdoches County. Associated with it are Allegheny Chinquapin, One-flower Hawthorn, Oklahoma Plum, Farkleberry, Oklahoma Prairie Clover, and Lazy Daisy. An attempt has been made to grow pines on this land, but every summer they die from lack of moisture.

Quercus marilandica
(black oak group)

Blackjack Oak

(Barren Oak, Jack Oak, Black Oak)

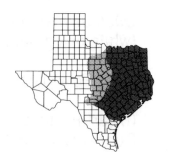

Two distinct forms of Blackjack Oak occur in Texas. Typical Blackjack Oak occurs on the east side of the arbitrary line seen on the accompanying map. It grows more than 50 feet tall and has large three-lobed, club-shaped leaves. Preferring very acid sands, sandy loams, and clays, this form of Blackjack Oak is an associate of Post Oak and is thus found in the Post Oak associations as well as the Shortleaf Pine—Post Oak—Southern Red Oak association and the Longleaf Pine—Sandjack Oak association.

The xeric or western phase of Blackjack Oak grows to 30 feet in height to the west of the line. Here this tree is found on sand or gravelly clay soils that are only slightly acidic. It is part of the oak-Mesquite-juniper parks and woods association of the Cross Timbers and Prairies, the Live Oak—Mesquite parks association of the Central Mineral Region, and the Live Oak—Mesquite—Ashe Juniper parks association on several of the hilltops on the Edwards Plateau.

Quercus michauxii
(white oak group)

Swamp Chestnut Oak

(Basket Oak, Cow Oak)

Swamp Chestnut Oak inhabits the mesic woodlands of eastern Texas in the Pineywoods and Gulf Prairies and Marshes in a 45-inch rainfall belt. It ranges from Marion County in the north to Brazoria County in the southwest. Swamp Chestnut Oak grows to almost 120 feet in height.

Swamp Chestnut Oak cannot tolerate constant standing water but does best with flooded conditions during the winter and only damp to intermittently inundated during the growing season. In fairly wet situations, Swamp Chestnut Oak is associated with Green Ash, Nuttall Oak, Willow Oak, Red Maple, Overcup Oak, and Black Gum. In drier situations, it occurs in the Loblolly Pine—Sweet Gum association with Water Oak, Sweet Gum, White Oak, Winged Elm, beech, American Hornbeam, and Flowering Dogwood. Its associates in the Bald Cypress—Water Tupelo swamp association are Water Hickory, Swamp Black Gum, Water Elm, Black Willow, Bald Cypress, and Water Tupelo. In more open areas, Swamp Chestnut Oak forms large acreages of browse and other pasture along with Dwarf Palmetto.

Quercus mohriana
(white oak group)

Mohr Oak

(Scrub Oak, Shin Oak)

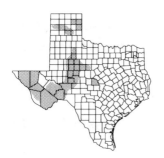

Mohr Oak is found west of the 100th meridian except for a few populations in Callahan, Runnels, San Saba, and Taylor counties. As one of the few grassland oaks that have evolved in midgrass to shortgrass prairies, it must therefore contend with prairie wildfires. It is a small rhizomatous tree growing to 20 feet tall, although it is often shrubby and creates mottes in the Rolling Plains, western Edwards Plateau, and most of the counties west of the Pecos River.

Mohr Oak has blue-gray, evergreen or persistent leaves and grows on the hard limestone and exposed caliche soils in a rainfall belt that receives 25 inches or less annually. It is most easily seen just south of Interstate Highway 20 in Callahan, Taylor, and Nolan counties on the limestone caprock of the Callahan Divide. It can also be seen in Big Spring State Park on the limestone hills, though there are fewer trees here. Some of the most scenic areas available for viewing Mohr Oak are just under the Caprock escarpment of the Llano Estacado on Texas Highway 256 in Briscoe County, the steep hanging cliffs of the Palo Duro on Texas Highway 207 in Armstrong County, and the Mulberry Creek road heading to Claude and going through the JA Ranch to Clarendon in Donley County.

Quercus muehlenbergii
(white oak group)

Chinkapin Oak

(Chestnut Oak, Yellow Chestnut Oak, Rock Chestnut Oak, Rock Oak, Yellow Oak, Chinquapin Oak)

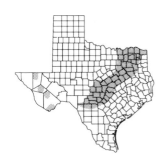

Chinkapin Oak grows to 90 feet in height, occurring on the well-drained, deeper soils of river and creek bottoms; on the limestone soils of the Blackland Prairies, Cross Timbers and Prairies, and Edwards Plateau; and also in small isolated groves in the mountains of the Trans-Pecos and the Post Oak Savannah of northeastern Texas. The state champion Chinkapin Oak is in Newton County, but it is not clear if it is a planted tree. This species is not common, although it is far from rare.

Chinkapin Oak is found with American Elm, hackberry, Bur Oak, Bois d'Arc, and Shumard Oak on the Cross Timbers and Prairies. On the Edwards Plateau it is associated with Texas Red Oak, Cedar Elm, Bur Oak, Escarpment Black Cherry, and Western Soapberry. In this area, the trees produce leaves that are shorter and wider than those on the Cross Timbers and Prairies. The acorns are second in size only to those of Bur Oak.

The distribution of this oak in the Trans-Pecos mountains is interesting. It is readily found along creek banks on the limestone Capitan Reef formation in the Del Norte, Glass, and Guadalupe mountains. In the Chisos Mountains, it occurs in small pockets of limestone. I have seen this tree in the heart of the Davis Mountains on what I considered to be limestone of unknown origin.

Quercus nigra (black oak group)

Water Oak

(Possum Oak, Spotted Oak, Duck Oak, Punk Oak)

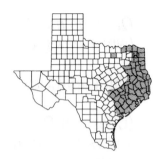

Water Oak grows rapidly and attains heights of almost 80 feet. It occurs in the swamps, low flats, and stream banks in the Post Oak Savannah, Pineywoods, and Gulf Prairies and Marshes, with a small isolated grove along a creek near Flower Mound in Denton County in the East Cross Timbers. This oak is part of a complex consisting of the Willow, Water, and Laurel oaks and their hybrids, all of which are difficult to identify in the field.

Water Oak belongs to the Loblolly Pine—Sweet Gum association, the Bald Cypress—Water Tupelo association in the Pineywoods, and the Pecan-elm forest association of the Gulf Prairies and Marshes. It is one of the dominant plants in the Willow Oak—Water Oak—Black Gum forest association of the southeastern Pineywoods and Gulf Prairies and Marshes. In the Post Oak Savannah, Water Oak is an integral part of the Water Oak—elm-hackberry forest association in the river bottoms of northeast Texas. In all of these associations, water-logged, oxygen-deficient soils that are neutral to quite acid are primarily responsible for the trees growing there.

Water Oak is a widely planted tree and, in its most typical form, has dark green, spoon-shaped leaves that vary in persistence from completely deciduous to almost totally evergreen.

Quercus nuttallii
(black oak group)

Nuttall Oak

(Red Oak, Red River Oak, Pin Oak, Striped Oak)

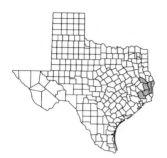

Nuttall Oak is one of the rarest oaks in Texas. It occurs in greater numbers in Alabama, Arkansas, Louisiana, Mississippi, and Missouri but is still not a common tree.

Nuttall Oak is usually not over 50 feet in height in Texas, although in the Mississippi River drainage basin it can easily reach more than 100 feet. In Texas, Nuttall Oak occurs on the Sabine River in Newton County, in the Neches River drainage area in Angelina, Tyler, Jasper, and Hardin counties, and along the floodplain of the Trinity River in Liberty County. It is easily seen on the north side of Texas Highway 105 and west of the Trinity River just west of Romayor. Here it grows on poorly drained clays. It does well in areas with winter flooding and year-round moisture, but it is highly intolerant of shade. Nuttall Oak is part of the Willow Oak—Water Oak—Black Gum forest and Bald Cypress—Water Tupelo swamp associations of the Neches, Trinity, and Sabine floodplains in the Big Thicket area.

Nuttall Oak is attractive and suitable for landscape plantings in areas that are waterlogged and oxygen-deficient. It is closely related to Northern Pin Oak, and the species are almost indistinguishable when they grow together in the same areas in Arkansas and northern Mississippi.

New nomenclature proposed for this tree of the swamps and acid lowlands of East Texas is *Quercus texana.* The vernacular should remain as "Nutall Oak." *It will not grow in the calcareous soils of Austin, Dallas, or San Antonio.*

287

Quercus oblongifolia
(white oak group)

Mexican Blue Oak

(Blue Oak)

Mexican Blue Oak was unknown in Texas until the early 1970s when it was found in the Bofecillos Mountains in Presidio County. It is also suspected of occurring in the Quitman Mountains in Hudspeth County; if it does, it might also be found on Eagle Mountain and other ranges in the southern Trans-Pecos.

When I first saw these oaks in a little box canyon high above Madera Falls, I could distinguish them almost a mile away because of the deep blue of their leaves. The oaks occupy the upper, drier end of the canyon, and *Fraxinus papillosa* (or *F. velutina*) line the small body of water around the spring. The state champion tree was recorded here, measuring only 28 feet in height.

I have seen small groves of this evergreen tree on conglomerate in dry creekbeds. It superficially resembles Lacey Oak and might be confused with Gray Oak.

Quercus phellos
(black oak group)

Willow Oak

(Pin Oak, Peach Oak, Swamp Willow Oak)

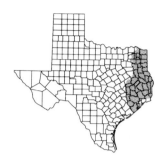

Willow Oak grows on the poorly drained, hardpan, upland soils of the Post Oak Savannah and on all types of floodplains in the Pineywoods, Gulf Prairies and Marshes from Brazoria County to the east, and also the stream bottoms and flooded drainageways of the Post Oak Savannah.

A graceful tree reaching almost 100 feet in height, it is easily confused with its close relatives, Laurel Oak and Water Oak. Willow Oak is deciduous and displays attractive golden leaves in the fall. It is almost always in the wetter soils of eastern Texas that can be inundated year-round but are usually flooded for six to eight months in the fall, winter, and spring. Its small acorns are eaten by wildlife and are especially important in the diets of various waterfowl.

Willow Oak is an integral part of the Pecan-elm forest association of the Post Oak Savannah and Gulf Prairies and Marshes, the Water Oak—elm-hackberry forest association of the northern Post Oak Savannah, the Willow Oak—Water Oak—Black Gum forest association in the Pineywoods, and the Loblolly Pine—Sweet Gum and Bald Cypress—Water Tupelo swamp associations.

Quercus pungens var. *pungens* (white oak group)

Sandpaper Oak

(Scrub Oak, Shin Oak, Scrub Live Oak, Encino)

Sandpaper Oak attains heights of only 15 to 20 feet, generally growing on limestone hillsides and dry creek and river banks. The leaves are crisped or rolled at the edges and are harsh to the touch, thus the common name. It occurs in its purest form in Culberson, El Paso, and Hudspeth counties; in Presidio and Brewster counties it hybridizes with Vasey Oak. It is part of the Montane Chaparral and juniper-Pinyon woodlands, extending upward in elevation into the true oak and pine woodlands of the higher mountain ranges in the Trans-Pecos. At lower elevations it will also occur along mostly seasonally dry watercourses in the riparian woodlands.

Sandpaper Oak closely resembles Vasey Oak, and in the southern Trans-Pecos it is difficult to separate these oaks because the entire population is a segregating hybrid swarm.

Typical Sandpaper Oak can be observed along any of the trails in Guadalupe National Park and just before entering Lincoln National Forest on the left side of the right-of-way on New Mexico Highway 137.

Quercus pungens
var. *vaseyana*
(white oak group)

Vasey Oak

(Scrub Oak, Shin Oak)

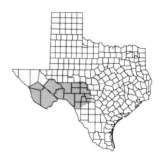

Vasey Oak is small, attaining only 40 feet in height, and has evergreen or persistent leaves that are a bright glossy green throughout most of the year. It is a premier tree for use in landscaping.

Found on the hard limestones of the southern and western Edwards Plateau and on igneous soil in Big Aguja Canyon on the Sproul Ranch in the heart of the Davis Mountains, Vasey Oak also occurs as a hybrid with Sandpaper Oak in Brewster and Presidio counties. On the western Edwards Plateau it is part of the Mesquite-juniper—Live Oak brush association. Vasey Oak is especially prevalent in Val Verde, Terrell, and Crockett counties. Almost any road north from Comstock, Langtry, Sanderson, Dryden, and Del Rio passes through small thickets of Vasey Oak. It attains its largest size in dry arroyos and along creek banks. It grows on the limestone hillsides and mesas in a Live Oak—Ashe Juniper woods association in the central Edwards Plateau. Vasey Oak is fairly common through Real and western Bandera counties but is less prevalent in Kerr County.

Quercus rugosa
(white oak group)

Netleaf Oak

Netleaf Oak is fairly uncommon, occurring only on Mount Emory in the Chisos Mountains of Big Bend National Park in Brewster County at elevations of 7,000 feet and above, and in a little-known canyon on the east slope of Mount Livermore in the Davis Mountains in Jeff Davis County. This is a striking oak of less than 30 feet in height, with thick, hard, rounded evergreen or persistent leaves. The acorns are on stems up to 2 inches long.

Netleaf Oak will be noticed by few people because of its scarcity. Unfortunately scientists and photographers will always go to the few oaks in the Chisos Mountains, seeking their specimens and photos. These trees are merely remnants of a long-ago population that was representative of this oak. Today these trees are severely diluted by hybridization with Gray Oak. Still they are convenient, if unrepresentative, because they hang over the South Rim Trail between the South Rim and Boot Springs and are accessible. Netleaf Oaks in the Davis Mountains are relatively pure but are on private property and high in one canyon on the east or southeast slope of Mount Livermore.

Quercus shumardii (black oak group)

Shumard Red Oak

(Swamp Red Oak, Shumard Oak, Spotted Oak)

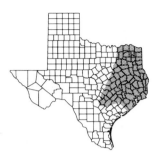

Shumard Red Oak is a large tree reaching 120 feet in height on the rich, moist bottomland soils of the East Cross Timbers, Blackland Prairies, Post Oak Savannah, Pineywoods, and Gulf Prairies. It is never found in large groves but usually occurs singly and widely spaced. It grows in the Red Oak—Cedar Elm—Bois d'Arc association of the Blackland Prairies, the Post Oak woods/forest and Water Oak—elm-hackberry association of the Post Oak Savannah, the Pecan-elm forest association of the Gulf Prairies, and the Loblolly Pine—Sweet Gum and Shortleaf Pine—Post Oak—Southern Red Oak associations of the Pineywoods.

One of the most puzzling oak complexes in Texas is the Shumard Red Oak—Texas Red Oak—Chisos Red Oak group (see plate 14). There is no doubt that they are extremely closely related, and much confusion exists in herbaria and in the field as to the correct identity of these oaks. For our purposes we will place Chisos Red Oak west of the Pecos, except for two canyons just east of the river in Val Verde County, where there are relict stands of this tree. Chisos Red Oak therefore doesn't bother too many people. We will place Texas Red Oak west and north of the Balcones Escarpment and the White Rock Escarpment just west of Dallas, and Shumard Red Oak is simply east of this line. Along the line from Dallas to Austin will be a great hybrid swarm of *Q. shumardii* x *Q. texana*. Pure Shumard Red Oak probably does not exist on the Edwards Plateau.

Quercus similis
(white oak group)

Bottomland Post Oak

(Delta Post Oak, Yellow Oak, Mississippi Valley Oak)

Bottomland Post Oak is a large tree of almost 100 feet in height that grows on the moist to wet second terraces of the Loblolly Pine—Sweet Gum association and the Willow Oak—Water Oak—Black Gum forest association. It grows alongside Green Ash, Swamp Chestnut Oak, Southern Red Oak, Black Gum, Shumard Red Oak, White Oak, Winged Elm, American Hornbeam, Sycamore, and Black Willow.

This common tree of the rich, moist bottoms of the southeast Texas Pineywoods and Gulf Prairies and Marshes is especially prevalent in the wet lowlands of Hardin, Liberty, Tyler, Jefferson, Orange, Jasper, Newton, Polk, and San Jacinto counties as well as parts of Sabine, San Augustine, Angelina, and Montgomery counties in the Big Thicket. Outside the Big Thicket it occurs in Harris, Chambers, and probably other counties.

Quercus sinuata var. *breviloba* (white oak group)

Bigelow Oak

(Shin Oak, White Oak, Scrub Oak, Scalybark Oak)

Bigelow Oak is called scrub or shin oak because it is generally a multitrunked tree of only 10 to 12 feet in height, although in rare instances it can approach 40 feet. This is a grassland oak and is found in the Blackland Prairies, West Cross Timbers and Prairies, the southern Rolling Plains, and all but the far western portion of the Edwards Plateau.

Bigelow Oak grows on hard limestone and forms thickets when it occurs in lighter soils or when its roots have been disturbed. It has many growth forms because it readily responds to differences in habitat and climate. Small groves of up to one acre occur along the Red River in Cooke County, where the trees are scarcely 3 feet tall. However, on the limestone escarpment east of Anna in Collin County and Van Alstyne in Grayson County, the trees are 12 to 20 feet tall and are widely spaced. The southern Grand Prairie and the Lampasas Cut Plains, between Hamilton in Hamilton County and Goldthwaite in Mills County, have vast acreages of Bigelow Oak that are approximately 10 to 12 feet tall and so thick that a person can hardly walk through them. These trees have many stems because they have been chained, which is a practice involving pulling a heavy anchor chain over the oaks and jerking some out of the ground, but leaving many rhizomes for subsequent sprouting. In the canyons of the Edwards Plateau and in Kerrville State Park, there are a few Bigelow Oaks that attain heights of 20 to 40 feet.

Quercus sinuata var. *sinuata* (white oak group)

Durand White Oak

(White Oak, Bluff Oak)

Durand White Oak grows to 90 feet in the east Texas Piney-woods, the Post Oak Savannah, and the Gulf Prairies. At the Balcones Escarpment of the Edwards Plateau, rainfall sharply decreases and the water-holding capacity of the shallow limestone soils is less. Selection by climate and soils over thousands of years has left a taller, more robust tree to the east (Durand White Oak) and a more xeric, dwarfed form to the west (Bigelow Oak). To the surprise of many these characters are more or less fixed. I have planted the 3-foot dwarfs from Cooke County alongside the 80- to 90-foot giants of Brazoria County. Ten years later the Bigelow Oak from the Red River Bluffs is only 3 feet tall and producing acorns, while Durand White Oak of the palmetto flats in Brazoria County is about 15 feet tall—and producing acorns.

Durand White Oak grows on the rich and wet, neutral-to-acid clays and limestone flats and grasslands of the eastern third of Texas but is sometimes confused with the taller-than-average Bigelow Oak on the Edwards Plateau.

Quercus stellata
(white oak group)

Post Oak

(Iron Oak, Cross Oak)

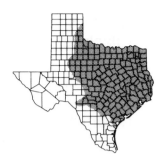

Post Oak is the widest-ranging oak in Texas, occurring in all areas except the High Plains and Trans-Pecos. It grows to more than 80 feet in height, but the majority range from 20 to 40 feet tall. It is possible that Post Oak is the most numerous of all Texas oaks, although arguments can be made for Southern Red Oak or Escarpment Live Oak having greater numbers.

Post Oak is confusing to identify because it has many growth forms. Some authors consider these forms varieties, but others lump them all together as Post Oak. Still others think each deserves the rank of species. Post Oak occurs in deep southeast Texas in the wet bottoms with *Quercus similis* (Bottomland Post Oak), on the deep sands of the Pineywoods and Post Oak Savannah with *Q. margaretta* (Sand Post Oak), in sands and sandy gravels on the central Texas Coastal Plains with *Q. drummondii* (Drummond Post Oak), and with *Q. boyntonii* (Boynton Post Oak) near Lufkin, a rhizomatous dwarf oak.

Post Oak is the dominant oak of the East and West Cross Timbers and the Post Oak Savannah. There are large numbers in the sandy, granitic soils of the Central Mineral Region of the Edwards Plateau and the Pineywoods of East Texas. It grows on slightly acid to highly acid sands and sandy loams in almost all areas. Across the high country of the Edwards Plateau and Real and Gillespie counties, it occurs on slightly acidic to neutral clay soil.

Quercus texana
(black oak group)

Texas Red Oak

(Spanish Oak, Spotted Oak, Red Oak, Rock Oak)

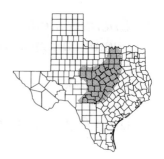

Texas Red Oak will reach 75 feet in height, though it usually is 30 to 50 feet tall. It grows to the west and north of the Balcones Escarpment in central Texas and west of the White Rock Escarpment (Interstate Highway 35), extending from Williamson County in the south to Grayson County in the north. In its purest form it is found on alkaline limestone and neutral to slightly acid gravels and sands of the West Cross Timbers, Grand Prairie, and Edwards Plateau.

There is a most confusing hybrid swarm of *Quercus texana* x *Q. shumardii* along the White Rock Escarpment—Balcones Escarpment line from the Red River through Dallas, Waco, Austin, and San Antonio, extending for several miles to the east on the Blacklands and Post Oak Savannah and several miles to the west in the Cross Timbers and Prairies and Edwards Plateau.

Pure stands of Shumard Red Oak occur to the east of the hybrid swarm, and Texas Red Oak occurs to the west in the heart of the central Edwards Plateau and Central Mineral Region; the Callahan Divide in Callahan, Taylor, and Nolan counties; and the western fringes of the West Cross Timbers. (See plate 14 for range map showing red oak complex.)

New nomenclature proposed for this oak is *Quercus buckleyi*. If we can't get a *nomina conservanda* for the binomial, I propose that we at least keep the vernacular of "Texas Red Oak."

Quercus turbinella
(white oak group)

Shrub Live Oak

(Turbinella Oak, Scrub Oak, Encino)

Shrub Live Oak grows to heights of 15 feet and has gray-blue evergreen leaves. It is an uncommon oak that is usually not shown on Texas plant distribution maps. However, it does exist in at least three mountain ranges in the Trans-Pecos.

Shrub Live Oak occurs in the Franklin Mountains in El Paso County and the Quitman Mountains and Eagle Mountain in Hudspeth County. It occurs at only moderate elevations of 4,000 to 4,500 feet and grows in igneous soil on rocky, rather steep hillsides. It is highly drought tolerant, and the acorns ripen extremely early, sometimes by middle June. Associates of Shrub Live Oak are *Berberis trifoliolata, Dalea pogonathera, Nolina erumpens, Poa fendleriana, Quercus intricata, Q. pungens* var. *vaseyana,* and *Yucca baccata.*

299

Quercus velutina
(black oak group)

Black Oak

(Yellow Oak, Quercitron Oak, Quercitron, Smoothbark Oak, Yellowbark Oak)

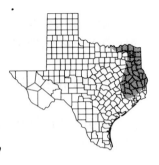

Black Oak grows to almost 90 feet tall, although 50 feet or less is the average. It is a striking species of the Pineywoods and Post Oak Savannah. Black Oak is fairly uncommon, occurring singly or in pairs but never in thickets and groves. It grows on sandy, gravelly upland ridges and terraces in soil that is always somewhat acidic and generally coarse-textured, such as sand, sandy loam, and gravelly sand. Black Oak is highly intolerant of shade and seems to be a poor competitor with other oaks. It forms a long taproot that helps it to survive in its droughty, sandy habitat.

One of eastern Texas' most attractive oaks, it has deep, rich green leaves in the summer and golden yellow fall color.

Black Oak is part of the Longleaf Pine—Sandjack oak association, the Shortleaf Pine—Post Oak—Southern Red Oak association, and the Post Oak woods/forest community in east Texas.

Quercus virginiana
(white oak group)

Live Oak

(Coast Live Oak,
Virginia Live Oak, Encino)

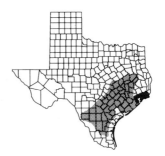

Live Oak grows to 50 feet tall and occurs east of the Brazos River in the Gulf Prairies and Marshes. It is easily confused with Escarpment Live Oak and other members of this series that occur in the southeastern United States. It is spatially segregated from the other species by the amount of rainfall that each receives. (See plate 15 for range map.)

A great complex hybrid swarm of *Quercus virginiana* and *Q. fusiformis* occurs from the west of the mouth of the Brazos River to the Balcones Escarpment of the Edwards Plateau, and as far north as Bell County, east into Houston County, and south to Aransas County. These trees are confusing to identify because they have so many different growth forms and leaf shapes.

Live Oak grows best on well-drained clay loams and gravelly clay loams. It does not tolerate poorly drained soils or extremely well-drained deep sand. Soil pH seems to be inconsequential, although it does best on neutral to only slightly acid soils. Temperature can be critical for Live Oak, for it was almost completely destroyed in the Dallas—Fort Worth area during the winter of 1983 when temperatures were below freezing for 296 consecutive hours (12⅓ days).

Rhamnus (buckthorn)

Rhamnaceae (buckthorn family)

Buckthorns total about 100 species in the temperate and tropical regions of both hemispheres. The majority of species occur in eastern Asia, with several in southwestern North America, Africa, Europe, and South America. The United States has 5 tree and 4 shrub species, and Texas has 1 tree and 3 shrub species.

Rhamnus caroliniana

Carolina Buckthorn

(Indian Cherry, Yellow Buckthorn, Yellow Wood)

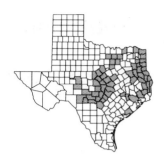

Carolina Buckthorn has been found in all areas of Texas except the Rolling Plains, High Plains, Rio Grande Plains, and Trans-Pecos. Birchleaf Buckthorn (*Rhamnus betulaefolia*) of the high mountain canyons in the Trans-Pecos is closely related to Carolina Buckthorn and intergrades with its eastern sibling in the western portion of the Edwards Plateau.

This small tree usually reaches heights of only 12 to 15 feet, although it sometimes approaches 40 feet, and grows under many diverse conditions of rainfall, soil, and temperature. In the bottomlands of east Texas, in a 55-to-60-inch rainfall belt, it grows in dense shade and highly acid sands and sandy loams. It also occurs in the highly calcareous bottomlands of the Blackland and Grand prairies, which are in a 30-to-35-inch rainfall belt. Farther west, in the Western Cross Timbers and the Edwards Plateau, this tree forms patches and groves on thin limestone hillsides where it receives full sunlight and only 15 to 30 inches of rainfall.

No one knows whether these three broad climatic- and soil-differentiated clones are genetically fixed for their requirements. Probably they are not that demanding or different, and one will grow with the other and vice versa. It is known, however, that there is a decided temperature adaptation—clones from Leakey in Real County are evergreen in Dallas and somewhat frost sensitive.

Rhus (sumac)

Anacardiaceae (sumac family)

The majority of sumacs are native to southern Africa, although some are found in both temperate and tropical areas of Asia, Europe, and North America. Several taxonomists describe around 120 species of *Rhus* worldwide. Others merge this genus with *Toxicodendron,* which includes Poison Sumac, Poison Ivy, and Poison Oak, making roughly 150 species worldwide. Here they will be considered separate genera. In the United States, there are roughly 15 species of *Rhus.* In Texas there are 4 shrubs with 2 species that are considered trees or at least treelike.

Rhus copallina var. *copallina*

Shining Sumac

(Wing-rib Sumac, Winged Sumac, Black Sumac, Mountain Sumac, Upland Sumac)

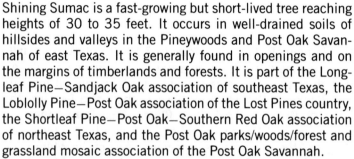

Shining Sumac is a fast-growing but short-lived tree reaching heights of 30 to 35 feet. It occurs in well-drained soils of hillsides and valleys in the Pineywoods and Post Oak Savannah of east Texas. It is generally found in openings and on the margins of timberlands and forests. It is part of the Longleaf Pine—Sandjack Oak association of southeast Texas, the Loblolly Pine—Post Oak association of the Lost Pines country, the Shortleaf Pine—Post Oak—Southern Red Oak association of northeast Texas, and the Post Oak parks/woods/forest and grassland mosaic association of the Post Oak Savannah.

The plants sucker readily, forming large clones. Birds are fond of the fruit and pass the seeds in their droppings along fencerows, so the turnrows of cultivated fields generally contain colonies of Shining Sumac.

This species produces male and female flowers on separate plants, with the female bearing dense red clusters of fruit. The winged, featherlike leaves turn brilliant red in autumn and make a showpiece on Interstate Highway 20 through Smith, Gregg, and Harrison counties.

Rhus lanceolata

Prairie Flameleaf Sumac

(Prairie Sumac,
Texas Sumac,
Lance-leaved
Sumac, Tree Sumac,
Limestone Sumac,
Prairie Shining Sumac)

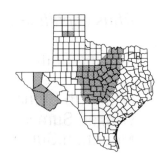

Prairie Flameleaf Sumac grows to 30 feet in height, usually on limestone or neutral clay, sand, and sandy loam soils, although at times it grows on acidic igneous soils. It inhabits the Blackland Prairies, the Cross Timbers and Prairies, the Edwards Plateau, the Rolling Plains (Palo Duro Canyon in Armstrong and Randall counties), and the higher mountain ranges of the Trans-Pecos. It is found west of the White Rock Escarpment (Interstate Highway 35) and west and north of the Balcones Escarpment. To the east of these two geologic divisions the tree will graduate into Shining Sumac.

Prairie Flameleaf Sumac will be found in many plant associations but is not a marker for any particular habitat. It will be found where the soil has been disturbed.

Robinia (locust)

Leguminosae (legume family)

There are ten to fifteen species of *Robinia* in the temperate regions of the United States and Mexico. The United States has four tree and four or five shrub species. Texas has only one species, *Robinia neomexicana,* which is a small tree in the Guadalupe Mountains in Culberson County. Black Locust (*R. pseudoacacia*) is native to Oklahoma but has become widely naturalized in many areas of Texas.

Robinia neomexicana

New Mexico Locust

(Southwestern Locust, Hojalito)

In Texas, New Mexico Locust is found only in the Guadalupe Mountains in Culberson County. It occurs at about 5,200 feet in the oak-Pinyon-juniper parks association, although it is more common at higher elevations—7,000 to 8,000 feet—in the Ponderosa Pine—Douglas Fir parks/forest association. Here it is associated with Madrones, Bigtooth Maples, and Knowlton Hop Hornbeams in McKittrick and other high canyons.

A small tree only 12 to 15 feet tall, it spreads vegetatively by rhizomes, forming vast thickets. It occurs on the hard limestone of the Capitan Reef formation. North of the park, in the Lincoln National Forest of New Mexico, it becomes almost an understory tree.

Sabal (palmetto)

Palmae (palm family)

About 25 species of *Sabal* occur in the Western Hemisphere. They are found mostly in the Caribbean and along the coast of South, Central, and North America. Six species are native to southern North America. Texas has 2 species: *Sabal mexicana* is a tree and *S. minor* is a shrub. There are a few tree forms of *S. minor,* but most authors state that these tall plants are the result of a high water table, frequent flooding, and shade. Here, the tall form of *S. minor* is considered an introgressed hybrid with *S. palmetto* and is not included. This tree form in the past has been linked with *S. palmetto* and a putative species called *S. louisiana.*

Sabal mexicana

Texas Palmetto

(Mexican Palmetto, Rio Grande Palmetto, Victoria Palmetto, Palma de Micharos, Texas Palm)

At one time Texas Palmetto occupied a narrow band along the Rio Grande from its confluence with the Gulf of Mexico to just above Hidalgo. Today, this 50-foot-tall tree is rarely found farther upriver than Santa Maria, and then, in much lesser numbers. The last remnant stands of the native groves of Texas Palmetto are protected in the Audubon Sabal Palm Grove Sanctuary in southern Cameron County.

Texas Palmetto has been widely planted in home landscapes in many coastal cities of Texas. It has been used as far north as Dallas, though less extensively because of its temperature requirements. Several were planted at the State Fair Grounds in 1936 for the Texas Centennial. They survived until the winter of 1983, when temperatures remained below freezing for 296 consecutive hours (over 12 days); however, attached "pups" survived. Farther south, in San Antonio, no damage was apparent to these native palm trees, although almost 100 percent of the exotic palms were killed.

Salix (willow)

Salicaceae (willow family)

Worldwide, the genus *Salix* contains around 300 to 400 species of trees and shrubs, found primarily in moist to wet areas of the northern temperate to arctic regions as well as the Andes Mountains as far south as Chile. There are roughly 80 to 90 species in the United States. Texas has 8 species, 3 of which are considered trees.

Willows are fast-growing, short-lived, and somewhat brittle, yet they are of great importance in erosion control on steep banks. They also are an important browse plant for many native species of wildlife.

Salix amygdaloides

Peachleaf Willow

(Almond Willow, Peach Willow, Southwestern Peach Willow, Wright Willow, Wright Peachleaf Willow)

Peachleaf Willow is a striking tree reaching heights of 40 feet. It is fairly uncommon, occurring in the higher elevations (3,000 to 4,500 feet) in the Panhandle but below 3,000 feet in the Trans-Pecos. It is easily recognized by its yellow twigs, green peach-leaf-shaped leaves that are silvery white underneath, and drooping branchlets. Its narrow-leaved form, *S. amygdaloides* var. *wrightii,* is the one most often seen in Texas.

Peachleaf Willow grows along waterways, whether they are wet or dry. It is also found around ponds or any water-holding depression. In Texas it occurs in three widely separated areas: the Canadian, Cimarron (Cold Water Creek), and Red River drainageways of the Northern High Plains and the Llano Estacado; the Pecos River drainageways in Culberson, Reeves, Loving, and Ward counties; and the Rio Grande from El Paso to Big Bend National Park.

Salix nigra

Black Willow

(Swamp Willow, Gooding Willow, Western Black Willow, Southwestern Black Willow, Sauz, Lindheimer Black Willow)

Black Willow is ubiquitous in its distribution. It can be found anywhere there is standing water, a flowing stream, a dry stream, or depressions where water may stand for short or long periods. There may be a few western, High Plains, and southern counties where Black Willow does not exist, as shown on the distribution map, but that seems unlikely. It is more probable that no herbarium specimen has been collected in those counties. It is difficult to determine if the Black Willows growing around every ranch and farm pond are native or naturalized. Some of the ponds were constructed almost as soon as the area was settled.

In the east Texas Pineywoods, Black Willow grows to well over 100 feet in height, but the state champion Black Willow from Big Bend National Park in the Chihuahuan Desert is less than 60 feet tall.

Included here is Gooding Willow (*Salix goodingii* var. *variabilis*) and Lindheimer Black Willow (*Salix nigra* var. *lindheimeri*). Gooding Willow was once considered a species of the Trans-Pecos, and Lindheimer Black Willow was considered a variety of the Black Willow with its center of distribution being the central Edwards Plateau.

Salix taxifolia

Yewleaf Willow

(Yew Willow)

Yewleaf Willow is an uncommon or rather rare tree in the Trans-Pecos region of Texas. It grows along streams of cool running water and periodically dry streambeds at elevations of 4,000 to 5,000 feet. This willow is readily identified by its small leaves, which resemble the leaves of the true yew (*Taxus* spp.). The leaves have a silvery gray cast that is quite distinctive when compared with the bright green of other willows.

Yewleaf Willow is recorded in Brewster, Jeff Davis, Presidio, and Terrell counties in the Trans-Pecos. In Brewster County, it is easily observed about 20 miles south of Alpine on Texas Highway 118. It grows in the drainageway of Calamity Creek, and small groves can be seen for several miles downstream. On the same highway heading into Fort Davis, there are small colonies of Yewleaf Willow in Musquiz Canyon. The Yewleaf Willows in the Chinati Mountains grow along seasonally dry streambeds in desert grasslands associations. In Texas, Yewleaf Willow grows in slightly acidic igneous soils.

Sambucus (elder)

Caprifoliaceae
(honeysuckle family)

Approximately 30 species of elder, both trees and shrubs, are found throughout the temperate and sub-tropical areas of the Americas, Asia, and Europe. Seven species are native to North America, of which 5 are trees and 2 are shrubs. Texas has 1 tree and 1 shrub species. *Sambucus* species are a valuable food source to many species of wildlife and are valuable for erosion control.

Sambucus caerulea (*S. glauca*)

Blue Elder

(Blue Elderberry, Blueberry Elder, New Mexico Elder)

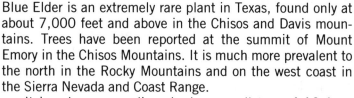

Blue Elder is an extremely rare plant in Texas, found only at about 7,000 feet and above in the Chisos and Davis mountains. Trees have been reported at the summit of Mount Emory in the Chisos Mountains. It is much more prevalent to the north in the Rocky Mountains and on the west coast in the Sierra Nevada and Coast Range.

It is a large spreading shrub or small tree of 12 feet. When it occurs in larger numbers, Blue Elder is important to wildlife because of the sweet, edible fruit. It is also valued for erosion control because it sprouts readily from the base.

Some authors are of the opinion that *Sambucus mexicana* (Mexican Elder) also exists in Texas. It is much planted in El Paso and other cities across the Trans-Pecos. It is part of a cottage nursery industry in that area. The plant is easily rooted from stem cuttings, and plants are sold out of homes and along the streets almost throughout the year in quart to gallon cans and other containers. The plant can be seen on many vacant lots, although they don't appear to be naturalizing, probably because of the lack of soil moisture.

Sapindus (soapberry)

Sapindaceae (soapberry family)

The genus *Sapindus* has about 40 species of trees and shrubs, most of which are native to Asia. The contiguous United States has 2 tree species, and there is 1 tree species in Hawaii. Texas has 1 species, which occurs in all ten vegetational areas, though it is rather rare in the Pineywoods.

Sapindus drummondii

Western Soapberry

(Wild Chinatree, Wild Chinaberry, Soapberry, Indian Soap Plant, Jaboncillo)

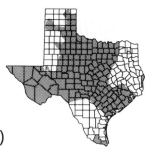

Western Soapberry most commonly ranges from 20 to 30 feet in height, although occasionally it may reach 50 feet. It occurs in all vegetational areas of Texas, though only sparingly in the Rio Grande Plains, Pineywoods, High Plains, and Post Oak Savannah. It is difficult to know for certain, but most likely the isolated groves on the High Plains and in the deep Pineywoods have been planted. This species is fairly general in its habitat, growing in areas with high or low humidity, high or low rainfall, and limestone or sandstone soils. However, it does tend to occur in moister sites in western Texas and does not grow in the swamps of eastern Texas. It also occurs more often on limestone than sandstone.

Male and female flowers occur on separate trees, and in the deep sands of the Rolling Plains, groves of one to ten acres can be found that are apparently of only one sex. One or several trees spread vegetatively by rhizomes, creating these large groves. The clusters of white flowers produced in May or June must be inspected closely to tell whether the tree is male or female. The female flowers produce large clusters of yellowish, transparent-walled fruit, each containing one shiny black seed, that hang through the winter. The fruit wall is rich in saponins, which were used by the American Indians as a cleansing agent. They taught the first settlers how to use this as a high-quality substitute for lye-based soap.

Sassafras (sassafras)

Lauraceae (laurel family)

There are only three species of *Sassafras* worldwide: one on the mainland of China, one in Taiwan, and one in eastern and southern North America. They are small to large, highly aromatic trees that bear male and female flowers on separate trees. Seed crops are borne every three to four years.

Sassafras albidum

Sassafras

(White Sassafras)

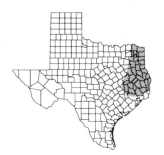

Sassafras is a small to medium tree growing to 20 feet in height, although it has been found as tall as 60 feet. It occurs on acid sands and sandy loams of the Pineywoods and Post Oak Savannah, as part of the pine-hardwood forest association (Loblolly Pine—Sweet Gum, Shortleaf Pine—Post Oak—Southern Red Oak, Longleaf Pine—Sandjack Oak) in the Pineywoods and of the Post Oak woods/forest and grassland mosaic and the Post Oak woods/forest association of the northern Post Oak Savannah.

The flowers of Sassafras are unisexual and bloom on separate trees. The trees reproduce vegetatively by rhizomes, creating large groves and mottes. They are almost impossible to transplant because of the sparse, far-ranging root system.

The fruit of Sassafras is a deep blue drupe on a bright red stalk. Upon ripening, it is quickly taken by many bird species.

Sophora (sophora)

Leguminosae (legume family)

The genus *Sophora* consists of approximately 70 species of unarmed deciduous or evergreen trees and shrubs as well as several herbaceous perennials. They occur in the warm temperate to tropical regions of both hemispheres. There are roughly 6 species native to the United States. Texas has 5 species: 1 deciduous tree, 3 evergreen shrubs (although many authors consider *Sophora secundiflora* a small tree), and 1 herbaceous perennial.

Sophora affinis

Eve's Necklace

(Texas Sophora, Pink Sophora, Necklace Tree)

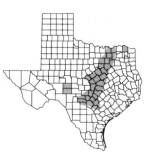

Eve's Necklace is a small tree usually less than 35 feet in height. It occurs on the Blackland Prairies, Cross Timbers, Grand Prairie, and Edwards Plateau, ranging from Grayson County on the Red River south to Uvalde, Medina, and Bexar counties with small populations to the west in Palo Pinto, Schleicher, and Sutton counties and east in Red River County. There may be other populations to the east and west on islands of calcareous or alkaline soils.

Eve's Necklace covers a range a few miles east and a few miles west of the Balcones Fault and follows the White Rock Escarpment from Williamson, Bell, McLennan, Hill, Ellis, Dallas, and Grayson counties to the Red River. The land has long been farmed and grazed, so it is difficult to know what plant communities and associations were there previously. Today most of the land is classified as crops association or native and introduced grassland association. Eve's Necklace is also common in right-of-way associations. In dense woods and shady stream banks, it forms a high climbing vine and is difficult to identify.

Styrax (snowbell)

Styracaceae (storax family)

There are roughly 120 species of *Styrax* worldwide, mostly in tropical to warm temperate areas of North America and Eurasia. Texas is the center of *Styrax* distribution in the United States, having 4 species with a variety. Of these, *Styrax grandifolius* is treelike, and the other species and varieties are usually shrubs. *S. youngae* is probably extinct in the wild in Texas but is cultivated in Dallas from seeds gathered in Mexico. Surprisingly, 2 species and a variety are western (west of the 98th meridian), and 2 species grow in the higher rainfall belt and acid soils of eastern Texas.

Styrax grandifolius

Bigleaf Snowbell

(Snowbell, Coast Snowbell, Storax)

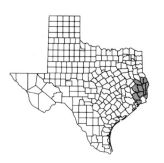

Bigleaf Snowbell is quite limited in its range in Texas, being found only in the Big Thicket of deep southeast Texas in the Pineywoods vegetational area. It is a small tree, averaging 12 to 15 feet in height, although it has been known to grow to 20 feet. On the mesic acid sands and sandy loams of Jasper, Newton, Sabine, San Augustine, Angelina, Tyler, Polk, Hardin, Liberty, and Chambers counties, it is a part of the Loblolly Pine—Post Oak association and Loblolly Pine—Sweet Gum association. It also occurs on the ridges in the Shortleaf Pine—Post Oak—Southern Red Oak association. It is especially prevalent in Jasper, Newton, and Sabine counties and generally is an understory tree growing in moderate to rather heavy shade.

Bigleaf Snowbell is not recognized in most manuals of Texas trees probably because it has been confused with *Halesia diptera,* a close relative. Snowbells (*Styrax*) and silverbells (*Halesia*) are easily confused at a casual glance, even when they are in flower, because they differ primarily in the number of petals per flower; *Styrax* has five and *Halesia* has four.

Symplocos (sweetleaf)

Symplocaceae (sweetleaf family)

The genus *Symplocos* is mostly tropical or subtropical with more than 350 species worldwide. Only one species, *Symplocos tinctoria* (Sweetleaf), is found in North America, and it also occurs in Texas.

Symplocos tinctoria

Sweetleaf

(Horse Sugar, Common Sweetleaf, Yellowwood, Wild Laurel)

Sweetleaf, a little-known but not uncommon tree of the Pineywoods, inhabits two interesting areas of the eastern forests: the old Longleaf Pine area of Jasper, Newton, Tyler, Polk, Hardin, and other counties in far southeast Texas; and the Caddo Lake drainageways in Harrison, Marion, and Cass counties in northeast Texas, where it is a dominant hardwood.

Sweetleaf is evergreen (or at least persistent-leaved) and grows to about 45 feet tall on the rich acid sands and sandy loams of the pine-hardwood forest association (Loblolly Pine—Sweet Gum, Shortleaf Pine—Post Oak—Southern Red Oak, Longleaf Pine—Sandjack Oak) and the young forest—grassland association of the Pineywoods.

Dense clusters of bright yellow flowers cover the tree from February to April, followed by blue-gray drupes from September to October. The leaves are sweet and heavily browsed by livestock and deer.

Taxodium (bald cypress)

Taxodiaceae (bald cypress family)

Only two species of this ancient genus now survive, and both are found in Texas. One species, *Taxodium mucronatum* (Montezuma Bald Cypress), is evergreen and is found from the Rio Grande south to Guatemala. The other, *Taxodium distichum* (Bald Cypress), is deciduous and ranges from Texas to the southeastern United States.

Taxodium distichum var. *distichum*

Bald Cypress

(Cypress, Southern Cypress, Swamp Cypress, Red Cypress, White Cypress, Yellow Cypress, Gulf Cypress, Tidewater Red Cypress)

Twenty million years ago, *Taxodium* occurred in Europe, Asia, and North America. Now the genus is found only in Mexico, the southeastern United States, and river valleys extending north to southern Illinois and Indiana. In Texas, Bald Cypress can be found in the Pineywoods, Gulf Prairies and Marshes, Post Oak Savannah, Rio Grande Plains, and Edwards Plateau, where it sometimes reaches heights of more than 100 feet.

In the Pineywoods, Bald Cypress is part of the Bald Cypress—Water Tupelo swamp association. In the lower Post Oak Savannah and the Gulf Coast Prairies and Marshes, it occurs in the river bottoms of the Pecan-elm forest association, and in the upper Post Oak Savannah and the northeastern Pineywoods it is part of the Water Oak—elm-hackberry forest association. On the Edwards Plateau it is found along running streams and rivers, such as the Medina, Guadalupe, and Pedernales, ranging west and northwest far into the Hill Country.

Although Bald Cypress will grow in relatively well-drained areas, it does better in the wetter areas. Cypress knees arise from the roots and measure a few inches to more than 6 feet tall. They protrude above the surface of the water and become hollow with age. The exact function of cypress knees is not known. It has been speculated that the knees help supply oxygen to the tree, but they also appear when the trees are planted in landscape settings.

Taxodium mucronatum

Montezuma Bald Cypress

(Mexican Cypress, Sabino, Ahuehuete, Cipres)

Montezuma Bald Cypress is an evergreen tree that reaches its northern limits on the banks of the Rio Grande and along resacas in Cameron and Hidalgo counties. The main difference between Montezuma Bald Cypress and Bald Cypress is the male flowers, which are borne in long racemes in the former and short clusters in the latter.

In the gardens of Chapultepec stands the Cypress of Montezuma, which by 1900 measured more than 168 feet tall and 50 feet in circumference. Another tree, El Gigante, grows in the churchyard at Santa María del Tule in Oaxaca and stands 140 feet tall and measures 150 feet in circumference. The tree is believed to be 1,500 to 2,000 years old.

In Texas, Montezuma Bald Cypress is usually under 50 feet tall. This tree of the subtropics has difficulty surviving the winters farther north than San Antonio, and even in moderate winters in Houston, it becomes deciduous.

Tilia (basswood)

Tiliaceae (linden family)

Tilia is a genus of about 35 species widely distributed in the northern temperate regions of Europe, Asia, and North America. There are either 3 or 4 species in the United States, with 1 or 2 species in Texas. Some authorities consider *Tilia floridana* a distinct species, but others consider it synonymous with *T. caroliniana*. Here it is considered the latter, giving Texas only 1 species.

Tilia caroliniana

Carolina Basswood

(Basswood, Linden, Carolina Linden, Florida Linden, Florida Basswood)

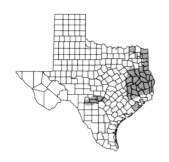

Carolina Basswood is a large tree, reaching heights of more than 90 feet. Though once quite extensive in its range, Carolina Basswood now occurs in only about seven or eight counties on the rich, deep, moist soils of the river bottoms and creeks of the Edwards Plateau in central Texas, and it is more widespread in the deeper, moister soils of stream banks, hillsides, and upland flats in the Pineywoods of east Texas.

Carolina Basswood flowers from April to June, with individual trees blooming for short periods of only about ten days. The flowers are perfect and fragrant, hanging in white clusters from a stalk attached to a leafy bract. They make excellent honey that is light in color but has a strong taste. Nectar production is erratic, so good honey production is possible in only about two out of five years. Also, there are so few trees in Texas that honey production from this source is no longer important.

Ulmus (elm)

Ulmaceae (elm family)

There are between 20 and 45 species of elm world-wide, found only in the temperate regions of the Old and New World in the Northern Hemisphere. Six species are native to North America, with 4 occurring in Texas. All species of elm in the United States are more or less susceptible to the deadly Dutch elm disease (*Ceratocystis ulmi*), which attacks the vascular system of the tree. It is not yet epidemic in Texas, as it is in other areas of the country. However, there are troublesome enclaves of Dutch elm disease in east Texas.

Ulmus alata

Winged Elm

(Cork Elm, Wahoo Elm, Witch Elm)

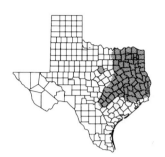

Winged Elm, usually less than 70 feet in height, is found in neutral to acid sands and sandy loams along river and creek banks, dry bluffs, hillsides, fencerows, and abandoned fields in eastern Texas.

It is native to the Pineywoods, Gulf Prairies and Marshes, and Post Oak Savannah, although small isolated populations occur in the Blacklands and the East Cross Timbers and Grand Prairie. There is a disjunct population in Erath County, almost 100 miles west of the Post Oak Savannah. A component of the Post Oak parks/woods/forest and grassland mosaic all across the Post Oak Savannah, Winged Elm will sometimes form dense thickets. It is part of the elm-hackberry association of the transitional Blackland Prairies and all phases of the pine-hardwood forest association of the east Texas Pineywoods.

Winged Elm flowers in early spring before the leaves are fully formed, and it is a prolific seeder, usually in alternate years. It sprouts readily from seed, grows rapidly, transplants easily, and is usually pest-free, with golden fall color.

Ulmus americana

American Elm

(White Elm, Soft Elm, Water Elm, Common Elm)

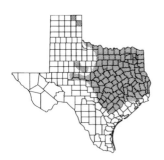

In Texas, American Elm can be found in all vegetational areas except the High Plains and Trans-Pecos. Except for a few populations in Bexar, Wilson, and Karnes counties, it is also absent from the Rio Grande Plains. It follows the Red River northwest into Hardeman County and grows on the banks of the Colorado River west into Coke County. It also occurs on the Callahan Divide of the Edwards Plateau and the surrounding redland soils of the Rolling Plains in Taylor County. In this western environment, which annually receives less than 24 inches of rainfall, American Elm is found only in river or creek bottoms and is a tree to 30 feet tall with small leaves. Two hundred miles to the east, it is more than 90 feet tall and has 3-inch-wide and 6-inch-long leaves.

American Elm will grow in many associations and situations. In Texas it occurs on neutral to acid sands and sandy loams as well as heavy clay soils that are alkaline. In the eastern part of the country, it grows in deep forests that receive almost 60 inches of rain per year, yet the western part of its range, in Coke and Hardeman counties, is dry, with less than 25 inches of rain. Throughout its range, American Elm is highly susceptible to Dutch elm disease.

Ulmus crassifolia

Cedar Elm

(Basket Elm, Scrub Elm, Lime Elm, Texas Elm, Olmo, Southern Rock Elm)

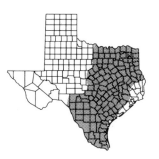

Cedar Elm can reach 90 feet, and it is the only native Texas elm that flowers and sets seed in the fall. Its leaves are small and sandpapery to the touch. It is prevalent on limestone soils of the Blackland Prairies, Cross Timbers and Prairies, Edwards Plateau, and Rio Grande Plains. It just may be as much a part of the slightly acid soils of the Post Oak Savannah, but it is not seen as often in the true Pineywoods.

Cedar Elm occurs in all areas of Texas except the Trans-Pecos, High Plains, and Rolling Plains. It is part of the Mesquite—Granjeno parks/woods association of the Rio Grande Plains; the oak-Mesquite-juniper and the Ashe Juniper parks/woods associations of the Cross Timbers and Prairies, the Live Oak—Mesquite parks, Live Oak—Ashe Juniper parks, Live Oak—Mesquite—Ashe Juniper parks, and Live Oak—Ashe Juniper woods associations of the Edwards Plateau; the elm-hackberry parks/woods association of the transitional Blackland Prairies; the Post Oak parks/woods/forest and grassland mosaic association of the Post Oak Savannah; the Pecan-elm-hackberry forest association of the northern Blackland Prairies and Post Oak Savannah; and the pine-hardwood forest association of the Pineywoods. In other words, Cedar Elm is common in all areas of the eastern half of Texas except the Longleaf Pine belt in the southeastern part of the state.

Ulmus rubra

Slippery Elm

(Red Elm, Gray Elm, Soft Elm)

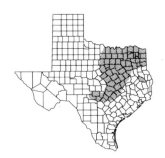

Slippery Elm is easily confused with American Elm. It is generally not as large as American Elm, although in Texas Slippery Elm has been found growing to 90 feet tall. It does not have the pronounced vase shape of American Elm but does grow in about the same area, although it is not nearly as prevalent. Its leaves have a characteristic sandpapery feel.

Although it grows in roughly the same area as American Elm, Slippery Elm doesn't occupy as much territory. It appears to be northern, especially in the Pineywoods area, where it hardly grows south of Caddo Lake in Harrison County. Slippery Elm also is not found in the western areas with American Elm.

Slippery Elm occurs in the Blackland Prairies, the Cross Timbers and Prairies, the northern Post Oak Savannah, the northeastern corner of the true Pineywoods, and some areas of the Edwards Plateau. In all of these areas, it grows on the deep, moist soils of riverbanks and shaded hillsides and does equally well in slightly acid to alkaline soils.

Vaccinium (blueberry)

Ericaceae (heath family)

The majority of blueberry species are shrubs, although a few are trees. There are approximately 150 to 300 species worldwide, mostly in the northern temperate regions of North America, Europe, and Asia, as well as the high mountains of tropical lands and islands south to the Andes. The United States has about 30 species. Of the 7 species in Texas, 1 is a tree and 6 are shrubs. The species are either deciduous or evergreen.

Vaccinium arboreum

Farkleberry

(Sparkleberry, Huckleberry, Winter Huckleberry)

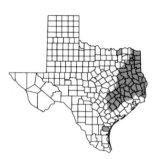

Farkleberry, a small evergreen or persistent-leaved tree or large shrub, reaches heights of 30 feet in clearings, abandoned fields, open mixed forests, and dry sterile hillsides as well as wet bottomlands of the Pineywoods and Post Oak Savannah. It is found in acid sands and sandy loams that are well drained. It also grows along moist stream banks and temporarily inundated areas.

There are disjunct populations with Red Bay, Southern Wax Myrtle, and Coast Laurel Oak in the sand dune areas of Aransas, Nueces, and San Patricio counties. It is usually an understory tree in the Post Oak woods/forest and grassland mosaic association and the Water Oak—elm-hackberry forest association of the Post Oak Savannah. It is also a component of the young forest/grassland and all phases of the pine-hardwood forest association of the Pineywoods.

Vauquelinia (vauquelinia)

Rosaceae (rose family)

Vauquelinia is a little-known genus of the southwestern United States and northern Mexico. Of the eight to ten species, only two are trees; the others are shrubs. Of the tree species, one occurs in Texas and the other in Arizona.

Vauquelinia angustifolia

Chisos Rosewood

(Narrowleaf Vauquelinia, Vauquel Bush, Guauyul, Palo Prieto)

Chisos Rosewood is a small, evergreen tree of only 10 to 20 feet in height. It is native only to the Trans-Pecos, where it is found at relatively low elevations (3,000 to 5,000 feet) in the dry canyons of the Chisos Mountains, in the Dead Horse Mountains, and in Presidio County, where it is extremely local in the Chinati Mountains and their foothills. It might be found in the Eagle and Quitman mountains when these ranges are thoroughly explored. Although it is quite local in distribution, it occurs in relatively dense thickets and cannot be considered rare. The tree is also found in Mexico.

Chisos Redwood is a good landscape plant and does quite well in the calcareous soils of the Blackland Prairies at least as far north as McKinney. Its most spectacular asset is its 7-inch-long, ¼-inch-wide, sharply toothed, dark green leaves. Dense clusters of fragrant, white flowers cover the tree in the spring, with the brownish tan capsules ripening in August.

Viburnum (viburnum)

Caprifoliaceae
(honeysuckle family)

Worldwide, *Viburnum* has more than 150 species, of which most are large shrubs or small trees. They are found in both temperate and subtropical regions of the Northern Hemisphere and the Andes in South America. The United States has about 15 shrub and 6 tree species. Some authors show Texas with 7 species, 4 of which are small trees in certain situations. Others list only 6 species, with varying interpretations as to which are trees and which are shrubs.

Viburnum rufidulum

Rusty Blackhaw

(Southern Blackhaw, Blackhaw, Bluehaw, Nannyberry, Southern Nannyberry, Rusty Nannyberry)

Rusty Blackhaw can be a small tree of almost 30 feet in height or a shrub of 10 feet. This species is found in all areas of Texas except the Rolling Plains, High Plains, and Rio Grande Plains, but it would not be surprising to discover it in shaded canyons in those three areas.

Rusty Blackhaw is generally an understory tree but is most attractive in the open in full sun. It can grow on almost any soil as long as it is fairly well drained. In shaded, moist areas of the Pineywoods, Post Oak Savannah, and Blackland Prairies, Rusty Blackhaw usually occurs singly, although there may be two or three in an area. In areas with less rainfall, however, such as the Cross Timbers and Prairies and the Lampasas Cut Plains, Rusty Blackhaw occurs on exposed calcareous hillsides in drifts and groves of sometimes up to 100 plants. In almost every case, plants on thin soils in a 30-inch rainfall belt will form treelike shrubs of 10 to 12 feet. However, in the hills and deep valleys of the Edwards Plateau and the Central Mineral Region, Rusty Blackhaw is usually a small understory tree up to 15 feet tall.

One of the most interesting range extensions of any plant in Texas is the small grove of Rusty Blackhaw in Horsesprings Canyon on the Sproul Ranch high in the Davis Mountains, 250 miles west of those plants on the Edwards Plateau.

Yucca (yucca)

Liliaceae (lily family)

The 35 to 40 species of *Yucca* are found exclusively in North America, including Mexico and the West Indies. Roughly 26 of the species are native to the United States, with approximately 19 in Texas. Three of the Texas species are possible hybrids. If it is determined that those 3 species are hybrids, then Texas would have 16 species, 6 of which are trees. In the near future, Faxon Yucca may be merged with Carneros Yucca, reducing the number of species in Texas to 15, with 5 tree species.

Yucca carnerosana

Carneros Yucca

(Giant Dagger, Palma, Palmilla, Spanish Dagger, Palma Barreta, Palma Samandoca)

Carneros Yucca is a small tree yucca reaching 20 feet in height. The state champion Carneros Yucca in Hudspeth County is 25 feet tall, but some people consider it a Faxon Yucca. Carneros Yucca is usually found on limestone soil at elevations between 3,000 and 5,000 feet only in Brewster County; it is the dominant yucca of Dagger Flat in Big Bend National Park. The greatest numbers of these yuccas are in the Dead Horse Mountains (Sierra del Carmens) in Big Bend National Park and on the flats and hills east of the Dead Horse Mountains in the Black Gap Wildlife Management Area of the Texas Parks and Wildlife Department.

The plant flowers only once every three to four years and produces flower clusters weighing up to 70 pounds. It is assumed that the intervening years are needed for carbohydrate buildup within the plant to support this large expenditure of energy.

It is likely that Carneros and Faxon yuccas will soon be considered one species.

Yucca elata

Soaptree Yucca

(Amole, Palmilla, Soapweed Yucca)

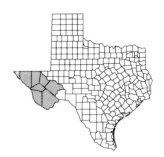

Soaptree Yucca is a multistemmed yucca that reaches heights of 20 to 30 feet, and some authors believe it lives to be 250 to 300 years of age. It is found in both alkaline (limestone) and acid (igneous) soils almost throughout the Trans-Pecos. However, it is more prevalent on the mesas and high grasslands at altitudes of 4,000 to 4,500 feet. One of the most stunning scenes in all the Trans-Pecos is viewed from farm-to-market road 1111 between Sierra Blanca and Cornudas when the Soaptree Yucca is in bloom. Several pastures in this high grassland have thickets of Soaptree Yucca, all about the same height, which indicates that the area has been overgrazed.

Most yuccas are easy to transplant because fibrous roots will grow thickly from the smooth, rounded knob at the basal end of the caudex or stem. Soaptree Yucca, however, has a taproot, making it difficult to transplant. Even small yuccas 2 to 3 feet high are extremely difficult to dig.

The inner bark of the roots and trunk is sometimes used as a substitute for soap, hence the common name.

Yucca faxoniana

Faxon Yucca

(Spanish Bayonet, Spanish Dagger, Palma)

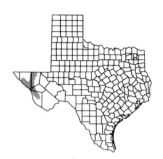

From the rimrock of the Vieja Mountains in Presidio County, Faxon Yucca forms what looks like a yucca woodland far in the distance. Here it is easily 25 feet tall, with some specimens approaching 40 feet.

Faxon Yucca occurs in the Creosote-Lechuguilla shrub association in Presidio, Jeff Davis, Culberson, and Hudspeth counties and is part of the Tobosa—Black Grama grassland association in Culberson and Hudspeth counties.

The low hills just west of Sierra Blanca along Interstate Highway 10 are covered with Faxon Yucca, most of which are only 10 feet high. The grasslands west of Valentine also contain Faxon Yucca but not in great numbers. Another place to view this giant yucca is in McKittrick Canyon in the Guadalupe Mountains. Some of the specimens on the canyon floor are more than 12 to 15 feet tall.

Yucca rostrata

Beaked Yucca

(Big Bend Yucca, Palmita, Soyate)

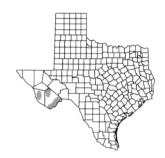

Beaked Yucca is a common yucca on the slopes of the Dead Horse Mountains in southern Brewster County. It is also the most common and tallest yucca in the Black Gap wildlife refuge. Small hillsides of Beaked Yucca are seen in the outlying foothills of the Santiago Range on the road into Big Bend National Park from Marathon.

The tallest Beaked Yucca that I have ever seen was 60 miles from this area, in the foothills of the Chinati Mountains in Presidio County. This particular yucca stood more than 35 feet tall and was growing in igneous soil. It had two pups 3 to 5 feet tall that remained standing after the main trunk was wind-thrown in 1986.

347

Yucca torreyi

Torrey Yucca

(Old Shag, Spanish Bayonet, Spanish Dagger, Palma)

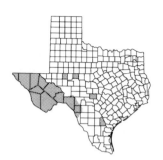

Torrey Yucca is found in the Trans-Pecos, in the western Edwards Plateau, and in Kinney, Uvalde, and Maverick counties on the Rio Grande Plains. It is closely related to Trecul Yucca, and where the two species come together in Uvalde and Maverick counties they are difficult to identify. Hybrids occur in this area, causing some authors to consider Torrey Yucca a variety of Trecul Yucca.

From a horticultural standpoint, Torrey Yucca is probably the least attractive of all the tree yuccas because of its unkempt appearance. It is easy to understand why the residents of the region call this yucca Old Shag. It can grow to 25 feet but is usually much shorter. I have seen this yucca as far east as the McGinley Ranch in Gillespie County and on the east bank of the Colorado River near Bronte in Coke County. It is ubiquitous in the Trans-Pecos.

Yucca treculeana

Trecul Yucca

(Spanish Bayonet, Spanish Dagger, Palma Pita, Palma de Datil, Palmito)

Trecul Yucca grows to about 15 feet in height and is the only tree yucca in Texas that is found exclusively east of the Pecos River, occurring in the Rio Grande Plains and the Gulf Prairies and Marshes. It extends as far east as Matagorda Bay and as far north as Bexar, Medina, and Uvalde counties. Trecul Yucca is closely related to Torrey Yucca and possibly to *Yucca baccata,* which is a stemless yucca of the Trans-Pecos and the western Edwards Plateau.

Trecul Yucca grows on Palmito Hill on Texas Highway 4 on the way to Boca Chica in Cameron County. It is here that the last battle of the American Civil War was fought on May 13, 1865.

349

Zanthoxylum (prickly ash)

Rutaceae (citrus family)

There are roughly 250 species of prickly ash worldwide. Most are tropical or subtropical, but some extend into temperate zones in North America and eastern Asia. There are 7 species in North America, with 4 occurring in Texas. One species is a tree, 1 is a shrub, and 2 can be considered either trees or shrubs.

Zanthoxylum clava-herculis

Hercules'-club

(Pepperbark, Toothache Tree, Tickletongue, Prickly Ash)

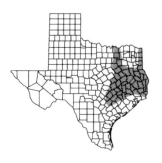

Hercules'-club can attain 50 feet in height but is more commonly 15 to 20 feet tall. It is a tree of the Blackland Prairies, Pineywoods, Gulf Prairies and Marshes, and Post Oak Savannah. It is widely scattered, growing on deep, heavy, alkaline clay soils in the Blackland Prairies, on acidic, almost sterile sands in the Post Oak Savannah and the Pineywoods of deep east Texas, and in neutral, well-drained clay soils in the Gulf Prairies and Marshes.

Hercules'-club attains its largest size and becomes most attractive on disturbed sites or abandoned cropland. It is common in woods' edge and fencerow associations, where it is quite clear that the seeds have been voided by birds and other wildlife while resting in the trees and on the wires.

Bibliography

Adams, R. P. 1973. Reevaluation of the biological status of *Juniperus deppeana* var. *sperryi* Correll. Brittonia 25:284–289.

Agricultural Research Service. 1960. Plant hardiness zone map, MP No. 814. U.S. Dept. of Agriculture, U.S. Govt. Printing Office. Washington, D.C.

Ajilvsgi, Geyata. 1979. *Wild flowers of the Big Thicket, east Texas, and western Louisiana.* Texas A&M Univ. Press. College Station.

Benson, L., and R. A. Darrow. 1981. *Trees and shrubs of the southwestern deserts,* 3rd edition, revised and expanded. Univ. of Arizona Press. Tucson.

Brown, C. A. 1972. *Louisiana trees and shrubs.* Claitor's Publishing Div. (Reprint). Baton Rouge.

————. 1972. *Wildflowers of Louisiana and adjoining states.* Louisiana State Univ. Press. Baton Rouge.

Carter, W. T. 1931. The soils of Texas. Texas Agricultural Experiment Station Bulletin 431. College Station.

Collingwood, G. H., and W. D. Brush. 1974, revised and edited by D. Butcher. *Knowing your trees.* American Forestry Assoc. Washington, D.C.

Correll, D. S., and M. C. Johnston. 1970. *Manual of the vascular plants of Texas.* Texas Research Foundation. Renner.

Correll, H. B., ed. 1963. *Wrightia, a botanical journal,* vol. 2. Texas Research Foundation. Renner.

Cory, V. L. 1936. Three junipers of western Texas. *Rhodora* 38:182–187.

———— and H. B. Parks. 1937. Catalogue of the flora of Texas. Texas Agricultural Experiment Station Bulletin 550. College Station.

Droze, W. H. 1977. *Trees, prairies, and people: A history of tree planting in the plains states.* Texas Woman's Univ. Denton.

Elias, T. S. 1980. *The complete trees of North America.* Van Nostrand Reinhold. New York.

Godfrey, C. L., G. S. McKee, and H. Oakes. 1973. General soil map of Texas. Texas Agricultural Experiment Station MP No. 1034, and USDA Soil Conservation Service. College Station.

Gould, F. W. 1962. Texas plants: A checklist and ecological summary. Texas Agricultural Experiment Station Misc. Pub. 585/Rev. 1975. College Station.

———, G. O. Hoffman, and C. A. Rechenthin. 1960. Vegetational areas of Texas. Texas Agricultural Experiment Station L-492. College Station.

Great Plains Flora Association. 1977. *Atlas of the flora of the Great Plains.* Iowa State Univ. Press. Ames.

———. 1986. *Flora of the Great Plains.* Univ. Press of Kansas. Lawrence.

Henrickson, J., and M. C. Johnston. 1986. Vegetation and community types of the Chihuahuan desert. In *Chihuahan Desert—U.S. and Mexico II,* J. C. Barlow, A. Michael Powell, and B. N. Timmermann, eds. Chihuahuan Desert Research Institute. Alpine, Texas.

Holden, W. C. 1970. The Espuela Land and Cattle Company: A study of a foreign-owned ranch in Texas. Texas State Historical Association. Austin.

Jones, F. B. 1977. *Flora of the Texas coastal bend,* 2nd edition. Mission Press. Corpus Christi.

Jordan, T. G., J. L. Bean, Jr., and W. M. Holmes. 1984. *Texas: A geography.* Westview Press. Boulder, Colorado.

Kartesz, J. T., and R. Kartesz. 1980. *A synonymized checklist of the vascular flora of the United States, Canada, and Greenland, vol. 2: The biota of North America.* Univ. of North Carolina Press. Chapel Hill.

Kearney, T. H., R. H. Peebles, and collaborators. 1960. *Arizona flora,* 2nd edition with supplement. Univ. of California Press. Berkeley.

Kennard, D. 1978. *Preserving Texas' natural heritage.* Lyndon B. Johnson School of Public Affairs, Univ. of Texas Press. Austin.

Lanner, R. M. 1984. *Trees of the Great Basin: A natural history.* Univ. of Nevada Press. Reno.

Little, E. L., Jr. 1971. Atlas of United States trees, vol. 1: Conifers and important hardwoods. USDA Forest Service MP No. 1146. U.S. Govt. Printing Office. Washington, D.C.

————. 1976. Atlas of United States trees, vol. 3: Minor western hardwoods. USDA Forest Service MP No. 1314. U.S. Govt. Printing Office. Washington, D.C.

————. 1977. Atlas of United States trees, vol. 4: Minor eastern hardwoods. USDA Forest Service MP No. 1342. U.S. Govt. Printing Office. Washington, D.C.

————. 1979. Checklist of United States trees, native and naturalized. USDA Forest Service Agricultural Handbook 541. U.S. Govt. Printing Office. Washington, D.C.

————. 1981. Atlas of United States trees, vol. 6: Supplement. USDA Forest Service MP No. 1410. U.S. Govt. Printing Office. Washington, D.C.

Lundell, C. L., ed. 1945. *Wrightia, a botanical journal,* vol. 1. University Press, Southern Methodist Univ. Dallas.

————. 1966. *Wrightia, a botanical journal,* vol. 3. Texas Research Foundation. Renner.

————. 1971. *Wrightia, a botanical journal,* vol. 4. Texas Research Foundation. Renner.

———— and collaborators. 1961. *Flora of Texas,* vol. 1 (1966), vol. 2 (1969), vol. 3 (1961). Texas Research Foundation. Renner.

Mahler, W. F. 1973. *Flora of Taylor county,* Texas. SMU Bookstore. Dallas.

————. 1984. *Shinners' manual of the north central Texas flora.* SMU Bookstore. Dallas.

Marbut, C. F. 1927. A scheme for soil classification. *Proceedings and Papers of the First International Congress of Soil Science,* vol. 4.

McMahan, C. A., R. G. Frye, and K. L. Brown. 1984. *The vegetation types of Texas, including cropland.* Texas Parks and Wildlife. Austin.

Miller, H. A., and S. H. Lamb. 1985. *Oaks of North America.* Naturegraph Publishers. Happy Camp, California.

Muller, C. H. 1951. The oaks of Texas. In *Contributions from the Texas Research Foundation,* C. L. Lundell, ed. Texas Research Foundation. Renner.

Nixon, E. S. 1985. *Trees, shrubs, and woody vines of east Texas.* Bruce Lyndon Cunningham Productions. Nacogdoches.

Nixon, K. C. 1984. A biosystematic study of *Quercus* series *Virentes* (the live oaks) with phylogenetic analysis of Fagales, Fagaceae and *Quercus.* Dissertation. Univ. of Texas. Austin.

Parks, H. B. 1937. Valuable plants native to Texas. Texas Agricultural Experiment Station Bulletin No. 551. College Station.

Pass, F., ed. 1979. *Texas almanac 1980–1981.* A. H. Belo. Dallas.

Peattie, D. C. 1953. *A natural history of western trees.* Bonanza. New York.

———. 1956. *A natural history of trees of eastern and central North America.* Bonanza. New York.

Pellett, F. C. 1978. *American honey plants, together with those which are of special value to the beekeeper as sources of pollen,* 5th edition. Dadant and Sons. Hamilton, Illinois.

Sargent, C. S. 1965. *Manual of the trees of North America,* 2nd edition, vols. 1 and 2. Dover Publications. Reprint. New York.

Sellards, E. H., W. S. Adkins, and F. B. Plummer. 1932. *The geology of Texas, vol. 1: Stratigraphy.* Univ. of Texas Press. Austin.

Shinners, L. H. 1958. *Spring flora of the Dallas–Fort Worth area.* SMU Bookstore. Dallas.

Simpson, B. J. 1986. *The oaks of Texas. Journal of Arboriculture* 12(12):302–304.

Soil Conservation Service. 1981. Land resource regions and major land resource areas of the United States. USDA Soil Conservation Service Agricultural Handbook 296, rev. Dec. 1981. U.S. Govt. Printing Office. Washington, D.C.

Texas Forest Service. 1987. *Registry of 193 champion big trees in Texas.* Texas Forest Service. College Station.

Turner, B. L. 1959. *The legumes of Texas.* Univ. of Texas Press. Austin.

Van Dersal, W. R. 1938. Native woody plants of the United States, their erosion-control and wildlife values. USDA Misc. Pub. No. 303. U.S. Govt. Printing Office. Washington, D.C.

———. 1942. *Ornamental American shrubs.* Oxford Univ. Press. New York.

Vines, R. A. 1960. *Trees, shrubs, and woody vines of the southwest.* Univ. of Texas Press. Austin.

Walker, L. A. 1984. *Trees: An introduction to trees and forest ecology for the amateur naturalist.* Prentice-Hall. Englewood Cliffs, New Jersey.

Warnock, B. H. 1970. *Wildflowers of the Big Bend country, Texas.* Sul Ross State Univ. Alpine.

————. 1974. *Wildflowers of the Guadalupe Mountains and sand dune country, Texas.* Sul Ross State Univ. Alpine.

————. 1977. *Wildflowers of the Davis Mountains and the Marathon Basin, Texas.* Sul Ross State Univ. Alpine.

Waterfall, U. T. 1972. *Keys to the flora of Oklahoma.* OSU Bookstore. Stillwater.

Williams, J. E. 1974. *Atlas of the woody plants of Oklahoma.* Oklahoma Biological Survey, Oklahoma Univ. Press. Norman.

Index